*Baudelaire and the
Aesthetics of Bad Faith*

Baudelaire and the Aesthetics of Bad Faith

Susan Blood

STANFORD UNIVERSITY PRESS
STANFORD, CALIFORNIA

Published
with the assistance
of the Frederick W. Hilles
Publication Fund of Yale University

Stanford University Press
Stanford, California
© 1997 by the Board of Trustees of the
Leland Stanford Junior University

Printed in the United States of America

CIP data are at the end of the book

Stanford University Press publications are
distributed exclusively by Stanford
University Press within the United States,
Canada, Mexico, and Central America;
they are distributed exclusively by
Cambridge University Press
throughout the rest
of the world.

For Roger

Acknowledgments

Two people in particular deserve thanks in more ways than I can tell for helping me complete this book. My adviser, Josué Harari, provided the kind of encouragement and keen, good-humored criticism I only wish more students could benefit from. My husband, Roger, patiently listened to each paragraph as it was being written, and always seemed to know when to speak and when to be silent. My students have been a constant source of stimulating conversation. Among the many colleagues and friends who have been supportive over the years, I want particularly to thank Suzanne Guerlac and Leah Ulansey—they have given my work the most careful reading and the most challenging criticisms.

I am grateful for the support of the American Association of University Women during the early stages of research. I would also like to thank the Morse Fellowship and the Mellon Fellowship, both at Yale University, for enabling me to complete the manuscript.

S. B.

Contents

A Note to the Reader, xi

Introduction, 1

ONE
The Two Baudelaires: Valéry's Canonization of
Les Fleurs du mal, 29

TWO
Defining and Defending Poetry: Sartre Versus Bataille, 57

THREE
The Caricatural Mechanism in Baudelaire's Poetry, 94

FOUR
The Allegorical Architecture of *Les Fleurs du mal,* 123

FIVE
Baudelaire Against Photography:
An Allegory of Old Age, 150

Conclusion, 173

Notes, 181
Bibliography, 199
Index, 205

A Note to the Reader

All translations from Baudelaire and other French sources are my own. In translating the poetry I have tried to be as literal as possible, both because my analysis depends upon a precise rendering of the original texts, and because I feel that some of the aesthetic quality of Baudelaire's poetry is tied to its literal meaning. Citations are taken from the Pléiade edition of Baudelaire's *Oeuvres complètes* (1975) and *Correspondance* (1973), and are abbreviated as OC and C, respectively. Valéry's works are similarly cited from the Pléiade *Oeuvres* (1957) and abbreviated as O. Complete information for these works can be found in the Bibliography.

*Baudelaire and the
Aesthetics of Bad Faith*

Introduction

Since the early twentieth century, Charles Baudelaire's poetry has been deeply implicated in attempts to define aesthetic modernism. Baudelaire himself, in *Le Peintre de la vie moderne* (The painter of modern life), was among the first French critics to use the term *modernité*. The definition of a specifically modern art preoccupied him in critical essays devoted to the works of Poe, Delacroix, and Wagner. He asked the same questions of each of these artists: "How is it that he produces a sensation of novelty? What does he give us which is more than the past has given us? He is as great as the great, as skillful as the skillful, but why does he please us more?" (OC, 2: 636). It is perhaps natural that these same questions would be asked of Baudelaire by the generation of writers that came of age half a century later, around the time of the First World War. This was a remarkable moment in several respects. The year 1913 has been called the annus mirabilis of French literature, since it saw the publication of Proust's *Combray* and Apollinaire's *Alcools*, and marked Valéry's return to poetry after a fifteen-year silence. While much has been said about the literary production of these years, less attention has been paid to the work of historical revisionism that was taking place simultaneously. The same writers who produced the modernist masterpieces of the early twentieth century were also engaged in a reevaluation of their literary predecessors. To cite André Malraux, the moment represented both a "revolution of the present" and a "metamorphosis of the past" (p. 9). No other figure from the past was more transformed by this critical process than Baudelaire. For his contemporaries, he appeared as a writer of secondary import, a lesser Romantic coming at the end of the movement's heroic phase. For the First World War generation, however, Baudelaire became more than a major figure: he was hailed as the originator of modernism and his poetry came to eclipse that of the heroic Romantics (Lamartine, Vigny, Hugo), who now seemed pallid in comparison. The reevaluation of Baudelaire thus accompanied a crucial reorienting of aesthetic values and the birth of the literary sensibility that we call modern.

The questions I seek to investigate in this book circle around the relationship between poetry and literary history. Walter Benjamin once claimed that Baudelaire's poetry was unique because of its self-conscious historical character: "His work cannot merely be categorized as historical, like anyone else's, but it intended to be so and understood itself as such" ("Motifs": 162). This observation seems consistent with the foregoing outline of Baudelaire's role in the formulation of twentieth-century modernism. *Les Fleurs du mal* must be read both as a work and as a kind of epoch-making critical event, as a literary-historical phenomenon which is less poetry per se than the myth of poetry. The reading of Baudelaire in the twentieth century has borne out Benjamin's claim in more than one instance. Just as the period of the First World War was accompanied by an intense rethinking of literary values, the Second World War prompted a similar type of questioning, and Baudelaire's standing in the field of literary history was once again brought under scrutiny. In 1944, Jean-Paul Sartre wrote his essay on Baudelaire, and the work set off a controversy of epic proportions. Sartre's philosophy of engagement pitted itself against the modernist myth of poetry, and lost. Baudelaire emerged from the battle in crisis-proof form—the consensus was that modernist poetry could not be subjected to ethical evaluation or even to the gaze of history. The paradoxical relationship of modernism to historical pressures thus became apparent: although it was the product of historical revisionism and crisis, modernism itself proved resistant to reevaluation. In a fascinating shift of historical perspective, Sartre's attempt

Introduction

to update the profile of Baudelaire was rejected as a reactionary undertaking.

It occurs to me, in reflecting on this scenario, that many of the implications of Baudelaire's situation in twentieth-century literary history have gone unrecognized. To begin with, the reaction against Sartre's essay was so intense that no one seemed to realize the historical ironies it revealed. Instead, the debate exacerbated a sense that literary criticism had to choose between two irreconcilable paths—on the one hand a historicist path (or a path we would now call historicist) which took into account biographical data and questions of context, and on the other hand a formalist position which upheld the prerogatives of pure poetry. After that point, to think about modernism in historical terms proved to be a heretical activity, an illegitimate transgressing of limits. The tension between two ways of viewing literature had become an obdurate opposition.

It is interesting that Theodor Adorno, in his 1962 essay "Commitment," associated this critical impasse with a cold-war mentality. He spoke of the opposition between what he dubbed "Sartrean goats" and "Valéryean sheep," and lamented the loss of a productive antagonism between the two: "Between these two poles the tension in which art has lived in every age till now is dissolved," he wrote (p. 178). Adorno's contention was that the positions represented by Sartre and Valéry could not so easily be separated, that committed art and art for art's sake were mutually dependent. This is the contention that I examine in the opening chapters of this book, with a particular focus on the reading of Baudelaire. I begin by investigating Paul Valéry's 1922 essay "Situation de Baudelaire," which codified the modernist profile of Baudelaire, and proceed to a discussion of Sartre's Baudelaire book and the controversy that surrounded it. By underscoring the resemblances between these two apparently opposing critical moments, I hope to give a different emphasis to the history of modernism in our century. The balancing act is a delicate one, because modernism, as I have mentioned, exists in an uneasy relationship to its own historicity. My tendency has been to rehabilitate Sartre, to demonstrate the ways in which Valéry's Baudelaire foreshadows Sartre's. This is not only because

Sartre's position has been suppressed in the history of modernism, but also because I believe that position is more fully aware of its own internal contradictions. Although Sartre's aggressive, polemical style seems to leave little room for nuance, his insistence upon the concept of bad faith places the question of self-contradiction at the center of his analysis.

Much of my own analysis involves a rethinking of bad faith along the lines that Adorno has drawn. Rather than suppose, as contemporary literary history has done, that bad faith is a strictly ethical concept pertaining to the philosophy of engagement, I have argued that bad faith must be understood in terms of the tension between engagement and aestheticism that Adorno regretted losing. If art indeed lives in such tension, this may explain why Baudelaire's bad faith was so productive of poetry. I have traced the structures of bad faith through Valéry's reading of Baudelaire back to Baudelaire's own poetry and aesthetic theories. My ultimate contention is that the modernist consciousness is a consciousness in bad faith, and that Baudelaire's privileged place in the history of modernism exists because of his bad faith, not in spite of it.

In order to appreciate how much this contention goes against the grain of high modernism, it would be useful to review the tenets of that position. The theory of high modern art is predicated upon notions of aesthetic authenticity. Such authenticity is guaranteed by a series of exclusions: art defines its authentic essence by excluding extra-aesthetic subject matter (be that matter ethical, historical, or scientific); the various arts in turn define themselves by excluding one another and exploring the possibilities of their independent media. This view of aesthetic authenticity has come to be associated with Kantian philosophy and its overall critical project. Although there are many commentaries on the relationship between Kant and aesthetic modernism, the most concise statement I have found on the topic is one made by Clement Greenberg in his essay "Modernist Painting":

Modernism includes more than just art and literature. . . . I identify Modernism with the intensification, almost the exacerbation, of this self-critical tendency that began with the philosopher Kant. Because he was the first to criticize the means itself of criticism, I conceive of Kant as the first real Modernist.

The essence of Modernism lies, as I see it, in the use of the characteristic methods of a discipline to criticize the discipline itself—not in order to subvert it, but to entrench it more firmly in its area of competence. (p. 193)

Although Greenberg's analysis focuses on painting, and Manet is established as the inaugural figure who sets aesthetic modernism on its way, the same arguments are used by Valéry in his discussion of modern poetry. Baudelaire is crucial to this discussion because his poetry is self-critical and thereby seeks to purify itself of alien elements. The result is a poetry that at last may be called "pure poetry" (this is Valéry's epithet for *Les Fleurs du mal*) and whose claims to aesthetic authenticity are justified. Throughout "Situation de Baudelaire," Valéry consistently associates pure poetry and modernity. In order for pure poetry to come into being, it must break with the past. For Baudelaire this meant distinguishing himself in a radical manner from his Romantic predecessors. Valéry calls this need to break with the past Baudelaire's "reason of state" and thereby distinguishes it from a mere psychological necessity. According to this line of thought, pure poetry is either modern or it does not exist at all—its very existence depends upon an imperative newness which seems to underwrite its authenticity.

My critique of this high modern position begins with the observation that the concept of authenticity cannot be sustained by the imperative for self-distinction. Sartre's work on Baudelaire gives ample demonstration of this fact, albeit from a psychological perspective. For Sartre, Baudelaire's pretensions to originality, his cultivation of dandified manners, and his declarations of solitude all masked the painful suspicion that he was not unique after all. If he had an authentic nature or an essence, this was something he could experience only through the eyes of others, not for himself. Baudelaire's bad faith stemmed from this predicament: he needed others in order to become himself, and could never fully acknowledge his dependency. His claims to authenticity actually deepened his bad faith; his authenticity was undermined by its very affirmation.

A similar logic may be applied to the discussion of modernism and to Valéry's portrayal of Baudelaire. The imperative to be new, which seems to give rise to authentic works of art, can also undermine their claims to authenticity. The very concept of modernity implies a relative mode of being—the new is defined in relation to the old. Modern art can never fully attain to the condition of authenticity since it can never fully contain its definition within itself. It may be that Valéry recognized this when he chose to speak of Baudelaire's reason of state. The imperative that gave rise to Baudelaire's poetry was a reason devoid of conceptual content: *Les Fleurs du mal* sought not to be this or that type of poetry, but simply to be. And in order to be, Baudelaire's poetry had to be different. In defining itself relative to other poetic accomplishments, pure poetry betrayed its authentic pretensions. This is the conclusion that was *not* drawn by the first readers of "Situation de Baudelaire," and was only later examined by Benjamin.[1] The structures of bad faith motivate what might be called the tragic passion of pure poetry: in order to be, pure poetry must betray itself. To borrow from a Sartrean vocabulary, the existence and the essence of pure poetry are fatally opposed.

Within Baudelaire's own thinking the bad faith of the modernist consciousness is even more clearly displayed. There are moments when Baudelaire sounds decidedly post-Kantian in arguing for the strict specificity of aesthetic values. In one of the projected prefaces to *Les Fleurs du mal* he makes the following statement: "I know that the impassioned lover of fine style is exposed to the hatred of the multitude. But no human respect, no false modesty, no coalition, no universal suffrage will constrain me to speak this century's incomparable jargon, nor to confuse ink with virtue" (*OC*, 1: 181). While the distinction between ink and virtue, or between aesthetic and ethical concerns, is made here categorically, the modernity of Baudelaire's position is not so apparent. His cultivation of aesthetic purity is opposed to the progressive ideology of his contemporaries. If his position is aesthetically radical it is also politically reactionary. I argue that the modernist impulse in Baudelaire is always accompanied by its antithesis, that the radical and the reactionary

Introduction

consistently coincide in his thinking. The kind of historical irony that plagued Sartre's book on Baudelaire—the conversion of a progressive-minded project into a reactionary one—is something that Baudelaire would have understood very well. The extent to which Sartre found himself caught in this irony was an indication of the depth of his engagement with Baudelaire's aesthetic thought, rather than a measure of his obdurate philistinism.

In Baudelaire's case, the bad faith of his position meant that his claims to be engaged in the production of pure poetry could always be denied. There is, for example, the declaration he made to his *conseil judiciaire*, Narcisse Ancelle, almost a decade after *Les Fleurs du mal* had come to trial and been condemned as an offense to public morality: "Must I tell even you, who did not guess it any more than the others, that in this *atrocious* book I have put all my *heart*, all my *tenderness*, all my *religion* (travestied), all my *hatred*? It is true that I will write the contrary, that I will swear by the gods that it is a book of *pure art*, of *monkeyshines*, of *jugglery*, and I will be lying through my teeth" (C, 2: 610, letter dated Feb. 18, 1866; original emphasis).

This kind of frank self-contradiction was not available to Sartre, but in a similar vein one could argue that the ethical focus of his work on Baudelaire blurs strangely, leaving open the question of his intentions. In the minds of many readers (probably the majority), Sartre had no interest in Baudelaire's aesthetic accomplishments and no sympathy for the man. Philip Thody expressed this view succinctly when he wrote, "There is little doubt that [Sartre] would have preferred Baudelaire to have been a third-rate early Socialist pamphleteer rather than a first-rate lyrical poet" (p. 148). For others, however, Sartre's book is a masterpiece of sympathetic identification and aesthetic insight. Annie Cohen-Solal paraphrased the last line of Baudelaire's poem "Au lecteur" (To the reader) in her description of this "important, strong, and largely misunderstood book in which Charles Baudelaire appears as Sartre's double, his kin, his brother" (p. 378).[2] Benjamin Suhl went even further by calling the work "the only monument possible" to Baudelaire (n. 63, p. 149). These contradictory reactions are not simply the result of careless reading. They point to a peculiar, self-negating mechanism that seems to infect Sartre's thinking when he speaks of Baudelaire. It is very tempting, and not at all inaccurate, to see Sartre as answering Baudelaire's request for a "hypocritical reader," one who would confirm his kinship to the author of *Les Fleurs du mal* by denying it. The concept of bad faith characterizes this reader-author relationship even more accurately than that of hypocrisy, since hypocrisy implies a greater degree of self-awareness or intentionality.[3] My sense is that Sartre lost himself in reading Baudelaire, that his intentions became rigorously undecipherable even to himself.

By departing from the canonical story, which interprets the struggle between Sartre and Baudelaire as a confrontation between pure poetry and the enemy of art, I intend to set the stage for a rethinking of Baudelaire's aesthetics. If we admit the possibility of a fraternal intimacy between Baudelaire and Sartre, or between pure poetry and its enemy, how might this affect our reading of *Les Fleurs du mal*? This is the question I address in Chapters 3 and 4. Whereas the high modernist reading of Baudelaire focuses on notions of aesthetic purity and self-critique, my reading emphasizes problems of aesthetic indeterminacy and what I call the poetry's self-caricaturizing mechanism. In Chapter 3 I examine Baudelaire's two prefatory poems, "Au lecteur" and "Epigraphe pour un livre condamné" (Epigraph for a condemned book), as keys to rethinking the aesthetic character of *Les Fleurs du mal*. These are "contractual" texts, ones in which Baudelaire establishes the conditions under which his poetry ought to be read. The reader who complies with such conditions will be rewarded with understanding. The one who does not comply will understand nothing and receive the poet's malediction. As Baudelaire says in "Epigraphe," "Jette! tu n'y comprendrais rien . . ." (Throw the book away! You won't understand a word . . .) and "Plains-moi! . . . Sinon, je te maudis!" (Pity me! . . . If you don't, I'll curse you!). Briefly, my argument is that the contractual poems mark the insertion of pure poetry in an intersubjective economy of meaning which threatens its authentic character. The threat is realized in an undercurrent of violence—this is poetry that curses and is cursed—which attests to the persistence of an alien subject (in this case the reader) whom the poet cannot fully purge or reduce to a modality of the self. Outside the contractual poems, the alien presence can be traced in what Barbara Johnson has called the "dialogical structure of most of *Les Fleurs du mal*" (p. 60). Although the relationship between an "I" and a "you" is common in lyric poetry, in Baudelaire it is experienced as both an obsession and an embarrassment, one which he attempts to cover over with violence. This is expressed in the sadomasochistic dynamic of a poem like "L'Héautontimorouménos" (The self-tormentor) in which the second person disappears, and the violence of the opening line "Je te frapperai" (I will strike you) is turned against the poet himself—"Je suis la victime et le bourreau" (I am the victim and the executioner). Johnson accounts for this twist by writing that "the second person is not really another person but the personification of the alterity of the self" (p. 60). The reduction of the other to the self, or an elimination of the I-you dialogue, is clearly a goal of the violence in "L'Héautontimorouménos." I would nuance Johnson's reading, however, by adding that the operation is never complete: *Les Fleurs du mal* never overcomes the dialogical structure that threatens the poetry's intelligibility. The violence of the poetic contract cannot be purged by a "purer" violence, one which would eliminate the other by destroying the self.

In the high modernist portrait of Baudelaire such a pure violence would be understood as the self-critiquing moment of authentic poetry. In my reading, the impure violence that I attribute to *Les Fleurs du mal* (impure because it never succeeds in negating itself) is related to the poetry's capacity for self-caricature. Far from leading to a purification of the poetic medium and the definition of specific poetic properties, the caricatural mechanism of *Les Fleurs du mal* displays the poetry's inspecificity and openness to extra-textual determinations (e.g., its acknowledgment of the reader's role in investing it with meaning): just as "Epigraphe pour un livre condamné" can be read as a reduction and caricature of "Au lecteur," others of *Les Fleurs du mal* can be seen as alternative renderings of each other, tragic and comic, pathetic and ironic, by turns. This kind of indeterminacy must be taken into account if we are to articulate the concept of Baudelaire's aesthetics; and such indeterminacy may be linked to the structure of bad faith which, as Sartre tells us, is accompanied by a "fundamental impossibility of taking oneself entirely seriously" (*L'Etre et le néant*: 102).

In Chapter 4 I extend my analysis of poetic caricature to account for one of Baudelaire's most successful mystifications, his claim that *Les Fleurs du mal* could only be understood by readers who managed to unlock the poetry's "secret architecture." The force of such a claim is, once again, to remove the locus of meaning outside the individual poem: the prefatory pieces and the secret architecture together constitute an external rule of intelligibility for the poetry. Through my reading of the poem "Danse macabre," I argue that Baudelaire's secret architecture becomes a caricature of poetry as such, by pointing up the inability of poetry to totalize meaning within itself. The tone of high seriousness with which Baudelaire and his advocates, like Barbey d'Aurevilly, speak of the secret architecture, the way in which the architecture seems to produce a tremendous intensification of meaning, can be interpreted as the flip side of a caricature that divests its subject of meaning. This convergence of gravity and levity is, of course, symptomatic of bad faith: I venture to say that it constitutes the aesthetic character of bad faith, or even that it constitutes bad faith as an aesthetic character.[4]

Reading *Les Fleurs du mal* in search of an architecture should produce rather different results than reading the poetry from modernist premises. As codified by Valéry, the modernist view of Baudelaire privileges the poem "Correspondances," which is taken to represent in miniature the sum of Baudelaire's poetics. Henri Peyre has argued in his book *What Is Symbolism?* that the valorization of "Correspondances" and the designation of Baudelaire as a precursor of the Symbolist aesthetic was the work of twentieth-century literary historians (I follow up this contention in my discussion of Valéry).[5] What is intriguing about the critical moment Peyre diagnoses is the way that it reproduces in its own operation the symbolic character it attributes to Baudelaire: "Correspondances" is set in a symbolic relationship to the rest of Baudelaire's oeuvre by becoming the part that contains the whole within itself; this critical act of symbolization takes place at the same time that the notion of *correspondances* comes to represent the symbol itself. I argue in Chapter 4 that an architectural reading of *Les Fleurs du mal* works against this kind of dual symbolization. Viewed architecturally, other, aesthetically less successful poems than "Correspondances" begin to acquire critical importance: in my own reading, "J'aime le souvenir de ces époques nues" (I love the memory of those naked epochs) and "L'Ennemi" are seen to be significant for the position they occupy in *Les Fleurs du mal*, although they hardly fulfill an aesthetic ideal for poetry. In other words, an architectural reading reveals a disparity between poetic meaning and poetic beauty, a disparity which prevents any individual poem from standing symbolically for Baudelaire's poetry as a whole. Instead, meaning and beauty approach one another without quite coinciding (this is particularly apparent for a poem like "J'aime le souvenir"), thus marking the failure of symbolic synthesis.

Such a reading is closely linked to my analysis in Chapter 1, where I discuss the problem of aesthetic difference in Valéry's description of Baudelaire's poetics. Valéry's attempt to remake Baudelaire in the Symbolist image never succeeds in defining *Les Fleurs du mal* as an aesthetic totality: the symbolic correspondence of what Valéry calls "le son et le sens" (O, 1: 611) (and what I have called beauty and meaning) is always deferred in Baudelaire. Aesthetic difference is thus experienced as a temporal suspension of symbolic fulfillment. It should not surprise us then to find that the architecture of *Les Fleurs du mal* engages a thematics of temporality: such a thematics runs directly counter to the totalizing claims of the symbol, demonstrating these to be in bad faith. For Valéry, the temporal threat to the symbol's good faith is not quite conscious: it occurs in his need to locate the aesthetic experience of Baudelaire's poetry in memory. For a reader like Benjamin, the temporal dimension of Baudelairean *correspondances* is affirmed explicitly, and explicitly distinguished from Symbolist aesthetics: "There are no simultaneous correspondences [in Baudelaire], such as were cultivated by the symbolists later. The murmur of the past may be heard in the correspondences, and the canonical experience of them has its place in a previous life" ("Motifs": 182). With typical economy, Benjamin affirms here two distinctions at once: first, and most obviously, he reopens the historical distance that Valéry had closed off between Baudelaire and the Symbolists; and second, he discerns within the Baudelairean symbol itself a temporal difference, "the murmur of the past." This dual distinction openly undoes the dual symbolization that Peyre points to in Baudelaire's twentieth-century reception.

In the closing chapter, Benjamin appears more directly in my work as I discuss his critical appraisal of Baudelaire's denunciation of photography in the *Salon de 1859*. Although my argument offers a critique of Benjamin's critique, it does so from a thoroughly Benjaminian perspective: whereas Benjamin saw in Baudelaire's denunciation an error of judgment, I have seen the attempt to articulate an allegorical temporality. Rather than accuse Baudelaire of having betrayed modernism by reacting against the aesthetic claims of photography, I have argued that his reaction is symptomatic of an effort to understand the conditions of possibility of modernism. In the chapter "Modernism" from "The Paris of the Second Empire in Baudelaire," Benjamin praises Baudelaire for the allegorical insight that enables him to see modernity as a kind of antiquity.[6] This insight is still operating in Baudelaire's discussion of photography, which he treats as both novel and primitive. If we are to take seriously Benjamin's characterization of Baudelaire as an allegorist, then we should not be surprised to find here, as elsewhere, a reactionary moment at the heart of Baudelaire's most progressive aesthetic insights. The allegorical perspective unleashes this kind of temporal paradox by revealing modernism's bad faith, particularly in relationship to its own historicity (high modernism both posits and hides from its own historical specificity).

Another symptom of allegory can thus be seen in a peculiar destabilization of historical terminology. This occurs in the *Salon de 1859* with Baudelaire's treatment of "The Queen of Faculties": the imagination. The imagination, which is typically affiliated with a Romantic aesthetics, is enlisted by Baudelaire to defend the Classical conventions of art. Valéry runs into a similar disturbance in the Classic/Romantic distinction as he attempts to classify Baudelaire's poetry. Although Valéry does not formulate the issue as such, his essay demonstrates that the unequivocal modernity of *Les Fleurs du mal* is linked to an equivocal presentation of historical categories. It is worth noting, too, that although both Valéry in "Situation de Baudelaire" and Baudelaire in the *Salon de 1859* use a post-Kantian framework for their arguments, the former produces a modernist aesthetic perspective while the latter is perceived as reactionary. This reveals an overarching allegorical structure in the history of Baudelaire's reception: if the relationship between post-Kantianism and modernism is not a necessary one, then the grounds upon which Baudelaire has been promoted to the fountainhead of literary modernism are not stable. Other histories of Baudelaire may be told, remain open for the telling. The canonical story of Baudelaire's aesthetic success is rigorously an allegory, since it retains the potential to reverse its own narrative.[7] Put another way, the story cannot transcend its own temporality: it itself is engaged in a temporal predicament even as it recounts the flight of Baudelaire's poetry from the temporal into the symbolic realm.

From the preceding observations we may conclude that Benjamin's work on Baudelaire has already gone far to critique the modernist profile of the author. If the extent of the critique has not generally been recognized, this may be due to the fact that Benjamin has been more influential in comparatist circles than in strictly French ones. There is also the obvious difficulty of his work which, combined with a certain asystematic character, has made the work hard to situate in the context of Baudelaire criticism, most of which is quite polemical and explicit as to its methodological orientation. Nevertheless, if we begin simply with Benjamin's designation of Baudelaire as an allegorist, and if we remember that, since Goethe, allegory and symbol have been opposed to one another in discussions of the aesthetic, then the subversive character of Benjamin's subtle work becomes apparent.⁸ It is almost brazen to cast the father of Symbolism as an allegorist, to take the patron saint of twentieth-century modernism and return him to his nineteenth-century context, to the Paris of the Second Empire. Because I do not discuss Benjamin's work at length in this book, I would like to summarize here what I see as unsynthesized aspects of his influence on Baudelaire studies.

Broadly speaking, post-Benjaminian criticism of Baudelaire falls into two categories. The first category could be called historicist criticism since it seeks an understanding of Baudelaire in relation to nineteenth-century social conditions and currents of thought. Richard Burton's *Baudelaire and the Second Republic* represents this critical trend most thoroughly. Burton's preface gives an extremely helpful overview of historicist work on Baudelaire, so I need not repeat his exposition here. I simply mention his comment that most of this work has been done by German scholars and that their focus has been on the years 1848–1851, since these are the years in which Baudelaire seemed to take an active interest in political events. (After Louis Napoléon's coup d'état in 1851, Baudelaire said he had been "physically depoliticized" (C, 1: 188). What the historicist trend avoids in Benjamin is the critical confrontation with allegory. This is not surprising because, as we have seen, allegory involves a disturbance of historical categories. The indeterminacy of Baudelaire's aesthetic thought (Is it radical or reactionary?) is also evident in his political thinking, making it difficult to interpret his historical significance in any simple manner. Burton acknowledges this difficulty but suggests the following solution in a reading of the prose poem "Assommons les pauvres" (Let's beat up the poor):

It is perhaps as an anticipation of this *fin de siècle* meeting of the categories of "left" and "right" and their eventual amalgamation in something close to fascism that the historical significance of "Assommons les pauvres" may be said to lie. The very fact that the text can be plausibly interpreted either as an incitement to revolutionary violence (in a left-wing, proto-Marxist sense) or as a nihilistic *reductio ad absurdum* of all forms of leftism already locates it at or close to the point—so fateful for the twentieth century—where the opposition between left and right ceases to be operable. (p. 363)

The historical method has here been turned most intriguingly on its head. The attempt to determine the meaning of Baudelaire's corpus by situating it within its socio-political context has resulted in a sudden reversal: now Baudelaire is seen, not as the reflection, but as the anticipation of a historical reality. One could say that his poetry has been invested with the power of *generating* the context in which it would find meaning. This kind of reversal resembles others I examine in various efforts to "situate" Baudelaire: once Valéry has located Baudelaire's canonical position, Baudelaire can become the "author" of subsequent poetic productions including Valéry's; once Benjamin has read *Les Fleurs du mal* then he may claim that the poetry engenders its own readership. At issue is a suspension, or a reversal, of determination, similar to what I discuss in Chapter 3, with my reading of "Le Soleil" (The sun). As Baudelaire's poetry engages with historical determinants, these become subject to the peculiar mechanism I have called "caricatural." Since the analogy between poetry and context is not fully conceptualized, it remains unstable; the historical ground can, as a consequence, lose its gravity and become the airy projection of poetry. To return to Sartrean terminology, facticity and freedom interpenetrate with the indeterminacy characteristic of faith; this explains the metaphysical lightness ("légèreté métaphysique")[9] that can suddenly relieve the historical fact of its weightiness. What we have here is not an instance of pure poetic freedom as it might be understood from a post-Kantian perspective, however. As I argue at the end of Chapter 3, the caricatural mechanism that "lightens" facticity does not thereby transcend it: a caricatural aesthetics, while it critiques its situation, remains situated.

The attempt to think through the kind of reversal I have just outlined has given rise to the second category of post-Benjaminian criticism on Baudelaire. Although this type of criticism is also concerned with historical and sociological questions, it sees these as aesthetically mediated: hence the emphasis on the concept of allegory, whose aesthetic impurities enable referential and representational concerns to intervene in the articulation of a poetics. Clearly, my own work is sympathetic to this critical trend. The risk of such a criticism is that allegory can become a kind of catch-all concept where, to quote Baudelaire, "accounts, poems, love letters, and legal briefs" are subsumed together in an unthought relationship.[10] In other words, this second type of criticism runs the risk of the first, with the added disadvantage that one might learn less along the way. At its best, however, the investigation of allegory has produced work that cuts closest to the bone of Baudelairean aesthetics.

Hans Robert Jauß, in his analysis of Baudelaire's second "Spleen" poem, locates allegory at the site of several mediations—between text and context, or between poetics and aesthetics (to borrow the distinction Paul de Man uses in his critique of Jauß).[11] While Jauß claims that there is no "objective mimetic relation" between text and context in Baudelaire's case, *Les Fleurs du mal* can still be read as a concrete reflection of social-historical processes "through the subjective mediation of an allegorical meaning" (p. 173). This is what Jauß sees as happening when Benjamin reads a collapse of the forces of production into "Rêve parisien" (Parisian dream), or when Wolfgang Fietkau sees a response to Louis Napoléon's coup d'état in "Le Cygne" (The swan). The allegory refers without representing, thereby describing a crucial split in linguistic function: reference is redeemed at the expense of representation. For Jauß this implies simultaneously a redemption of the historical-materialist method of interpretation. The inability to synthesize linguistic functions that my work traces and that characterizes the allegorical mode is in evidence here. There is also an important slippage in the concept of allegory from a specific feature of Baudelaire's poetry into an interpretive method: allegoresis. Jauß' discussion moves indifferently from one to the other, with an ease that should not surprise us if we take seriously Baudelaire's claims that his poetry depends upon its readership in order to *be*: in other words, Baudelaire's poetics itself slips towards an aesthetics, that is, towards a calculation of reader response which presents the poetic fact as always/already interpreted.

It might be useful here to summarize de Man's critique of Jauß, not so much with a view to its overall implications, but with a specific focus on the question of Baudelairean allegory. For de Man, it is possible to speak of allegory and something like historical materialism in the same breath, but not because of the "subjective mediation" that Jauß appeals to:

> Allegory is material or materialistic, in Benjamin's sense, because its dependence on the letter, on the literalism of the letter, cuts it off sharply from symbolic and aesthetic syntheses. "The subject of allegory can only be called a grammatical subject"... Allegory names the rhetorical process by which the literary text moves from a phenomenal, world-oriented to a grammatical, language-oriented direction. It thus also names the moment when aesthetic and poetic values part company. (Introduction to Jauß, *Toward an Aesthetic*: xxiii)

Where Jauß' allegoresis involves a convergence of "aesthetic and poetic values," de Man's allegory names the moment when these part company. The grammatical subject of allegory must not, in de Man's estimation, be confused with the phenomenal subject of consciousness, that is, with the subject of an aesthetics whose domain is that of the sensory or the perceptual. For de Man, Jauß' theory of reception is fundamentally an aesthetics: its emphasis on the response of the reader indicates its dependence upon the phenomenal world of perception. When Jauß speaks of allegory, he does not have in mind the language-oriented concept that de Man privileges. De Man thus distinguishes between a classical concept of allegory (represented by Jauß) which is engaged with phenomenality, and a more radical concept which is not phenomenal but material, because of its "dependence on the letter." Ultimately, de Man will situate his own reading squarely in the second camp, so that one imagines he would not confer the name of allegory on what he has sketched out as the classical concept. De Manian allegory, under the aegis of Benjamin and Hegel, comes to stand in a constitutive opposition to all aesthetic syntheses.

The question becomes, where can we locate Baudelairean allegory in this critical nexus? It is true that Baudelaire, like Hegel, associates allegory with what we could call the grammatical subject. In *Le Poème du hachisch*, Baudelaire traces the process of intoxication in "a partly excitable, partly choleric temperament" (*OC*, 1: 429), and argues that such a process develops the allegorical sense ("l'intelligence de l'allégorie") to astonishing proportions (p. 430). The heightened allegorical intelligence transforms perceptions of every sort, including the perception of grammar: "Grammar, arid grammar itself, becomes something like an evocatory sorcery" (p. 431), Baudelaire writes. While the association between allegory and grammar is thus being made, it would be difficult to argue, as de Man does, that their affiliation has nothing to do with aesthetic delight. Under the spell of allegorical evocation, the parts of speech acquire a distinctly phenomenal allure: "Words resuscitate, clad with flesh and bones: the substantive, in its substantial majesty, the adjective, a transparent garment that clothes and colors it like a glaze, and the verb, an angel of movement, which sets the sentence in motion" (p. 431). Elsewhere, Baudelaire has claimed that the intelligent combination of grammatical parts—"such a substantive with such an adjective"—can express "any sensation of sweetness or bitterness, beatitude or horror" (*OC*, 1: 183). In other words, grammar can be aesthetically manipulated to produce a sensory response in the reader. In theory, at least, such an understanding of allegorical intelligence is a far cry from the one advanced by de Man: "Everyone has always known that allegory, like the commodity and unlike aesthetic delight, is, as Hegel puts it, 'icy and barren'" (Introduction to Jauß: xxiii).

We might turn to the poem "L'Ennemi," which I discuss in Chapter 4, to determine whether Baudelaire's practice of allegory corresponds to his theoretical program. Clearly, much of the poem could stand as an illustration of de Man's concept of allegory. On every level the poem resists aesthetic and symbolic syntheses. As the allegory of the seasons of life is developed according to a literal logic, the poem's representational coherence is destroyed. As the lyric subject attempts to engage in self-reflection, what it uncovers is an "obscure Enemy," which cannot be represented and which calls into question the limits of consciousness. The Enemy may thus be read as a grammatical subject, a name lacking in predicates ("obscure" in this sense would simply confirm the lack of specification) and resisting the recuperative efforts of the conscious subject. Does this mean, then, that the poem belies Baudelaire's own speculations on allegory? I argue that it does not, for reasons that are most apparent in the closing stanza:

> —Ô douleur! ô douleur! Le Temps mange la vie,
> Et l'obscur Ennemi qui nous ronge le coeur
> Du sang que nous perdons croît et se fortifie!
>
> —O woe! O woe! Time eats life,
> And the obscure Enemy that gnaws at our hearts
> From the blood that we lose grows and gains strength!

These lines have sent many exegetical wheels spinning in efforts to identify the Enemy. A large part of the mystery, I believe, stems from the overt parallelism between "Le Temps mange la vie" and "l'obscur Ennemi . . . nous ronge le coeur." Strangely, the figure whose meaning was perfectly clear becomes obscure as it is repeated and explicated. Both the figure and its repetition are allegorical, but each in a particular way. A distinction similar to the one de Man makes between a conventional and a radical mode of allegory might be useful in defining the differences. "Le Temps mange la vie" is readable because we recognize it as a conventional allegory and do not expect it to render up a sensory image of the phenomenal world. Instead, it functions much like the linguistic sign to designate an idea it in no way embodies.[12] What happens as the figure is repeated could be described as both a literalization *and* a phenomenalization (these are the two processes that de Man separates to mark the distance between himself and Jauß). The verb *manger*, which we first read figuratively, becomes literalized: the activity of ingestion is now depicted as a gruesome violence ("qui nous ronge le coeur") which draws blood.[13] There is nothing "icy and barren" about this final figure. It elicits a strong aesthetic response, albeit a negative one, which is actually heightened by the

Enemy's resistance to representation: we panic all the more because we know we are bleeding but we don't know where.[14] The repetition of the allegory makes it both less readable and more aesthetically powerful. All of this boils down to saying that a radical mode of allegory may be cut off from the symbolic synthesis of meaning and representation and still involve the aesthetic and the phenomenal in some way.

My reading of "L'Ennemi" suggests that the model of allegory at work in Baudelaire's poetry may be more complex than either Jauß or de Man acknowledge. If the poem describes a painful breakdown of the conscious subject, it also moves towards the affirmation of a collective identity: in the final stanza, the predicament of the isolated subject has become "our" predicament. To paraphrase de Man paraphrasing Hegel, the "I" of this poem may have trouble saying "I," but it has no problem saying "we."[15] In fact, the harder it is to say "I," the easier it is to say "we"; the more obscure "my" relationship is to the Enemy, the more transparent "my" relationship is to "you." There is a simultaneous loss and gain of symbolic synthesis as the poem's allegorical meaning unfolds. This is not the first time we have encountered this particular dual structure. Earlier I alluded to the peculiar dialogism of *Les Fleurs du mal*, where the "I-you" relationship describes a complex figure of partial syntheses; and in Chapter 1, Valéry's notion of *poésie pure* will be seen to involve the symbolic synthesis of sound and meaning at the expense of a connection between poetic and everyday language. A rigorous account of Baudelairean allegory would need to respond to this kind of dual articulation. Such an account would enable us to think more critically about Baudelaire's celebrated aesthetic dualism. I attempt something along these lines with the observation, in Chapter 1, that the symbolic reading of *Les Fleurs du mal* has produced, but not represented, a history of Baudelaire's poetry: in other words, the attempted elimination of aesthetic difference has resulted in an occulted historical difference. In light of the preceding analysis, this kind of dual structure could be called allegorical.

It is not surprising that many critics, in grappling with Baudelairean allegory, respond to its duality by postulating the existence of *two* allegories. De Man, as we have seen, initiates his discussion by distinguishing between a classical and a critical mode of allegory. Marie Maclean, in her book on Baudelaire's prose poems, defines what she calls "open" and "closed" allegory (p. 164). In "Mémoire et mélancolie," Ross Chambers analyzes the relationship between "a *contextualizing* conception of allegory" and "a *textualized* conception" as he sifts through different readings of "Le Cygne" (p. 175, original emphasis). Chambers' essay is worth examining more closely, because it focuses explicitly on the connection between a historical mode of interpretation and a text-based analysis that borrows its methods from semiotics and rhetorical reading.

"Le Cygne" lends itself particularly well to this type of investigation. It insists, more than any other of Baudelaire's poems, upon the absolute specificity of its context. With the line, "Comme je traversais le nouveau Carrousel" (As I was crossing the new Carrousel), the poem acquires an unusually exact location in time and space.[16] "What mattered to me," Baudelaire wrote in his dedicatory letter to Hugo, "was to capture quickly all the suggestive potential of an accident, an image . . ." (*OC*, 1: 1007). An accident being, by definition, the most specific of events, the accidental character of "Le Cygne" specifies its context with ultimate precision. (We might even speak of this poem as Baudelaire's one *oeuvre de circonstance*, provided that the term be understood with a kind of philosophical rigor.) At the same time, however, "Le Cygne" subjects its context to a relentless process of irrealization, or allegorization. "Je ne vois qu'*en esprit* tout ce camp de baraques, / Ces tas de chapiteaux ébauchés et de fûts . . ." (I only see *in spirit* this whole camp of huts, / These heaps of rough-hewn capitals and columns. . . , my emphasis). The décor of the new Carrousel, the site of the accident of "Le Cygne," only appears "in spirit." The poet claims, in the second part of the poem, that his obdurate melancholy transforms all objects of perception—"new palaces, scaffoldings, blocks, old suburbs"—into allegory. Things are thus no longer things, but ghostly signs that point to a meaning beyond themselves in what Chambers calls "a limitless semiosis" (p. 171). In sum, "Le Cygne" seems both to engage and to suspend the phenomenal world, tempting the critic to apply a mixed methodology to account for the poem's peculiarities.

Chambers' distinction between contextualizing and textual allegory corresponds roughly to the distinction between Jauß and de Man. The contextualizing tradition—which Chambers notes is practiced most frequently by "certain German-speaking critics" (p. 172)—sees in "Le Cygne" "an encoded but perfectly readable allusion to the political events of 1848–1851 and to their consequences" (p. 172). Contextualizing allegories are perfectly readable once one knows the code that would enable their deciphering. In this instance it is possible to read the figure of the escaped swan as an allegory of the working classes, whose members were released from an oppressed condition during the 1848 Revolution and took to the barricades, thus finding themselves, like the swan, *sur le pavé* (in the streets, with a connotation of homelessness). The expression "Comme les exilés, ridicule et sublime" (Like exiles, ridiculous and sublime) can be decoded similarly, as a reference to the difference between the Second and First Empires in France: the First was sublime, the Second ridiculous, echoing Napoléon's own adage "Du sublime au ridicule, il n'y a qu'un pas." While the game of decoding can become quite involved, its intricacies are never due to an inherent linguistic complexity. Understood as contextualizing allegory, the language of "Le Cygne" owes its indirection to political censorship, to the danger of 1859 of expressing solidarity with obstinate exiles like Hugo, or nostalgia for the events of 1848.

The linguistic indirection of *textual* allegory, on the other hand, is not due to external pressures. Chambers explicitly identifies this type of allegory with de Man and with those North American critics who have been influenced by him. Textual allegories get at meaning indirectly because they are constitutively incapable of containing the process of signification. Thus, the various figures in Baudelaire's poem—Andromaque, the swan, the negress, the orphans, the sailors—point to one another in an open-ended gesturing at meaning. It is impossible to say that one figure means another because we cannot isolate a single figure from the series and claim it as the final referent. Each figure is called upon, not only to *be* but to *mean*, and thus is marked by a kind of existential absence.

The subtlety of Chambers' reading is that he sees the two types of allegory as converging. Through the thematics of exile and memory, the political allegory points to an impossible desire, "un désir sans trêve," to return to a time or place which was always/already marked by absence and loss. The poet's fertile memory evokes many figures of the past, but these are all figures of exile who, in turn, must remember something they no longer have. The dynamics of memory in the poem, while they evoke a political context, may thus also be read as an allegory of the "limitless semiosis" that results from a purely textual analysis. Conversely, the endless search for meaning that is produced by the semiotic reading becomes a kind of meaning in itself, which in turn can be contextualized. As Chambers puts it, "If one cannot exhaust the limitless semiosis set off by the spectacle of the swan, the common characteristic of all these allegorical figures—their exile, the lack which irremediably corresponds to their desire—enables one to say that the swan still has a meaning. The meaning is this very impossibility of closure, this lack which belongs to the swan ("qui y *a sa place*"), as Derrida says in his critique of Lacan's "Seminar on *The Purloined Letter*" (p. 175, original emphasis). By attending to that elusive moment when the two allegories converge, Chambers has brought the discussion of Baudelairean allegory to its most developed point.[17]

This complex treatment of allegory is crucial to Chambers' analysis of the peculiar historical character of modernism. As Chambers sees it, modernism is characterized aesthetically by the semiotic open-endedness of textual allegory. It is this characteristic that leaves modernism vulnerable to charges of meaningless game-playing or nihilism. To counter such charges, Chambers argues that "the new 'open' textuality that characterizes literary modernism is inseparable from a contextualizing self-referentiality which requires the reader to grasp this very textuality in terms of a historical moment" (p. 175). The self-referential gesture of the modernist text is thus understood as simultaneously "contextualizing," as containing indirectly a kind of historical consciousness.

The critical challenge becomes to *think* the modernist moment because, as I have argued, such a moment both posits and conceals its historicity. We cannot grasp its historical character simply by wanting to—some indirection is required in order to seize for understanding a moment which obliterates its own conditions of possibility. It is for this reason that a contextualized reading of modernism cannot be identical to a more traditional study of literature in context. What Chambers calls "a contextualizing self-referentiality" does not produce meaning by the placing of text in context; rather, it produces context through self-reference, leaving context as a byproduct of the hermeneutic process.

This may explain why it is easy to produce different contexts for Baudelaire's poetry. My own study of Baudelaire's canonization emphasizes a twentieth-century context, as does Burton's analysis of "Assommons les pauvres." Fredric Jameson makes the case for a multitude of contexts in the opening of his article "Baudelaire as Modernist and Postmodernist." Thus, even the historicization of Baudelaire is open to a kind of aesthetic free play. There is evidence of this free play in Baudelaire's own historical self-consciousness. His denunciation of photography, for example, can be read as an anti-modernist *prise de position*; or, it can be read as an exercise of aesthetic freedom in the face of historical determinants. Under the pressure of denunciation, photography becomes, not the material condition of aesthetic innovation, but the symptom of aesthetic regression, and Baudelaire's own position modulates from reactionary to progressive. By insisting on the primitive, cultic character of the photograph, Baudelaire produces an alternative context both for himself and for the object of his evaluation. With this free production of context, Baudelaire's denunciation reveals a modernist intuition despite the anti-modernism of its ostensible content. Its historical character is both self-conscious and indeterminate, a combination that I argue is implicit in Chambers' definition of modernism.

In order to demonstrate that this is, indeed, the historical character of modernism, we will need to look at Chambers' closing discussion of the cogito as it appears in "Le Cygne." The expression "je pense" (I think) occurs at both the beginning and the end of the poem. For Chambers, this expression is an invitation to read "Le Cygne" in conjunction with a Cartesian notion of the subject and of consciousness. The Cartesian cogito describes a subject that, according to Chambers, is "autonomous and compact," while the subject of "Le Cygne" is dispersed and approaches self-understanding only through the mediation of "the vast community of exiles" (p. 183). Baudelaire's poem is modern because it calls into question the autonomy of consciousness.

While Chambers claims that the difference between an autonomous and a decentered subject is a historical difference, his analysis clearly shows that more is at stake in the distinction. By organizing the historical scenario in terms of cognition, Chambers enables the historical difference to be judged according to a true-or-false system of evaluation. Under these circumstances, the classical cogito fares badly. If the cogito can lay claim to autonomy, this is only because it fails to recognize its own duplicity. The truth we are dealing with here is that consciousness is always unhappy, that the effort to seize the self for cognition will always divide the self from itself. So, if the subject thinks it is autonomous, it is in truth deluded, even hypocritical, "if by hypocritical we mean 'unconscious of its own duplicity'" (p. 184). Interestingly, then, the cogito finds itself in a condition of epistemological uncertainty—it is consciousness bought at the price of unconsciousness. This condition is also culpable. By calling the subject of the cogito "hypocritical," Chambers implies that it is somehow responsible for its predicament, that it is not purely and simply determined by historical circumstances.

The modern subject, in contrast, gains a kind of ethical stature by waking up to the duplicities of consciousness. It cannot overcome these duplicities, but at least it acknowledges them and, in so doing, it cleanses itself of responsibility. One is reminded of Baudelaire's own praise of "la conscience dans le Mal" (consciousness in Evil) in "L'Irrémédiable." It is apt that the plight of the modern subject be figured by a swan, with its connotations of purity and innocence. It is similarly fortunate that, in French, the textual play between *cygne* and *signe* enables Chambers to transpose the duplicities of consciousness into an allegory of signification: "What has left its cage with the publication of this poem, and what can never again be restrained, repressed, returned to its cage, is precisely *the duplicitous character of signs*, a character that the text itself displays in exemplary fashion" (p. 185, my emphasis). Once duplicity is seen as an inevitable function of signification, then the duplicitous subject can no longer be incriminated. Despite the fatal separation of the subject from itself, there is a kind of lyrical liberation associated with the failure of the cogito: something has fled from its cage and, in Chambers' words, it can never again be confined, repressed, or put back. Consciousness is still unhappy, but it has become a *happy* unhappy consciousness in a successful act of failed cognition. Although it is never possible to rid the subject of its epistemological uncertainty, it is possible to be acutely conscious of such uncertainty. What characterizes the modern subject, then, is a simultaneous gain and loss of cognition. The historical consciousness of modernism is fundamentally paradoxical, caught between knowing and not knowing.

As I have mentioned, the modern subject cannot be understood (better yet, its paradoxes cannot be resolved) simply by placing it in context. It is true that the modern subject recognizes its historical entrapment. All Baudelaire's exiles in "Le Cygne" are victims of history, whether they are prisoners of war, playthings of empire, or both. But as Chambers notes, the figure of entrapment in the poem is itself infected with the paradoxes of the subject: the swan's flight from its cage is a liberation which is also an entrapment, and the two movements can never be separated. By *recognizing* its historical entrapment, the modern subject is also exercising a freedom. Even when Chambers argues for the situation of "Le Cygne" in a Second Empire context, the cognitive paradoxes remain. In fact, the Second Empire ultimately functions as another figure of duplicity which both knows and does not know itself. Far from serving as the historical ground which will stabilize the semiotic indeterminacy of

Baudelaire's poem, the Second Empire is itself lacking historical grounding: it is the inauthentic empire par excellence, a false semblance of other empires. The historical meaning that is produced by placing "Le Cygne" in such a context can only be expressed as a crisis of historical meaning.

The complexities that arise from the attempt to historicize modernism can be understood quite simply. The modern subject, in order to define itself as such, must have an uneasy relationship to its own historicity. Modernism requires both the recognition and the refusal of historical location. If there is no refusal of history there can be no modernism, no production (however mystified) of the irreducibly new. To return to the vocabulary I have used throughout my work, the historical consciousness of modernism must be in bad faith. This is why Chambers' analysis finally turns upon what Sartre would call the amphibological concepts of innocent duplicity or genuine (because historically localizable) inauthenticity. The self-deceiving movement of consciousness accepts the power of history to exculpate but resists its power to determine.

In Chambers' allegorization of the modern subject, this movement of consciousness is equivalent to the flight of the swan. The flight is a flight from one mode of self-deception (hypocrisy) into another, more unstable mode. This other mode, which I affiliate with bad faith, is more difficult to define because its self-difference infects the very categories of definition. A hypocrite, for example, may not be what he seems; but hypocrisy does not disturb the categorical distinction between being and appearance. The flight of the swan is another matter. It mobilizes a whole series of distinctions: freedom becomes enslavement, self becomes other, past becomes present. As the swan flees its cage in the purest effort at self-coincidence, "le coeur plein de son beau lac natal," it becomes the emblem of an inevitable alienation, "mythe étrange et fatal," estranged from itself in its affirmation of self.[18] The conceptual instability that is set in motion by the swan's flight returns us to the problematics of bad faith.

It is remarkable that Chambers should rediscover bad faith in his historicist reading of Baudelaire. Sartre was accused by many critics, including himself, of neglecting history and relying too heavily upon an atemporal articulation of bad faith in *Baudelaire*. Chambers' essay, however, demonstrates that Sartre's "amphibological concept" is still at work in the most recent attempts to rethink Baudelaire and his crucial relationship to modernism. This suggests that Sartre did indeed grasp Baudelaire's poetry in its historicity and that bad faith may serve as a kind of Ariadne's thread, enabling one to trace a complex interrelationship between art and history. The following pages are devoted to exploring the consequences of this thesis, both for the reading of Baudelaire and for the understanding of his historical place.

CHAPTER ONE

The Two Baudelaires
Valéry's Canonization of 'Les Fleurs du mal'

Few, if any, French authors are in a position to rival Charles Baudelaire for the role he plays in what we might call the canon of French letters. His poetry and his quirky critical essays are crucial to most histories of modern art in Europe. "Today there is general agreement that *Les Fleurs du mal* are one of the living sources, doubtless the principal source, of the contemporary movement in poetry." This was Marcel Raymond's assessment in 1933, and the arguments he derived from it in *De Baudelaire au surréalisme* (p. 11) have become the standard fare of literary histories since that time: through Baudelaire, one can make sense both of divergent poetic movements in France (from Mallarmé to Rimbaud, and Valéry to Breton), and of literary innovations outside the country (T. S. Eliot, in pointing to Baudelaire's work as his own "living source," called it "the greatest example of modern poetry in any language"[1]). It is difficult to imagine what histories of aesthetic modernism would look like, what story they would tell, without Baudelaire to mark their opening chapter.

Given this situation, students of Baudelaire are often surprised to find how shaky his reputation could be among his nineteenth-century contemporaries. Of course, it is common for truly novel poetry to shock or annoy, at least initially. But in Baudelaire's case, the surprising fact is that he irritated so many readers with what they perceived as his banality: "As if Baudelaire had discovered or invented vice, as if vice itself had only been born yesterday . . . he acquired a unique reputation for *Satanism*. . . ." Ferdinand Brunetière thus complained about Baudelaire's pretensions to originality: "He's only a roominghouse Satan, a table d'hôte Beelzebub. If you take away a half-dozen poems from *Les Fleurs du mal* . . . all that remain are clichés; and Baudelaire's procedures for renewing them owe less to *Satanism* than to old-fashioned rhetoric" (p. 697, original emphasis). Maxime Du Camp similarly called Baudelaire's originality "a little too contrived,"[2] and recounted what must be considered an emblematic anecdote of his meeting with the poet, whose hair had recently been dyed green: "Don't you see anything out of the ordinary in me?" Baudelaire asked his acquaintance. "No, I don't," Du Camp answered. "But I have green hair, and that's not very common." "Everyone's hair is more or less green," was Du Camp's response (Pichois and Ziegler, 249).

Contemporary accounts of Baudelaire abound with this kind of anecdote: they display, with varying degrees of bemusement and condescension, the conviction that the man and his mystifications, whether personal or poetic, should not be taken too seriously. I do not mean to suggest that no one saw past the green hair and the forced rhetoric to that which we now take to be Baudelaire's major poetic accomplishment; but those who did so were conscious that theirs was a minority opinion, and prided themselves on the rare quality of their judgment. Charles Asselineau summed up the minority position when he said of his friend, "This Baudelaire is a real touchstone: he invariably offends imbeciles."[3]

By calling Baudelaire a touchstone, Asselineau was putting his finger on a point of considerable importance: for contemporary admirers, Baudelaire's ability to divide his readership was part and parcel of his aesthetic appeal. A curious reversal, whereby the one judging becomes the object of judgment, is at work in the process of aesthetic estimation understood in these terms. The prestige of Baudelaire's poetry thus lay in its apparent power to look back at its reader and to separate aesthetes from "imbeciles." Given this division of the readership, it is not surprising that nineteenth-century accounts of Baudelaire's poetry are often starkly antithetical: the same poetic object is passed off as profound and superficial, powerful and weak, original and antiquated. There seems to be no mediating between the threadbare Romanticism that Brunetière sees in Baudelaire and Asselineau's radical touchstone. One has, consequently, the impression of two very distinct Baudelaires, who share no characteristics.

Against the background of Baudelaire's nineteenth-century reception, the story of his canonization in the early twentieth century is all the more peculiar. In 1917, *Les Fleurs du mal* came into the public domain and cheap editions of the poetry began to proliferate. As Henri Peyre tells it, this publishing event coincided fortuitously with the advent of the First World War and the formation of a generation "prematurely sensitive to this bitter poetry": "Very soon the eloquence of the Romantics, Hugo's cymbal-clanging and even his visionary mysticism, the contrived eccentricities of certain symbolists, were all sacrificed to this new god. Baudelaire was directly consecrated as a Classic, included in the program for examinations, recited by heart in colleges" (Peyre, *Connaissance de Baudelaire*: 10–11). The articles of Marcel Proust and Charles Du Bos in 1921, and of Paul Valéry in 1924, three authors whom Peyre cites as "guides d'opinion" (p. 157), delineated the features of what would become the twentieth century's reading of Baudelaire. Baudelaire's canonization, or what Peyre calls his consecration as a Classic, thus involved simultaneous activity on several fronts: he became widely read, institutionalized ("included in the program for examinations"), and critically categorized, in what must strike us as a kind of literary conspiracy since the separate activities converged so neatly.

Just as Valéry used a metaphor of statehood when he alluded to the "reason of state" (*O*, 1: 600) at work in the production of Baudelaire's poetry, one is tempted to speak of a poetic Manifest Destiny in the case of its canonization. Baudelaire's assumption of his canonical position was so speedy and unequivocal that it has left literary historians with very little to say. No one asks how a controversial poet could become popular, how a belated Romantic could become a Classic, or how two Baudelaires could become one; and yet all this was accomplished in the blink of an eye by Baudelaire's canonization, by a mechanism so dazzling that it has erased itself from view. The nineteenth-century reception of *Les Fleurs du mal* has consequently been so discredited that the question of how Baudelaire got from there to here has been deprived of any historical seriousness. What I mean by this is that it is not considered a question: the twentieth-century transformation of Baudelaire is received as a foregone conclusion, as Baudelaire's coming into his own, not through any real historical processes, but through a kind of aesthetic destiny which has revealed the poetry's true and enduring physiognomy. Baudelaire's canonization appears as a moment of aesthetic revelation in which the contingencies of history have been transcended.

It is my purpose here to attempt a reading of that self-obliterating historical moment which performed the canonization of Baudelaire. The stakes of such a reading are several. On the most general level, I am interested in investigating the processes of literary history as such. As I have mentioned, Baudelaire has been cast as the absolute origin of a certain literary history, the one that tells the story of our modernity. This history has come to supplant others, ones that were more common in the nineteenth century and that were likely to place their point of origin with Victor Hugo. In and of itself, this shift is a fascinating one: Hugo and Baudelaire do not function as origins in the same way, and a comparison of their respective "originalities" would be well worth carrying out. Although I do not conduct a full analysis here, I would suggest that Baudelaire's status as the origin of literary modernity is intimately linked to the unmediated duality that led to his contemporaries' perception of two Baudelaires. In other words, the story of the one Baudelaire and of his historical legacy, of how his poetic work diversified and gave us Mallarmé and Rimbaud, Valéry and Breton, is bound up with an original duality. The story, then, of the one Baudelaire must be read, not as the transcendence of the two, but as their historical inscription.

This literary historical problem, the problem of Baudelaire's originality, thus raises other questions which are pertinent to a consideration of the poet's canonization. If my hunch about Baudelaire's status as origin is correct, then there is a kind of deception involved in the canonizing process: that process conceals its own condition of possibility or, put differently, the story that it tells is at odds with its own activity of telling. Perhaps this should not surprise us, because there is an innate tension in the concept of canonization itself. That concept marks a separation within the notion of aesthetic origination, so that the moment of aesthetic production, the moment when the poet conceives a poem and puts pen to paper, can no longer be accepted as a simple or absolute origin. It is an open question how this activity of aesthetic production relates to the moment of canonization: one would like to think that the canonization of an author is the ultimate fruit of aesthetic production, the product of the product, or the work of the work. It would then be possible, at least in some sense, to be the author of one's own canonization. But even in this most reassuring scenario, the moment of canonization marks a rift in the activity of aesthetic production. The work of the work cannot be identical to the work of the author: the latter is discursive and open-ended, while the former (if we accept it as a possibility) can only be a pure gesture of self-positing. In other words, a work can impose itself within the canon by virtue of qualities we might associate more with military than with cognitive activity—power, endurance, and so on,—but a work cannot rewrite itself. Without stretching things too much, we can borrow J. L. Austin's terminology and say that the work of the work is fundamentally performative. Although the work of the work might lead to a descriptive or to constative activity, it has no descriptive component in and of itself. The canonical authors are not canonical because we can describe them as lyrical or as impersonal, as Classic or as Romantic: they are in the canon and *then* we describe them, often with conflicting predicates.

The particular interest of Baudelaire's canonization has to do, I argue, with the clarity with which it reveals the problematic features of canonization as such. The rift between authorial production and the moment of canonization is marked, in Baudelaire's case, by a series of antitheses: Romantic versus Classic, derivative versus original, minor versus major, two versus one. If the description of a single author can be reversed in this way through the process of canonization, then clearly descriptive or constative categories do not determine that process, but are secondary to it. This point is easy enough to grasp. What is more difficult to see is the way in which Baudelaire's poetry seems to prefigure its own canonization and carry within itself the rift between authorial production and historical inscription. The descriptive indeterminacy of *Les Fleurs du mal*, its ability to receive conflicting predicates, is not merely revealed by literary history before and after Baudelaire's canonization. That indeterminacy was already present for Baudelaire's contemporaries, as their perceptions of two Baudelaires suggests. This means that what we might take to be a purely historical problem (how one generation appropriates and reconceives its predecessors), in this instance functions as the extension of an aesthetic problem (how one poetic corpus divides its readership). Viewed in this way, Baudelaire's duality and his divided readership have not disappeared. The divided readership, which was first understood in *aesthetic* terms (as the difference between people with good and bad taste), still exists for us, only in *historical* terms (as the difference between nineteenth- and twentieth-century readers). The tendency is to treat all of Baudelaire's contemporaries as imbecilic readers, and to define twentieth-century aestheticism against this uncomprehending foil.[4]

What I have called the deception involved in the canonizing process thus acquires intensified significance in the case of Baudelaire. As I previously mentioned, the story of Baudelaire's canonization tells of a parting of ways between aesthetic and historical categories, of an aesthetic transcendence of historical contingency. And yet, if my preceding observations are accurate, what enables the canonical story to be told is a particular complicity between aesthetic and historical phenomena. This complicity can be understood in several ways—as the historical translation of an aesthetic question; as the peculiar instance of an author engendering his own canonization by writing his poetry into a literary history; or as the predication of aestheticism on historical grounds, the grounds that would mark a difference between the nineteenth and the twentieth centuries. Once again, the canonical story is in conflict with its own conditions of possibility; only here, the stakes have been raised: as we negotiate the relationship between one and two Baudelaires, the more general question of the relationship between aesthetic and historical categories is at play. In some sense, this latter question is *the* critical question of canonization as such.

I have been guided in my thinking on this topic by two essays, both of which are crucial to the development of Baudelairean studies. The first is Paul Valéry's "Situation de Baudelaire," one of the essays to which Peyre attributes the critical canonization of Baudelaire. The essay is striking in several respects. Perhaps the most significant is the fact that many of its ideas have become such clichés that we no longer associate them with Valéry. This is not equally true of the essays by Du Bos and Proust (the two other essays cited by Peyre), which retain specific signatures. It is amusing, for example, to recall that Valéry was behind the idea of Baudelaire's dual posterity (both intellectual and sensual currents of French poetry are said to stem from him) when we read Marcel Raymond's *De Baudelaire au surréalisme*: Raymond accepts the dual posterity as a received idea of the critical community at the same time that he excoriates Valéry by name as lacking in critical insight. The anonymity of Valéry's ideas testifies to the success of his canonizing enterprise: the ideas have imposed themselves with the kind of ambiguously authored force I have associated with canonization.

Valéry's essay is also unusual in that it sets out, not primarily to *describe* Baudelaire, but to *situate* him. In other words, the essay's explicit intention is to articulate Baudelaire's canonical position. It is the misunderstanding of this intention that has led critics like Raymond to dismiss "Situation de Baudelaire" while being influenced by it. True, the description of Baudelaire that Valéry gives can be oddly tendentious: sometimes one has the impression that Valéry's focus has slipped, and that he is in fact describing Mallarmé, or even himself. And yet, if we understand canonization as thematizing a rift in the notion of aesthetic production, this peculiar displacement of authorship should not surprise us. If canonization is fundamentally performative rather than descriptive, we might even expect it to pursue its performance by a displacement of description. This would lead to the conceptual oddity that Valéry introduces at the end of his essay, where he claims that, if we wish to be fair, we must consider Baudelaire the author of other poets' works (I will examine this claim later in greater detail). Here the rift in the concept of authorship has been taken to the extreme, an extreme that marks Valéry's essay at its most crucial moments. Rather than dismiss this extremism as fanciful or hysterical, I would like to view it as a consequence of the canonizing goal Valéry set for himself. The remainder of this chapter will be primarily devoted to a reading of "Situation de Baudelaire," whose peculiarities are illuminating for the critical problems attending the activity of canonization.

The second essay that has contributed to my thinking on Baudelaire's canonization is Walter Benjamin's "On Some Motifs in Baudelaire." This piece is crucial because it initiates (albeit in an elliptical fashion) my own reading of Valéry's essay. Benjamin's engagement with Valéry is of particular interest because, in many respects, "On Some Motifs in Baudelaire" is written from a pre-Valérian vantage point: Benjamin insists upon Baudelaire's duality, on the division of *Les Fleurs du mal* into an aesthetics of *correspondances* and an aesthetics of *spleen*, which are radically incommensurate. Far from transcending historical contingency, such a dual aesthetics enables Baudelaire to "[hold] in his hands the scattered fragments of genuine historical experience" ("Motifs": 185). Aesthetic and historical categories are profoundly intertwined in Benjamin's analysis. It is not clear, for example, whether Benjamin's statements on history are grounded in the aesthetic categories furnished by Baudelaire's poetry, or vice versa. In any event, we are far from the canonical division of categories that Valéry's essay seems to advocate.

Despite the apparent differences of position, Benjamin turns to Valéry to frame his own reading of Baudelaire's poetry:

In his "Situation de Baudelaire" Valéry supplies the classical introduction to *Les Fleurs du mal*. There he says: "The problem for Baudelaire was bound to be this: to become a great poet, yet neither Lamartine nor Hugo nor Musset. I do not claim that this ambition was a conscious one in Baudelaire; but it was bound to be present in him, it was his reason of state." There is something odd about speaking of a reason of state in the case of a poet; there is something remarkable about it: the emancipation from experiences [*Erlebnissen*]. Baudelaire's poetic output is assigned a mission. He envisioned blank spaces which he filled in with his poems. His work cannot merely be categorized as historical, like anyone else's, but it intended to be so and understood itself as such. (p. 162)

Benjamin's gloss of "Situation de Baudelaire" brings to the surface one of several anomalies in Valéry's thought: if we are to take the notion of Baudelaire's "reason of state" seriously, then we must conclude that he first of all staked out his position in the canon and only secondarily filled this "blank space" with writing. This is a sheer reversal of the normative view of canonization as I have attempted to define it: the work no longer performs its canonization through a kind of secondary authorship. Baudelaire's authorial relationship to his canonization is primary and unmediated. This leaves his poetry in a peculiar situation since it now becomes the secondary product. Baudelaire's poetry is not seen as his unalienated possession, as an immediate lyrical expression: this is in part what Benjamin means when he speaks of that poetry as being emancipated from experiences. While this might seem to constitute a devalorization of poetry and its claims to essentiality, it actually increases the historical seriousness of *Les Fleurs du mal* in Benjamin's eyes. In the normative view of poetic canonization, the problem of authorship, the rift between the immediate production and the historical inscription of a work, need not appear. This is because the rift occurs *between* the work and its canonization and can easily be put down to the anonymous functioning of history—a self-obliterating history, as I have suggested, which erases itself as it performs its function. In Baudelaire's case, where historical inscription *precedes* the work, the problem of authorship cannot similarly escape detection. By its very nature, the work cannot obliterate itself, so it cannot conceal the authorial rift that constitutes it as a work. Consequently, its historical inscription must appear as part of its aesthetic character. In this sense, *Les Fleurs du mal* "cannot merely be categorized as historical" like any other poetry: its historicity is not anonymous, but bears Baudelaire's signature.[5]

It should be apparent from the foregoing that Benjamin's appropriation of the Valéry piece is diametrically opposed to the canonical appropriation as outlined by Peyre. It is tempting to read the historicist emphasis in Benjamin as either subversive and a-canonical or as willfully reactionary—to some extent it is both. But, rather than read Benjamin as the historicist challenge to Valéry's aestheticism, what I hope to show in the following pages is an internal tension in "Situation de Baudelaire" which is revealed by Benjamin's analysis. If there is a challenge posed by that analysis, it comes, not from outside the canonizing process, but from within. Ultimately this has implications for the interpretation of Baudelaire's poetry. Once the collusion between historicist and aestheticist modes of interpretation is made apparent, then it should be possible for us to read *Les Fleurs du mal* in the fullest possible sense: as imbeciles *and* aesthetes (to return to Asselineau) capable of discerning the simultaneous profile of *two* Baudelaires.

"Situation de Baudelaire" was originally given as a lecture in February, 1924. Part of its declamatory tone can doubtless be attributed to this circumstance. The essay begins with the resounding statement "Baudelaire est au comble de la gloire" (Baudelaire is at the height of glory) and proceeds, through a series of loosely connected reflections, to prove that "if there are, among our poets, greater and more powerfully gifted poets than Baudelaire, there is none more *important*" (O, 1: 598, original emphasis). In the course of his proof, Valéry manages to collect and/or to formulate the elementary clichés that now compose Baudelaire's canonical profile: *Les Fleurs du mal* inaugurates the poetics of modernity, it fulfills the anti-didactic, anti-historical program for poetry that Poe outlined in *The Poetic Principle*; Baudelaire is the poet *cum* critic, his writing is not spontaneous but self-reflexive; his work gives rise to two poetic currents, one running through Verlaine and Rimbaud, who borrow his themes and his sensibility, the other running through Mallarmé, who continues his intellectual and formal preoccupations; the charm of *Les Fleurs du mal* comes from the rigorous separation of poetic diction from ordinary language, a separation which prefigures Symbolism, and so on.

Despite the varying implications of these remarks, they have a common conception of the aesthetic—what is beautiful in Baudelaire's poetry is its scrupulous detachment either from the prior tradition of French versification (therein lies its modernity) or from the prosaic use of language, which would involve ethical or merely anecdotal elements. Valéry's aesthetic assumptions owe much to Mallarmé and the latter's contribution to the doctrine of *poésie pure*: pure poetry is poetry that has been cleansed of foreign matter and reduced to an essence.[6] Thus Valéry remarks: "*Les Fleurs du mal* contain neither historical poems nor legends; nothing that is based upon a narrative. There are no philosophical tirades. Politics is absent. Descriptions are rare, and always *significant*. But everything is pure charm, music, powerful and abstract sensuality. . . . Luxury, form and pleasure [*luxe, forme et volupté*]" (pp. 609–10, original emphasis).

As I have already mentioned, this collection of clichés is seldom traced back to Valéry's essay. Because of its powerful canonizing performance, the essay has erased itself as a specific, textual phenomenon. This is consistent with the description of canonization as a self-obliterating, historical moment. But the fact remains that we still have access to Valéry's text, and this enables us to *read* Baudelaire's canonization in a way that is not possible with authors whose canonization is not textually underwritten. Therefore we can ask whether Valéry's essay, read textually, supports its canonizing performance, whether the clichés it produces are in accord with the mechanism of textual production. It is reasonable to expect genuine incompatibilities between the positive gesture of canonization and discursive, textual complexity. In this instance, I argue that a textual reading reveals the operation of the historical category in the essay's production of aesthetic aperçus.

From the very beginning, "Situation de Baudelaire" is characterized by an inconsistency of tone. As I have noted, there is much declamation in the piece, but this alternates with quieter, digressive passages. One almost has the impression that Valéry lacked the energy to sustain a declamatory mode, that he needed the digressive pauses to catch his breath. The first example of the lapse in tone occurs at the opening of the essay and involves the question of Baudelaire's translatability: "This little volume of *Les Fleurs du mal*, which does not come to three hundred pages, is esteemed by literate people in the balance with the most illustrious and vast works. It has been translated into most of the European languages: this is a fact I shall dwell upon for a moment, for I believe it is without precedent in the history of French letters" (p. 598). What follows is a digression on the nearly universal untranslatability of French poetry: the latter is both too subtle and too simple in its conception to be perceptible to "those individuals who do not have an intimate and original acquaintance with our language" (p. 598). This limitation does not necessarily hold for French prose, which has had some appeal for foreigners. Valéry cites the example of Victor Hugo, whose novels have proved popular abroad but whose poetry remains a national phenomenon. Thus a clear opposition is laid out between poetry and an intimate national character on the one hand, and prose and an international accessibility or translatability on the other. The digression ends once this opposition has been articulated, and Valéry returns to his declamatory tone: "But with Baudelaire, French poetry finally leaves the boundaries of the nation. It is read throughout the world; it commands attention as the very poetry of modernity . . ." This is the tone of the canon-maker or canon-proclaimer, and yet, in the wake of the preceding digression, Valéry's statement takes on a complex coloration. The simple sense that French poetry has achieved a kind of ultimate recognition with Baudelaire, that the two *gloires* are synonymous, is accompanied by a risk: by allying its fortune with that of Baudelaire, French poetry has stopped behaving like itself. Its step outside the boundaries of the nation must simultaneously alter its intimate character and raise the question of its distinction from prose. If French poetry has suddenly become translatable, what has happened to the "overly pure design," and the "overly elegant and nuanced diction" (p. 598) which separated it from prose? A tension which is not only stylistic but conceptual begins to play between the assertive and digressive moments of Valéry's essay: the opposition between poetry and prose, or between the familiar and the foreign, is mobilized so that categorical distinctions become most unstable at the moment when Valéry's tone is most assured. By itself this tension tends to undermine the canon-making project, because affirmation and categorization are at odds with one another: canonical regulation requires *both* processes and their separation smacks of absurdity. But there is even more at stake in this peculiar division of the canon-making process.

The categorical distinctions between poetry and prose or between the familiar and the foreign are not incidental to the construction of Valéry's essay. One might even argue that these categories supply the canonical portrait of Baudelaire with its basic content. As Valéry claims later in the essay, Baudelaire's prosody is characterized by the fact that it is "scrupulously distinct from prose" (p. 602). The doctrine of *poésie pure*, whose aureole Valéry wishes to place around Baudelaire's head, depends upon the possibility of distinguishing poetry from prose. This distinction entails the second one (familiar/foreign) insofar as prosaic subjects—history, science, ethics—are *foreign* to poetry, which is among "the creations of one's *intimate* being" (p. 609, my emphasis). In fact, the doctrine of *poésie pure*, as Valéry presents it, coincides with a generalized production of categorical differences: "Poe understood that modern poetry had to conform to the tendency of an age that has seen the modes and spheres of activity become more and more distinct from each other, and that it could claim to realize its proper object and to produce itself, so to speak, *in a pure state*" (p. 609, original emphasis).

So the canonical story goes: the purification of poetry takes place as the difference between what is proper and improper to all "modes and spheres of activity" is defined. This is why Valéry is careful to nuance his comments on Baudelaire's interest in music:

"It is remarkable that the same man, to whom we owe this return of our poetry to its essence, is also one of the first French writers to be passionately interested in music properly speaking" (p. 611). One must not assume that a poet's passion for music arises from a natural affinity between the two arts: if Baudelaire (remarkably) turned to music, it was in the interest of confirming its difference from poetry and understanding music "properly speaking." Only with this qualification firmly in mind are we able to understand Valéry's allusion to music's influence on poetry in the generation that succeeded Baudelaire: "What was baptized Symbolism can be very simply summed up in the intention shared by several families of poets to take back from music their own property [*reprendre à la musique leur bien*]" (p. 612).[7] The Mallarmean project of investing poetry with "musical" properties is thus seen, not as a borrowing which might be more or less legitimate, but as a restoration of stolen goods, a return to legitimacy of both music and poetry. Such a project, in Valéry's analysis, continues and consolidates Baudelaire's own aesthetic undertaking, which began the work of categorical delineation in "this return of our poetry to its essence."

In light of the preceding remarks, any disturbance of categories in the description of Baudelaire's poetics must appear anomalous, at the very least. It is unlikely that Valéry, with his celebrated critical consciousness, would permit this kind of anomaly out of simple recklessness or muddled thinking. The likelihood is even smaller when we realize that a tension between the canonical portrait of Baudelaire and its categories occurs at the crucial point of Valéry's essay: this is the moment when Valéry recounts, as an "exceptional circumstance" of Baudelaire's situation, the latter's encounter with the work of Edgar Allan Poe (p. 599).

Baudelaire's discovery of Poe is critical for a variety of reasons. Without Poe, Valéry contends, the Baudelaire we know might never have existed: "[Baudelaire] was born sensual and precise; the demands of his sensibility led him to the most scrupulous investigations of form; but these gifts would have made him only an emulator of Gautier, or an excellent artist of the Parnassian school, if he had not, due to his inquiring turn of mind, had the good fortune

The Two Baudelaires

to discover a new intellectual world in the words of Edgar Poe" (p. 599).[8]

Interestingly, the encounter with Poe transforms Baudelaire into himself. From this point onward Baudelaire will possess his canonical identity. Before Poe, what we see is a minor figure, described anonymously as "un émule de Gautier" or "un excellent artiste du Parnasse," determined fully by the contingencies of literary history. After Poe, we have a poet whose importance propels him outside historical determinations. This can be seen, first by a comparison of Baudelaire and his contemporaries, which reveals for Valéry an absolute incommensurability: ". . . if we take care to compare this collection [*Les Fleurs du mal*] to other poetic works of the same period, we will not be surprised to find Baudelaire's works remarkably consistent with Poe's precepts, and thereby remarkably different from Romantic productions" (p. 609). It is important that we not read Baudelaire's conformity to Poe's precepts as the substitution of one determining factor for another. The relationship between Baudelaire and Poe is not the subject of literary history, as the relationship between Baudelaire and Gautier is. The former relationship does not involve emulation or imitation, but a curious exchange in which the categories of self and other acquire a dialectical mobility: "*Baudelaire, Edgar Poe exchange assets. Each one gives to the other what he has; he receives what he does not have*" (p. 607, original emphasis). This dialectical exchange reduces any attempt to write a history of influence to absurdity: Poe, as much as Baudelaire, benefits from "this magical contact between two minds" (p. 599), and therefore cannot play the role of historical predecessor in any simple sense. Like Baudelaire, Poe becomes himself through contact with another subject. That is why Valéry cites the opening line of Mallarmé's "Tombeau d'Edgar Poe," "Tel qu'en Lui-même enfin l'éternité le change" (Such as into Himself at last eternity changes him), and argues that "this expanse that changes the poet into himself . . . it is Baudelaire's act, his translations, his prefaces, that open and guarantee it to the ghost of the wretched Poe" (p. 607).

If the discovery of Poe propelled Baudelaire from his historical context by making him irreducibly different from his contemporaries, it also contributed to his curious position with respect to later literary productions. Valéry writes:

> Today we see that after more than sixty years the resonance from Baudelaire's single and scarcely voluminous work still fills the entire sphere of poetry, that it is present to all minds [*présente aux esprits*], impossible to neglect, reinforced by a number of remarkable works that derive from it, that are not its imitations but its consequences, and that therefore to be fair one would have to add to the thin volume of *Les Fleurs du Mal* several works of the highest quality and a set of the most profound and refined investigations that poetry has ever undertaken. (p. 610)

Here again we have a scenario which in no way corresponds to standard literary history. One does not get from Baudelaire to more recent poetic endeavors by means of a chronological progression: Baudelaire's work is continually "présente aux esprits" and shows no signs of receding into a historical background. Consequently, later works must be seen, not as developing from *Les Fleurs du mal*, but as adding to it, as being more *fleurs du mal*, that is, if we are really to be fair ("pour être équitable"). Although the self/other dialectic is not explicit here, as it was in Valéry's discussion of Poe, a similar appropriation of other subjects for the self is taking place: Rimbaud, Mallarmé, perhaps Valéry himself, all become the authors of a "reinforced" *Fleurs du mal*. This they do, not by imitating Baudelaire, but by pursuing their own poetic interests as a *consequence* of his work. Again, both Baudelaire and the writers who follow him benefit from this intersubjective exchange. They find their idiom, while he becomes a strangely generalized subject, the author of other people's works. This extension of the Baudelairean subject resembles what Valéry called the "expanse" that Baudelaire gave to Poe by translating him into French. Such an expanse, which is also Mallarmé's eternity in "Tombeau," cannot be conceived in conventional historical terms. The progression from Baudelaire to later writers is to be understood, not as a temporal phenomenon, but as the movement from general principle to particular consequence in a logical deduction. It is thus Baudelaire's generality that explains his "spiritual fertility," because as Valéry says later about Poe, "The characteristic of the truly general is to be fertile" (p. 606). At first glance it may seem as though the discovery of Poe, as peculiar as it is in Valéry's treatment, is perfectly compatible with the canonical view of Baudelaire advanced by the essay. Many of the canonical features are directly attributable to Poe, as Valéry takes care to emphasize. But this is precisely the problem. What status should be given to a categorical poetics that results from a mobilizing of the categories of self and other? Should we neglect the fact that Baudelaire's "intimate" style—which Valéry sees as appropriate to pure poetic expression—is mediated by contact, not only with another subject, but with one born "beneath a very different sky" (p. 605), an alien? The same play between the foreign and the familiar that troubled Valéry's critical exposition at the beginning of "Situation de Baudelaire" recurs here at the essay's focal point. The issue of translation is raised with similar complexities in both places as well: just as Baudelaire's translatability confirms his poetic importance while it casts a suspicious light on the purity of his poetic accomplishment, the translation of Poe, his passage into a foreign tongue, simultaneously guarantees his self-identity. How can we reconcile this valorization of translation, with its strong double valency, and the doctrine of *poésie pure*, which excludes all foreign matter? It is something quite unexpected to find a legendary literary purist like Valéry showing enthusiasm for translation; most purists hold the essence of poetry to be untranslatable. So we must try to take stock of what is involved in the apparent *contresens* of the essay.

A first observation might be that we have landed upon a more explicit formulation of what I earlier called a division in the canon-making process. On the one hand that process furnishes a basic conceptual content, which is the *poésie pure* doctrine. On the other hand, it is translation which is the vehicle of that content, which imposes it and sustains its canonical position. Without translation, the *poésie pure* doctrine would have no claims to generality and hence to the aesthetic "fertility" that gives it its importance; with translation, however, that doctrine's claims to conceptual validity are constantly threatened. In other words, the doctrine's ability to be conceptualized is separated from its ability to be generalized (or practiced—this is in part the meaning of generalization for Valéry[9]). Of course, this is not at all the ideology of the *poésie pure* doctrine, which would like to owe its generality to its conceptual rigor alone, and hence to stand freely as a self-evident truth. But Valéry's analysis makes it plain that the doctrine cannot perform this kind of self-canonization, that it must split from itself in order to assure its canonical position.

This being the case, we are authorized to reinterpret that crucial moment when Baudelaire's poetry is said to acquire its true aesthetic (canonical) identity by breaking with history. This moment may be understood in terms of the poetry's reception, as the twentieth century's "forgetting" of Baudelaire's nineteenth-century readership, or in terms of its production, as Baudelaire's turning away from his French contemporaries under the spell of Poe. In either event, the moment of poetic becoming pretends to separate the aesthetic from history in a definitive way.[10] Yet, if we follow the cue of the preceding discussion, what we find instead is the separation of the aesthetic from itself. The very energy with which Baudelaire's poetry imposes itself in an affirmation of aesthetic purity is an impure energy, disruptive of the aesthetic totality. The detailed analysis of Baudelaire's canonization thus reveals a much more complex operation than we had originally perceived: the affirmation of aesthetic separateness remains, but it is an affirmation in bad faith, which both conceals and displays its difference from itself. The canonization does not sustain the history/aesthetics split in a categorical way, because that split is a mere reflection of aesthetic difference; aesthetic difference both appears and disappears in its own reflection, the reflection is also a camouflage which enables the aesthetic to pass for a beautiful totality while it continues to stand in opposition to itself. Thus, the historical category, far from being exterior to the aesthetic in a decisive way, stands as the necessary moment of mediation through which the aesthetic defines itself. (The logical structure of this relationship is similar to what transpires between Baudelaire and Poe in the definition of their respective self-identities.) In assessing the preceding remarks and their implications for the history/aesthetics relationship we can draw the following conclusions:

First, the necessary occurrence of history is *not* categorical insofar as it is generated by aesthetic difference, that is, the relationship of the aesthetic to itself. This brings us to the second point: Historical necessity, while it characterizes the aesthetic, does not ground or explain it. More specifically, an adequate aesthetic description of *Les Fleurs du mal* (Benjamin's work comes to mind here) will inevitably raise the question of history, without history's standing as the cause of poetic production. For example, for Benjamin, the description of the poetry is centered around the difference between *correspondances* and *spleen*. This difference requires the mediation of history to achieve its full articulation, and Benjamin goes so far as to claim that "Baudelaire in "Spleen" and "Vie antérieure" [the latter poem displaying an instance of *correspondances*] holds in his hands the scattered fragments of genuine historical experience" ("Motifs": 185). We cannot conclude, however, that history explains the difference between *correspondances* and *spleen*, which remains an aesthetic difference, produced by the poetry and not by historical circumstances. Consequently, Benjamin will continue to affirm that Baudelaire's "*correspondances* . . . are not historical data" (p. 182) and that the time that becomes palpable in the experience of *spleen* lies "outside history" (p. 184).

Third, the priority given the aesthetic in the foregoing analysis must not be confused with a simple aestheticism. What is crucial to the articulation of the history/aesthetics relationship is aesthetic *difference*. This will always undermine the attempt to totalize the aesthetic; it will therefore destabilize traditional aestheticist positions, like the doctrine of *poésie pure* or the privileging of art for art's sake. Whatever is seen from the traditional standpoint as exterior to the aesthetic (usually history or ethics) cannot be sustained in its exteriority and becomes engaged in the aesthetic's self-estranging mechanism.

Fourth, these observations can be confirmed and expanded by

returning to the text of Valéry's essay. We have already noted aesthetic difference at work in the tension between the performance and the conceptual content of Baudelaire's canonization: the *poésie pure* doctrine achieves canonical status only in translation, and the affirmation of an aesthetic totality thereby undergoes a first destabilization.

But aesthetic difference continues to wreak havoc with the *poésie pure* doctrine on a strictly conceptual level as well: this occurs in the course of Valéry's attempt to add to that doctrine by introducing the concept of poetic *charme*. The term was clearly important for Valéry, because two years earlier, in 1922, he had called a volume of his own work *Charmes ou Poèmes* (this was the first version of the collection now entitled *Charmes*). In the Baudelaire essay, poetic charm is evoked to account for the disproportionate impact of *Les Fleurs du mal*—"the true fertility of a poet is not measured by the number of his verses, but rather by the extent of their effect" ("Situation": 610)[11]—and to explain the aesthetic power of the poem "Recueillement" (Meditation). On the latter subject Valéry writes: "Of the fourteen lines of the sonnet "Recueillement," which is one of the most charming pieces in the work, I am always surprised to count five or six which are undeniably weak. But the first and the last lines of this poem display such a magic that the ineptness of the middle goes unfelt and can easily be taken for null and non-existent" (p. 610).

The critical response to this commentary has been, predictably enough, to speculate on which verses might be the weak ones (the second stanza is generally indicted). But such an analysis begs the more fundamental aesthetic question, which again is a question of disproportion: Baudelaire's poem is charming because the whole is not equal to the sum of its parts; its *effect* (like the effect of *Les Fleurs du mal* in literary history), far from being dependent upon an appreciation of its positive qualities, can actually obliterate the perception of those qualities ("the middle . . . can easily be taken for null and nonexistent"). What poetic charm describes, then, is a division in perception so that the poetic object cannot be perceived as a totality. In the case of "Recueillement," this means that the reader either experiences the poem's incantatory magic or enumerates its defects, but cannot integrate these two activities. The aesthetic appreciation of the poem is not a matter of adding up its good and bad qualities and seeing the balance tilted in one direction or the other: the aesthetic difference is such that good and bad cannot be placed on a common scale. It should be obvious how unsettling such aesthetic disproportion must be for the *poésie pure* doctrine: in order to purify poetry one has to identify its defects and eliminate them; but this simple activity takes on unexpected complications when poetic beauty conceals those defects and thus preserves them in a kind of aesthetic blind spot. Even when the blinding powers of beauty are resisted, say, by critics who have noted the weaknesses in the second stanza of "Recueillement," the elimination of defects is no longer a simple operation. Because the interrelation of beauty and defect is beyond our perception, the elimination of the latter might alter the former in unpredictable ways. Michael Riffaterre has argued that, for "Recueillement," the beauty of renunciation that is expressed in the closing tercets requires the conventional platitudes of the second stanza to achieve their full impact.[12] We are very close here to an Hugolian aesthetics of the sublime and the grotesque. Valéry's concept of *charme*, which was introduced as an ultimate refinement of the *poésie pure* doctrine, has lead to that doctrine's conceptual antithesis.

This contradiction of the *poésie pure* doctrine from within its own conceptual development can be explained in terms that Valéry himself sets up. After using the words "charm" and "miracle," Valéry admits that "these are terms that must be used cautiously because of the force of their meaning and their ease of employment" (p. 610). He then goes on to suggest a more technical mode of analysis which could substitute for the use of such volatile terminology. The analysis is based, not surprisingly, on an assertion of linguistic difference: "[This analysis] would show that language contains emotive resources mingled with its practical and directly signifying properties" (p. 611). Once we understand that language is divided into two unsynthesized properties, we are in a better position to appreciate the role of the poet: "The duty, the task, the function of the poet are to reveal and activate these powers of movement and enchantment, these stimulants of our affective life and intellectual sensibility, which in everyday language are mixed up with the signs and means of communication of ordinary, superficial life" (p. 611). This notion of the poet's task seems perfectly consistent with the *poésie pure* doctrine: by accentuating the nonsignifying properties of language, the poet marks a distance from "le langage usuel," which is the medium of everyday communication. It is easy to imagine, then, that pure poetry would signify nothing at all, that it would involve the complete separation of language's two properties. But this is not what Valéry says, nor even what he implies. The accentuation of language's nonsignifying component, far from eliminating signification, aims at the synthesis of what Valéry calls "le son et le sens" (sound and meaning). Poetic language is pure (or happy or powerful or profound—these are all adjectives Valéry uses in his description) because its goal is to overcome linguistic difference:

> Cette parole extraordinaire se fait connaître et reconnaître par le rythme et les harmonies qui la soutiennent et qui doivent être si intimement, et même si mystérieusement liés à sa génération, que le son et le sens ne se puissent plus séparer et se répondent indéfiniment dans la mémoire.
>
> This extraordinary utterance makes itself known and recognized by the rhythm and the harmonies which support it and which must be so intimately, and even so mysteriously linked to its generation, that sound and meaning can no longer be separated and reply to one another indefinitely in memory. (p. 611)

There is a great deal at stake in this remark. The self-reflexive character of poetic language, which is revealed in the proximity of cognition and recognition ("se fait connaître et reconnaître") as well as in the closeness of such language to its own production, is rapidly connected to the victory over linguistic difference. By itself, this connection merits careful examination but, for now, it is Valéry's formulation of linguistic synthesis that interests us—"que le son et le sens ne se puissent plus séparer et se répondent indéfiniment dans la mémoire."

We should note first that this desirable union of sound and meaning is equated by Valéry with what he calls the construction of a language within language: "The poet devotes himself to and expends himself in defining and constructing a language within language" (p. 611).[13] So the closer poetic language comes to achieving its goal, the more distinct it will be from "le langage usuel." While this seems like a natural corollary to the rest of Valéry's analysis, it actually adds complexity to the notion of linguistic synthesis. The poetic operation is, in fact, two-fold: the very process whereby sound and meaning are brought together exacerbates the rift between poetry and ordinary language. Ironically, perhaps, this makes the question of linguistic difference more visible than it was before the poet undertook the task of linguistic synthesis. The process of synthesis simultaneously produces difference, and there may be an awareness of this peculiar counterproductivity in Valéry's admission that the poetic operation "is never completed since it is not strictly possible" (p. 611). One might similarly question Valéry's reasons for describing the synthesis of sound and meaning as an indefinite echo-effect in memory—"le son et le sens . . . se répondent indéfiniment dans la mémoire." Here, sound and meaning do not fully coincide in the present; their interconnection is only perceivable over time and never acquires a definite status. If we can speak of synthesis at all, it is a deferred synthesis, one which is always on the verge of accomplishment. Thus, there is a kind of nostalgic dissatisfaction at the heart of the poetic enterprise: the goal of poetry is almost, but not quite attainable, and it is this slight reservation that heightens the sense of poetry's value and gives greater luster to its purity.[14] A shift of emphasis has taken place, so that the failure of poetry to eliminate linguistic difference and, hence, the *technical* impossibility of poetic purity, become the guarantee of another type of purity which we might call psychological, ethical, or sentimental. Poetic value is measured by the purity of intention rather than by any positive accomplishment; or, stated more paradoxically, poetic purity is redeemed by poetic impurity, by recourse to an extra-poetic register of value.

Linguistic difference persists. Sound and meaning can never be either fully separated from one another or fully synthesized. This is why poetic purity will always be conceptually unstable for Valéry. It explains the recurrence of discursive meaning (in this instance, an ethical or psychological measure of purity) within a poetic ideology that defines itself by the categorical exclusion of such meaning. Interestingly, when Valéry tried some years later (in 1938) to redefine Symbolist poetry, he dropped the Mallarmean slogan "reprendre à la musique notre bien" (to take back from music our own property), and claimed that whatever the Symbolists had in common, it "[did] not reside in the sensible characteristics of their art. There is no Symbolist aesthetic." Those who sought after poetic purity were united, so Valéry argued, not by shared aesthetic goals but by a similar *ethical* stance: "*They were brought together by a shared resolution to renounce the approval of the majority [le suffrage du nombre]*." The technical innovations of the Symbolists can be understood only "by a consideration foreign to aesthetics, but genuinely ethical. . . ." ("Existence du symbolisme": 690–92, original emphasis). The displacement of purity from an aesthetic to an ethical register is explicit here, betraying the instability of the linguistic medium.

This instability must influence Valéry's use of historical terminology because, as I have argued, that terminology reflects the dynamic of aesthetic difference. We have already examined Valéry's description of Baudelaire's break from his predecessors after the discovery of Poe. In this version of the break, historical questions seem to be bypassed in favor of a generalized aesthetic logic. But this is not the only version of the story that Valéry tells. At one point the break is explained in terms of Baudelaire's desire to distinguish himself from the Romantics as a group; at another point Baudelaire's "je ferai donc autre chose" (I will therefore do something else) is aimed solely at Victor Hugo. In other words, the break from the predecessors as a literary-historical event is disseminated throughout Valéry's text: in its most critical form (the Poe discovery), the event is markedly historical (the discovery has the character of pure accident); yet this historical event undermines the authority of literary history, as we have seen in the contradiction of

Baudelaire's canonization. When Valéry recounts the same event in its minor forms, the contradiction is not so apparent. To begin with, the historical character of the event is much less pronounced—Baudelaire's break with Hugo could just as easily be cast in psychological terms, for example. And the outcome of the event does not invalidate the use of historical terminology. Yet even in these minor instances, that terminology is disturbed. The clearest example of such disturbance occurs when Valéry defines Baudelaire's break with Romanticism as a kind of Classicism: ". . . Baudelaire, although Romantic in his origins and even in his tastes, can sometimes take on the appearance of a *Classic . . . a Classical writer is one who carries a critic within himself, and who associates it intimately with his labors*" (p. 604, original emphasis). At first glance this remark might seem consonant with traditional literary history—Baudelaire would be characterized as having neoclassical tendencies, harkening back to the literature of the seventeenth century. However, Valéry does not use the term "classical" in a historically descriptive way. Classicism is, for him, primarily conceptual—it is the concept of aesthetic critique. As such, its entry into history follows a *logically* determined pattern, and not a historically determined one.

The historical occurrence of Classicism must thus be seen as incidental to its aesthetic logic. This explains the absurdity, from a historical standpoint, of Valéry's subsequent statements: "*All Classicism supposes a prior Romanticism.* All the advantages that are attributed to a "Classical" art, all the objections that are made against it, are relative to this axiom. *The essence of Classicism is to come afterwards*" ("Situation": 604, original emphasis). It matters little that what we call Classicism precedes the Romantic movement in real chronology: the true aesthetic character of Classicism is "to come afterwards." This becomes its historical character as well, insofar as the secondary position implies a temporal component, coming afterwards assumes a local, historical movement. Such a historical movement is evidently necessary to Valéry's understanding of Classicism, but its historicity is just as evidently subordinate to the problem of aesthetic definition. Valéry's reversal of the Classic/Romantic relationship reveals the historical ungroundedness of the terms.

With a clearer idea of the potential complicity between history and the aesthetic in the description of Baudelaire, we can return to some of the questions raised at the opening of this discussion. The existence of two, historically distinct Baudelaires, one belonging to the nineteenth century and misunderstood, the other rehabilitated and popularized by the twentieth century, can now be reexamined. I mentioned earlier that Baudelaire's formal rehabilitation by the Cour de Cassation in 1949 involved the affirmation of such a historical disjunction; if we look at the text of the court's decision, however, it becomes plain that the historical disjunction is predicated upon an aesthetic judgment. The *arrêt d'annulation* dated May 31, 1949, reads: "if certain depictions succeeded, by their very originality, in alarming the minds of some readers at the time of the first publication of *Les Fleurs du Mal*, and if they appeared to the first judges as offensive to good morals, the arbitrary nature of such an assessment has been clearly shown, in that it confines itself to the realist interpretation of these poems, and ignores their symbolic meaning."[15]

What dominated the court's line of reasoning was not simply the "différence d'époques,"[16] to use Claude Pichois' expression; if the first judges of *Les Fleurs du mal* found the poetry offensive and later readers did not, this was less because standards for "good morals" had changed, than because of differing aesthetic approaches to the poetry. The first judges took the poetry for a piece of realism while later readers presumably understood its symbolic character. Just as the ethical assessment of *Les Fleurs du mal* is dependent upon this aesthetic choice, so, too, the poetry's status in history. It follows from the court's argument that, in order to make the two Baudelaires appear and confirm their historical separation, twentieth-century readers would have to reverse the aesthetic choice of the first judges and neglect any realist vein in the poetry, to enable concentration on its "symbolic meaning." This is a perplexing state of affairs since it establishes an unexpected complicity between history and Symbolism, a complicity which requires the exclusion of realist interpretation. It would imply that we moderns could never produce Baudelaire in his historical difference if we thought to read his ragpickers, beggars, and old women as authentic inhabitants of nineteenth-century Paris. Only the Symbolist reading would be productive of historical difference. Although I must concur with these conclusions (because I myself have drawn them), I have to add that the production of historical difference does not lead to the understanding of that difference in this instance. Something more is needed if we are to appreciate the historical meaning of the twentieth-century aesthetic choice.

Our analysis of aesthetic difference and its relationship to the concept of *poésie pure* should provide a clue to that meaning. The choice to exclude "the realist interpretation" from our reading of *Les Fleurs du mal* cannot be made with an entirely clear conscience. Just as Riffaterre would hesitate to exclude the "defective" second stanza from "Recueillement," not knowing what the consequences might be for the poem's charming aesthetic effect, we should be wary of assuming that a purely symbolic interpretation, without a realist moment, is possible. Valéry's inability to conceive of a language completely purified of discursive meaning should make us skeptical of our chances to eliminate the realist moment; that moment must be reduced, of course, and it is the process of reduction that constitutes the symbolic interpretation. But such a process "is never completed since it is not strictly possible." The open-ended aspect of symbolic interpretation, its inability to eliminate linguistic difference once and for all, gives it a temporal dynamic and, thus, a potential historical meaning.

That potential has been partially realized and has produced a change in our understanding of the two Baudelaires. The nineteenth century's *homo duplex*[17] whose poetry sprang from a series of dualisms (good and evil, high and low, *Spleen* and *Idéal*, and so on) and who starkly divided his readers, has been transformed by the process of symbolic interpretation. The negative, scandalous side of that original duality has been progressively reduced; Baudelaire's difference from himself has been translated into a history of his reception. From this perspective, his conquest of popular opinion can be seen for what it is—both a historical fact and an aesthetic calculation. The history of this conquest, by amplifying and revealing the poetry's aesthetic difference, proves to be the history that engages the aesthetic truth of *Les Fleurs du mal*.

CHAPTER TWO

Defining and Defending Poetry
Sartre Versus Bataille

Sartre's book on Baudelaire was originally published in 1946. From the beginning, Sartre intended it to be a minor work. In 1944 he had completed the monumental *L'Etre et le néant* (Being and nothingness), and his Baudelaire piece was meant to be a kind of case study, illustrating the principles of existential psychoanalysis laid out in the larger treatise. The study was published with a suitable lack of pretension as the introduction to the *Point du jour* edition of Baudelaire's *Ecrits intimes* (Intimate writings). It is intriguing that, given the work's unassuming beginnings, it should have been perceived as the epitome of Philistine presumption and should have provoked a literary scandal of singular proportion. Henri Peyre put this down to the "vigor" of Sartre's analysis, "[which] had the merit of giving rise to a discussion in which some of today's finest critics participated. . . ." (*Connaissance de Baudelaire*, 41–42). Michel Contat and Michel Rybalka went further in their explanation: "Since Baudelaire had become a national institution and the very symbol of poetry, the essay caused a scandal and was violently attacked on all sides. What Sartre was above all condemned for—in spite of the limits he himself had set to his study—was having spoken only of the man and ignored the 'fact of being a poet'" (*The Writings of Jean-Paul Sartre*, 1: 147).

This explanation touches on several factors that prevented *Bau-*

delaire from remaining of limited importance. In 1946 the Société des Gens de Lettres de France (Society of French Men of Letters), with the impetus of public opinion and the passage of a new law, had demanded the rehabilitation of Baudelaire in the courts. The 1857 trial and condemnation of *Les Fleurs du mal* was reviewed by the Cour de Cassation (Supreme Court of Appeal), and the adverse judgment was officially reversed in 1949. All of this is to say that the recognition of Baudelaire as "a national institution and the very symbol of poetry" also involved a desire to undo the historical accident of his condemnation. Sartre could not have picked a more volatile moment for launching his attack on Baudelaire, even if the terms of his ethical analysis differed radically from those used in the original judgment of the poetry. Not only was that analysis absurdly out of place historically speaking, it also seemed to violate, as Contat and Rybalka observe, the integrity of poetry in a general sense. This is a particularly interesting point, because it turns on the question of the limit between the man and his work. What is somewhat unexpected in the reaction against Sartre is that he was accused, not of transgressing that limit but of thinking he could maintain it and speak "only of the man." Curiously, then, by refusing to transgress a limit, Sartre was seen to be violating poetry.

The logical anomaly of this reaction is even more apparent when we remember that Baudelaire had already been embroiled in a *l'homme et l'oeuvre*[1] controversy several decades earlier when Proust had decided to tackle Sainte-Beuve and the latter's biographical method of literary criticism. By conflating the man and the work, Proust argued, Sainte-Beuve managed to misjudge the major literary figures of the nineteenth century, including Baudelaire. Baudelaire's aesthetic accomplishment could only be recognized and respected for what it was if his poetry were understood as having nothing to do with the man he appeared to be. In other words, the defense of Baudelaire in this early gesture at rehabilitation involved an extreme affirmation of poetic specificity. It is all the more remarkable, then, that Baudelaire the man should become "the very symbol of poetry" for a later generation intent upon defending him. My thesis is that Sartre's analysis scandalized because it revealed the peculiar mechanism whereby a man becomes a symbol and the definition of poetry transforms specificity into generality and limit into limitlessness. The reaction against Sartre proved that "poetry" is at stake elsewhere than in poems.

Before considering this thesis in any detail, it is useful to review the basic contentions of Sartre's book. The examination of Baudelaire's life is undertaken with a specific philosophical goal in mind: Sartre wishes to demonstrate that, contrary to received opinion, the misfortunes that attended Baudelaire wherever he went were not a series of inexplicable accidents, but the result of what Sartre calls Baudelaire's "original choice of himself."[2] The thought that Baudelaire was somehow different from his own life, that there was a disproportion in the man himself so that he was more than the man he was, is inadmissible to Sartre. "Is he so very different from the existence he led?" Sartre asks. "What if he deserved his life? What if men, contrary to received opinion, always have the life that they deserve? These questions must be examined more closely" (p. 18).

As Sartre looks closer he finds what he considers the crucial moment in Baudelaire's life, the moment when Baudelaire made a decisive choice of the person he would be. This took place after the remarriage of the poet's mother (Baudelaire was six years old). Until that time, mother and son had been living in perfect communion: "J'étais toujours vivant en toi, tu étais uniquement à moi. Tu étais à la fois une idole et un camarade." (I always lived in you, you were mine alone. You were both an idol and a chum.)[3] Sartre cites this declaration of the adult Baudelaire to his mother as proof that the young child had no sense of individual identity, that he and his mother made up an indifferentiated super-person who could never feel lonely or insufficient in any way. When Caroline Baudelaire married Captain Aupick, her son was cast into a painful state of solitude and experienced self-consciousness for the first time. In Sartre's analysis, this self-consciousness conveys no knowledge of a true or essential individuality. What Baudelaire experienced was an empty individuality, or what Sartre calls "formal singularity": "The child has recently acquired the conviction that he is not just anybody; now he becomes just anybody by acquiring this conviction. He is other than the others, that much is certain; but each other person is similarly other. He has undergone the purely negative experience of separation and his experience has borne upon the universal form of subjectivity, a sterile form which Hegel defines by the equation I = I" (pp. 23–24).

We must be careful here not to confuse the definitive moment in Baudelaire's life with either his mother's remarriage or his experience of self-consciousness. As Sartre maintains, these are the adventures of "n'importe qui" (anybody). What really made Baudelaire Baudelaire was not such banal experiences, but his response to them. Although his mother's marriage was a gratuitous event, something that might or might not have happened and that did not directly concern him, Baudelaire chose to see it as the consequence of his own unhappy destiny: "He laid claim to his solitude, so that at least it would come from himself, so that he would not have to submit to it passively. He *experienced* that he was *other*, by the sudden revelation ('dévoilement') of his individual existence, but at the same time he accepted responsibility for that alterity, with humiliation, rancor and pride" (p. 21, original emphasis). By embracing solitude, Baudelaire hoped to transform "formal singularity," which is the common lot, into the mark of a deeper, *essential* singularity. It is at this point, and not at the moment of his rude awakening to individual consciousness, that Baudelaire chose his personal destiny: "Sentiment de *solitude* dès mon enfance," Baudelaire writes in *Mon coeur mis à nu* (My heart laid bare). "Malgré la famille—et au milieu des camarades, surtout—sentiment de destinée éternellement solitaire" (A feeling of *solitude* dating from childhood. In spite of the family—and in the midst of companions, above all—a feeling of an eternally solitary destiny).[4]

The paradoxes that accompany this original choice of Baudelaire abound. First, and most obviously, the idea of choosing a destiny amounts to a conceptual absurdity. Was Baudelaire, or was he not, the primary agent in his own life? For Sartre, the stakes in answering this question are high. He must convince us that Baudelaire's passive submission to destiny was actively chosen, and that subsequently Baudelaire concealed his agency from himself. That agency must appear and then disappear, enabling Baudelaire both to retain control over his life and to deny accountability for himself. In other words, Sartre must show that Baudelaire was in bad faith. The demonstration proceeds by an analysis of the notion of solitude. Baudelairean solitude, Sartre claims, has little to do with "the great metaphysical solitude that is everyone's lot" (p. 65). This greater solitude involves the recognition that one cannot seek justification for oneself from somebody else: "No man can shift the responsibility of justifying his own existence onto other men" (pp. 65–66). Baudelairean solitude, on the other hand, is measured against the presence of others: "He claims to be *other*, that is true, but *other among others*; his disdainful alterity remains a social tie to those whom he despises, they have to be there to recognize it. This is testified to by the curious passage from *Fusées* (Rockets): 'Quand j'aurai inspiré le dégoût et l'horreur universels j'aurai conquis la solitude' (When I have inspired universal disgust and horror, then I will have conquered solitude)" (p. 66). Interestingly, this passage also seems to complement the fragment from *Mon coeur mis à nu*: there, Baudelaire's agency was at least partially hidden. Here, the boast "j'aurai conquis la solitude" is the trumpeting of individual agency. Sartre supplements his analysis with references to Baudelaire's letters and Asselineau's report that his friend could never bear being alone longer than an hour. Baudelairean solitude thus appears as an intersubjective phenomenon, finding its definitive form, as Baudelaire himself tells us, "in the midst of companions, above all."

Although Sartre restricts himself to Baudelaire's journals and letters in the effort to define Baudelairean solitude, his analysis resonates (here I am following Michel Leiris)[5] in the poetry as well. There is, for example, the curious declaration from the prose poem "Les Foules" (Crowds): "Multitude, solitude: termes égaux et convertibles pour le poète actif et fécond. Qui ne sait pas peupler sa solitude, ne sait pas non plus être seul dans une foule affairée" (Multitude, solitude: equal and convertible terms for the active and fertile poet. Whoever does not know how to people his solitude, also does not know how to be alone in a busy crowd) (OC, 1: 291). The various elements of Sartre's analysis are concentrated here with admirable economy. The intersubjective basis for Baudelairean solitude is acknowledged by the latter's "convertibility," by the equivalency established between the isolated individual and the bustling crowd. The question of agency, that is, of whether solitude is inflicted by destiny or chosen by the *solitaire*, is left in suspense, obscured by the notion of "convertibility." Some kind of destiny seems to be suggested by the opening line "Il n'est pas donné à chacun de prendre un bain de multitude" (It is not given to everyone to take a bath of multitude), but this is immediately nuanced. The conversion of multitude into solitude and vice versa is described in terms of a powerful individual agency: the poet who performs this conversion is "actif" and "fécond," possessing a knowledge that translates directly into action—"Qui ne *sait* pas peupler sa solitude, ne *sait* pas non plus être seul dans une foule affairée" (my emphasis). I argue that the way in which "Les Foules" manages to convert the solitary destiny of the *poète maudit*[6] into something decidedly different is typical of Baudelaire's aesthetics. From Sartre's perspective, this conversion is a mark of bad faith: the tone of tragic inevitability is indulged in and exploited for aesthetic effect, but there is no real inevitability. Just as the tone was chosen by a free agent, it can be revoked—the tragic teeters on the verge of comedy. What Sartre calls the "metaphysical lightness" (p. 220) of Baudelaire's world is apparent in the potential light-heartedness of even those poems where solitude and the weight of destiny are proclaimed most pathetically—"Bénédiction," "L'Albatros," and "Le Guignon" (Bad luck), for example.[7]

If we accept that Sartre's analysis resonates with Baudelaire's poetic works, then the scandal of *Baudelaire* needs to be rethought. On the one hand, we must question whether Sartre himself was in good faith in suggesting that the diagnosis of bad faith concerned *l'homme* and not *l'oeuvre*. As I mention in the Introduction, the second part of Sartre's book undertakes a definition of "the Baudelairean poetic fact" (p. 219), which follows rigorously from the biographical study. On the other hand, whether or not Sartre intended to engage Baudelaire's poetry, why should the poetic resonances of his analysis cause such offense? Maurice Blanchot addresses this question in his judicious essay, "L'Echec de Baudelaire" (Baudelaire's failure). After citing the poem "Le Gouffre" (The abyss), in which Baudelaire declares, "Hélas! tout est abîme,—action, désir, rêve,/Parole!" (Alas! all is abyss,—action, desire, dream,/Speech!), Blanchot writes, "We cite this well-known text simply to show that the philosophical terminology of the commentary is scarcely innovative with respect to the attitude that it comments upon, and consequently could not betray it" ("L'Echec": 137). What Baudelaire calls the "abyss" is simply what Sartre calls "existence," Blanchot claims; this leaves little room for scandal, and makes Sartre more open to charges of banality than of affrontery. It is quite easy to follow up Blanchot's observation and find points of direct correspondence between poet and philosopher: Sartre's description of consciousness—"the long, monotonous procession of his states of mind" (p. 28)—seems to be an echo of Baudelaire's "Spleen"—"Et de longs corbillards, sans tambour ni musique,/Défilent lentement dans mon âme" (And long hearses, without drum or music,/Proceed slowly in my soul) (*OC*, 1: 75); Baudelaire's perfumes provide a neat figure for Sartre's concept of false essences, and when the poet writes, "A mon destin, désormais mon délice,/J'obéirai comme un prédestiné" (To my destiny, henceforth my delight,/I shall obey like a man predestined) ("Le Léthé"; *OC*, 1: 156), he sums up the paradox of a freely chosen destiny with a single simile. All this is to say that if Sartre did not speak extensively of Baudelaire's poetry, he could easily have done so. Why, then, should his neglect of poetry become the point of scandal?

Clearly, what Sartre's critics have called his neglect of poetry must mean something other than his failure to address Baudelaire's poems, something other even than his insensitivity towards them. If Sartre was culpable in speaking "only of the man," it was because he refused to admit a particular notion of poetry. As I suggested earlier, this notion exceeds the limit between the man and the work, opening up the possibility for a man to become the symbol of poetry. Moreover, if a man can become a symbol, then a man can become more than a man; he can exceed himself. This is where Sartre's analysis conflicts most directly with a certain notion of poetry. By suggesting that Baudelaire was not so different from the life he lived, by harnessing the poet into a strict equivalency with himself, Sartre was attacking neither the man nor his work, but the rights of both to be other than themselves. There is a lack of charity evident in this gesture, and I do not defend Sartre's tone, which is deliberately provocative in many respects. But it is intriguing to note that Sartre was not taken to task primarily for his lack of generosity in the face of human foibles; he was accused, instead, of a lack of generosity towards poetry. What this implies is a definition of poetry *as* disproportion and excess, not only in the realm of letters but in the realm of human behavior as well. Sartre's analysis hit a kind of collective nerve and revealed the peculiar privileges that poetry had acquired, often without the knowledge of those who undertook its defense.

One of Sartre's critics, however, was quite conscious of the exorbitant notion of poetry that surfaced in the course of the *Baudelaire* debate. He was Georges Bataille, whose review of Sartre's book is now a chapter in *La Littérature et le mal* (Literature and evil). From the beginning of his critique, Bataille affiliates poetry with the concept of excess. In discussing Sartre's treatment of Baudelaire's "original choice," Bataille writes: "Before judging [his choice] to be unfortunate, we ought to ask ourselves what sort of choice it was. Was it made by default? is it only a deplorable error? Or, on the contrary, was it made out of excess? in a wretched manner, perhaps, but decisive nevertheless? I even wonder: is not such a choice, in its essence, that of poetry? Is it not *that of man himself*?" (pp. 42–43, original emphasis).

The implications of this passage are various and subtle. Bataille accepts the validity of reading Baudelaire's life in terms of an original choice, but seems to distance himself from the ethical overtones of Sartre's analysis. Instead, he pleads for a suspension of judgment, something he will call for throughout his essay. The suspension of judgment enables a hypothetical substitution to take place: the choice we might have attributed to an ethical error on Baudelaire's part can be posed as the possible result of an *excess*. Bataille is unclear as to what kind of excess this might be, but in setting the terms "default" and "excess" against one another, he succeeds in minimizing the ethical connotations of both. The option between his reading and Sartre's thus becomes an affair of more-versus-less: the intent is to establish a neutral zone within Sartre's terminology, and we can see that whatever else the concept of excess might mean, it bears the burden of this task. In the series of rhetorical questions that lays the groundwork for Bataille's argument, "excess" suspends the Sartrean line of reasoning so that "poetry" can take the place of censorial judgment, and "man" can take the place of "poetry" ("Is not such a choice... that of poetry? Is it not *that of man himself?*" p. 43). The apparent antagonism between poetry and judgment (the former seems equivalent to the latter's suspension), which might recall a post-Kantian affirmation of aesthetic limitation, actually leads to a totalization of the aesthetic. Not only has the limit between a man and his poetry been lifted: in the course of Bataille's exposition, Baudelaire's choice is dehumanized, so to speak, detached from whatever constituted him as an individual subject, only to become the choice of man in general. It is poetry that mediates this passage from a man to man, that estranges a man from his humanity in order to make him excessively human. For Bataille, Baudelaire's status as the symbol of poetry entitles him to stand symbolically for man as well.

It is important to note that Bataille, even while he lays out the definition of poetry as excess, retains an essentialist vocabulary: "Is not such a choice, *in its essence*, that of poetry? ... [F]reedom— if I may be permitted to state a proposition before justifying it—*is the essence of poetry . . .*" (pp. 40–41, my emphasis). This vocabulary marks a crucial departure from Sartre, for whom poetry, or any other exercise of human freedom, is an *inessential* activity. In Sartre's philosophical system, freedom and essentiality are incompatible concepts. So, for Sartre Bataille's assertion that freedom might be the essence of poetry places poetry at a point of conceptual absurdity. One could argue that this constitutes a telling critique and that poetry thus stands as the excluded term of Sartre's system. This surely is consistent with the frequent accusation that Sartre did not understand poetry and could not account for it philosophically. But, if we return to examine Sartre's philosophical system where it is presented most thoroughly, that is, in *L'Etre et le néant*, we will find that the locus of conceptual absurdity is scarcely excluded from systematic articulation: it simply passes under another name and is called, not poetry, but bad faith.

Far from lying outside the system, bad faith is crucial to Sartre's definition of "human reality" (p. 83). He begins his discussion of bad faith by indicating that the antithetical concepts of being and nothingness are inseparable in human consciousness: "Consciousness is a being conscious of the nothingness of its being" (*L'Etre et le néant*: 82).[8] It is in an effort to enter into "the intimacy of consciousness" and to explicate its antithetical structure that Sartre embarks on his description of bad faith. The latter produces conceptual absurdity on many levels, beginning with the designation of bad faith as both "essential to human reality" (p. 83) and freely chosen: "One does not submit passively to one's bad faith . . . it is not a *condition* [un état]. But consciousness itself assumes the shape of bad faith [*la conscience s'affecte elle-même de mauvaise foi*]. There must be an original intention and a project of bad faith" (p. 84, original emphasis). The free essence that Sartre thus describes corresponds closely to Bataille's preliminary definition of poetry, despite the fact that that definition was undertaken in opposition to Sartre's system. In both instances, conceptual absurdity leaves room for the development of a disproportionate identity: the poetic subject, or the subject in bad faith, is free to be other than it is at the same time that it never ceases to be itself. Such an identity in excess of itself is what Sartre detects in expressions like "L'amour, c'est beaucoup plus que l'amour" (Love is much more than love) or "Tel qu'en Lui-même enfin l'éternité le change" (Such as into Himself at last eternity changes him).[9] I contend that, as Bataille proceeds with his definition of poetry, its correspondence to Sartrean bad faith only becomes closer and more marked.

Bataille pursues his analysis of poetic freedom by citing a lengthy passage from *Baudelaire*. It is in this passage that Sartre (unwittingly, according to Bataille) accounts for the paradoxical status of Baudelaire's poetry by positing two orders of freedom, a major and a minor. The first order of freedom is terrifying. It requires that an individual "transcending all orders which do not emanate from himself, ... emerge in the void, without God, without excuses, with a total responsibility" (*Baudelaire*: 88). Sartre equates this freedom with what he calls the human condition and claims that Baudelaire experienced it most profoundly and tried most assiduously to hide it from himself.[10] In concealing his frightening moral responsibility, Baudelaire discovered a more reassuring and limited means of exercising his freedom: he could accept unquestioningly the most rigid of moral codes (this is how Sartre understands Baudelaire's enthusiasm for Joseph de Maistre[11]) and then choose to defy it, to live in a state of constant revolt against a morality that he continued to affirm. In the passage cited by Bataille, Sartre associates this minor exercise of freedom with Baudelaire's creation of poetry:

> For freedom to be vertiginous, it must choose, in the theocratic world, to be infinitely wrong. Thus it is *unique* in a world entirely oriented towards the Good; but it must adhere completely to the Good, it must maintain and reinforce it, in order to plunge more thoroughly into Evil. And the individual who damns himself acquires a solitude that is a feeble image of the great solitude possessed by the man who is truly free. . . . In some sense, this individual creates: in a world in which each element is sacrificed to the grandeur of the whole, he brings into being singularity, that is to say, the rebellion of a fragment, a detail. Something is thus produced which was in no way prepared for by the rigorous economy of the world. It is a deluxe work [*une oeuvre de luxe*], gratuitous and unpredictable. Let us note here the relationship between Evil and Poetry: when, in addition, poetry takes Evil as its object, the two forms of limited creation ("création à responsabilité limitée") join and blend together, and we suddenly get a flower of evil. (*Baudelaire*: 88–89, original emphasis)

Understood in these terms, poetry can possess an essential freedom because its freedom is circumscribed by a world of essences, a world in which ethical choices appear to be as objectively determined as physical laws. This is the world that Baudelaire evokes in the final stanza of "Le Gouffre":

> Et mon esprit, toujours du vertige hanté,
> Jalouse du néant l'insensibilité.
> —Ah! ne jamais sortir des Nombres et des Etres!

> And my mind, always haunted by vertigo,
> Envies the insensibility of nothingness.
> —Ah! never to take leave of Numbers and Beings!

The world of essences, of Numbers and Beings, appears here in a curious light. It is presented as a refuge from the abyss, as a shield (albeit an insufficient one) against the terrifying experience of freedom. At the same time, however, it is clear that Baudelaire is fully conscious of the dialectical twist whereby Being becomes Nothingness. "—Ah! ne jamais sortir des Nombres et des Etres!" can be read either as the expression of an impossible desire or as the protest against an accursed condition. In the first instance, the world of essences would constitute a stable but unattainable refuge. In the second case, the very endlessness of Being would produce the vertigo of Nothingness and Nothingness would acquire the stability of Being, leading to the statement "mon esprit . . . / Jalouse du néant l'insensibilité." In either case, the solidity of the world of essences is not available to the poet. What this means in terms of Sartre's analysis is simply that Baudelaire could not sustain the exercise of a limited freedom in good faith: he could not hide the gratuitous nature of the world of essences from himself and thus could not continue to affirm essential privileges for poetry. The opening stanza of "Le Gouffre" gives confirmation of this fact:

> —Hélas! tout est abîme,—action, désir, rêve,
> Parole! et sur mon poil qui tout droit se relève
> Mainte fois de la Peur je sens passer le vent.
>
> —Alas! all is abyss,—action, desire, dream,
> Speech! and in my hair which stands on end
> Many times I feel the wind of Fear pass.

Here the abyss of freedom empties out all human projects, eliminating the distinction between action and language. From this perspective, poetry is deprived of its essential specificity and becomes only part of the larger equation between everything and nothing—"tout est abîme."[12]

It is noteworthy that when Bataille cites the passage from *Baudelaire*, he omits Sartre's restriction that the limited freedom afforded by revolt or by poetry is only possible "in the theocratic world," in the world of essences. Bataille thus eliminates the distinction between relative and absolute freedom, making Sartre's analysis of the former valid for the latter. As a consequence he need not follow Sartre in allotting a relative position to poetry and need not question poetry's essential privileges. It is at this point that Bataille stands Sartre on his head, so to speak, and affiliates poetry with what he calls a "sovereign attitude":

> Poetry can verbally trample on the established order, but it cannot replace it. When the poet's horror at a powerless freedom compels him into a virile engagement with political action, he abandons poetry. But he henceforth assumes responsibility for the order of things to come, he adopts the *mature attitude* [*l'attitude majeure*], laying claim to the *direction* of his activity: and we cannot fail to see that the poetic existence, in which the possibility of a *sovereign attitude* may be discerned, is in fact the *minor attitude* [*l'attitude mineure*], the attitude of a child, a gratuitous game. Freedom is, strictly speaking, an infantile power: for the adult engaged in the obligatory order of action, it is nothing more than a dream, a desire, a haunting memory. (p. 41, original emphasis)

The terms "major" and "minor" remain in Bataille's analysis, but they no longer refer to two orders of freedom. What Bataille calls "l'attitude majeure" involves the acceptance of ethical responsibility, but precisely at the expense of freedom. Only "l'attitude mineure," the refusal of responsibility that is epitomized by "the poetic existence," can realize the sovereign stance of freedom. It is intriguing that Bataille uses the same concepts we encountered in "Le Gouffre"—"action, désir, rêve"—only he continues to affirm essential distinctions between them. Poetry is "only a dream" in the adult world of action, and for this very reason poetry retains essential privileges. In Bataille's framework, desire does not translate into action or action into dream. One is reminded of another of Baudelaire's declarations: "—Certes, je sortirai, quant à moi, satisfait / D'un monde où l'action n'est pas la soeur du rêve" (—For a certainty, I will be satisfied to leave / A world in which action is not the sister of dream) ("Le Reniement de Saint Pierre" [Saint Peter's denial], 1: 122). This is the world in which Bataille situates

Baudelaire, a world in which poetry and action remain irreconcilable.

It is by affirming the irreconcilability of poetry and action that Bataille is able to pursue his most extended critique of Sartre. The distinction that Bataille sets up between "the prosaic world of activity and the world of poetry" (this is the title of a subsection in his essay) is offered as an alternative to the conceptual system Sartre establishes in the opening pages of *Baudelaire*. There Sartre attempts to distinguish between Baudelaire's original perception of the world and what is loosely labeled "our" original perception. "We" forget ourselves in contemplating the world while Baudelaire desires only to be conscious of his own contemplation: "Qu'importe ce que peut être la réalité placée hors de moi, si elle m'a aidé à vivre, à sentir que je suis et ce que je suis?" (Does it matter what the reality located outside of me might be, if it has helped me to live, to feel that I am and what I am?) ("Les Fenêtres" [The windows], 1:339).[13] Bataille is perfectly right in commenting that Sartre's staging of the problem "does not set out a profound opposition" (p. 45). It is absurd to suggest, for example, that "we" have never experienced moments when the reality of the world seemed tenuous or that Baudelaire, alone of all the human race, never once intuited a reality beyond the circle of reflexive consciousness. In order to remedy the potential absurdity of Sartre's analysis, Bataille proposes to reinterpret the Baudelaire/us opposition in the following terms: "One could not better nor more precisely represent the distance between poetic and everyday vision. We forget ourselves when the arrow points to the road, or the bookmark to the page: but this vision is not *sovereign*, it is subordinated to our search for the road (that we are going to take), or the page (that we are going to read)" (p. 44, original emphasis). Thus "our" vision is in fact *prosaic*, subordinated to a practical end, while Baudelaire's poetic vision—"Qu'importe ce que peut être la réalité?" (Does it matter what reality might be?)—is not contaminated with everyday purposiveness. Bataille emphasizes the point that prosaic vision entails an absolute separation between the perceiving subject and the objects of its world: both arrow and road are determined outside the subject and possess the tedious opacity of real things. With poetic vision, however, there exists "a relationship of *participation* between subject and object," such that subjective purpose and objective determination can no longer be ascertained. More specifically, Bataille argues that "the *participation* is current" (p. 48, original emphasis); that is, the objects of poetic vision are determined by neither the future nor the past. Poetic *presence*, both conceptual and temporal, is thus opposed to prosaic separation.

Bataille intends to strengthen his case for the poetry/prose opposition by pointing to a "glissement" (slippage) in Sartre's terminology. At one moment Sartre uses the term *transcendance* in reference to the perceiving subject. The subject is constituted as subject by transcending itself and its circumstances in an infinite movement. At another moment, Sartre appeals to an *objective* transcendence like that of the arrow or the bookmark, which lose themselves to indicate other objects. Bataille puts this subject/object slippage down to a "tangling up of thought" (p. 45) and claims that it indicates Sartre's blindness to the poetry/prose opposition. But one could argue equally well that the "tangle" of transcendence seriously disrupts that opposition. First, we should consider that the keystone to Bataille's critical edifice is less the distinction between poetry and prose than that between subject and object in "the prosaic world of activity." If the prosy, everyday man were to find even a fragment of his image in the arrows and the bookmarks of his world, his vision would become proportionately poetic. Now, in order to defend the utilitarian nature of prosaic reality, Bataille (following Sartre) must allow certain objects to be infected with the subjective property of transcendence: the arrow is only a prosaic object if it points beyond itself to the road, which in turn must not exist *en soi*, as its own end. Were this epidemic of transcendence to stop with an object that indicated only its own sovereign presence, we would find ourselves before an ultimate *poetic reality*: poetic, because it would be subordinated to no end other than itself, and real, because its determination would remain firmly outside the subject. Thus, if Bataille's original analysis is played out, the subject/object distinction passes from the prosaic to the poetic world. By the same token, utilitarian values and reality are no longer aligned. The arrow is useful only to the extent that it may be dematerialized: reality in and of itself is useless. If we return to the line from "Les Fenêtres" which provoked both Bataille's and Sartre's reflections, we may see more clearly that the rejection of reality does not lead, as Bataille would have it, to a sovereign, poetic stance, but to the fabrication of a "prosaic," practical ethos: "Qu'importe ce que peut être la réalité placée hors de moi, *si elle m'a aidé à vivre, à sentir que je suis et ce que je suis*" (my emphasis).

If Bataille misreads Baudelaire's declaration as a statement of pure poetic freedom, this is due to a double simplification. On the one hand, Bataille assumes that the reality in question is a stable one, corresponding to Sartre's "theocratic world." As we have previously observed, Bataille's notion of essential freedom is dependent upon this assumption. However, the reality of "Les Fenêtres" is not so stable, but varies with its frame: "Ce qu'on peut voir au soleil est toujours moins intéressant que ce qui se passe derrière une vitre. Dans ce trou noir ou lumineux vit la vie, rêve la vie, souffre la vie" (What one can see in sunlight is always less interesting than what transpires behind a windowpane. In that black or luminous hole, life lives, life dreams, life suffers). Not only does this variability affect reality—"what one can see"—in subjective terms, making it more or less interesting; what one can see also undergoes objective modifications, particularly those of number: "Celui qui regarde du dehors à travers une fenêtre ouverte, ne voit jamais *autant de choses* que celui qui regarde une fenêtre fermée" (Whoever looks outside through an open window never sees *as many things* as the person who looks at a closed window) (my emphasis). Now, one would most expect to find a declaration of poetic freedom in this opposition between the opened and the closed window. Once the spectacle of the real has been veiled, then the poetic imagination may operate without encumbrance. But, instead of marking the difference between prosaic and poetic vision, the figure of the window, opened and closed, describes only a "prosaic" difference of quantity: the onlooker may see more or see less. When Baudelaire has tired of pursuing the complex geometry of the real and offers his dismissal, "Qu'importe!," it is not because he has "seen through" external reality and is expressing contempt for its prosaic banality. The dismissal is more an admission of failure to know the real than the sovereign refusal of something not worth knowing.

The second, un-Baudelairean simplification of Bataille's analysis concerns his conception of the prosaic. Prosaic vision, as we have seen, is subordinated to external reality, while poetic vision is sovereign or free. Bataille's reflections on this topic owe much to Hegel and his discussion of the poetry/prose distinction in the *Aesthetics*. Hegel finds the distinction crucial to his articulation of aesthetic freedom and, in treating the question of prose, focuses on the arts of historiography and oratory:

> The historian . . . must relate what confronts him and as it confronts him without reinterpreting it or giving it poetic form. Therefore no matter how much he may struggle to make the centre and single concatenating bond of his narrative the inner sense and spirit of the epoch, the people, or the specific event which he describes, he still has no freedom to subordinate to this purpose the circumstances, characters, and events confronting him, even if he shoves to one side what in itself is purely accidental and meaningless; to these circumstances etc. he must give free play in their external contingency, dependence on other things, and uncounselled arbitrariness. (pp. 988–99)

Although oratory appears in many ways to be a freer art than historiography, because what the orator expresses "is always his own free judgment, his own mood, and his subjective immanent end in which he can be vitally absorbed with his whole self" (p. 990), still the orator is subject to external circumstances—"his hearers' degree of education, their capability for understanding, and their character" (p. 993). Moreover, the art of oratory does not constitute an end in itself; it is subordinated to a practical purpose that lies outside the artistic presentation of the speech.

The details of Hegel's position, although Bataille does not evoke them, strike me as interesting because they enable the introduction of Baudelaire into the poetry/prose discussion. It is particularly clear from Hegel's analysis of oratory that the notion of prosaic enslavement need not be fatal, as Bataille makes it appear. Oratory is enslaved, not just to past "circumstances, characters, and events," but also to living subjects and their prejudices: these it can transform, at least to some extent, even while it must respect them. In other words, oratory can act upon the very circumstances that determine it. This complex notion of prosaic enslavement is pertinent to our understanding of Baudelaire's aesthetics. As I discuss in the next chapter, Baudelaire's presentation of his poetry is largely "oratorical": his compulsion to guarantee the intelligibility of his work through poetic "contracts" with his readers gives evidence of that fact. Walter Benjamin has gone so far as to argue that Baudelaire's poetry succeeded in shaping its own readership, thereby engendering the circumstances favorable to its reception: "The kind of reader [Baudelaire] envisaged is described in the introductory poem, and this turned out to have been a far-sighted judgment. He was eventually to find the reader at whom his work was aimed" ("Motifs": 155). A peculiar mixture of circumstantial constraint and aesthetic freedom (which Hegel calls *prosaic*) can thus be uncovered at the heart of Baudelaire's *poetic* praxis.

Hegel's notion of historiography does not seem to admit the same degree of aesthetic free play, and one might make the case that Bataille implicitly follows historiography as his model for prose. This would presumably keep the lines between prose and poetry distinctly marked, preventing the kind of slippage I have just suggested. If we turn to Baudelaire, however, who himself theorized on the relationship between history and freedom, we will find a different notion of historiography at work. In the forty-seventh fragment from *Mon coeur mis à nu* Baudelaire defines history, not as a set of circumstances, but as "l'identité des deux idées contradictoires, liberté et fatalité" (the identity of two contradictory ideas, freedom and fate). Although Baudelaire does not mention here the writing of history as a distinct activity, I argue that his notion of history implies a written component. This is due to the fact that he equates historical processes with the cognition/performance of a *law*: "Pour que la loi du progrès existât, il faudrait que chacun voulut la créer; c'est-a-dire que quand tous les individus s'appliqueront à progresser, alors, et seulement alors, l'humanité sera en progrès"

(In order for the law of progress to exist, everyone would have to want it to exist; that is to say, once all individuals apply themselves to progressing, then and only then will humanity be in progress), (1: 707). There is no separation in this formula between the cognitive activity whereby one would discern a law in historical events and the generation of the events themselves. The two activities determine one another in an open-ended movement, thus eliminating the possibility of a purely passive historian enslaved to circumstance. Instead, the writing of history is invested with considerable aesthetic freedom ("liberté" cannot be separated from "fatalité"), closer to what we saw in Hegel's treatment of oratory. This suggests that "prose" for Baudelaire might have different connotations than it does for Bataille, that the prosaic might play a larger role in Baudelaire's aesthetics than Bataille's analysis would admit.

To pursue this hypothesis, we can turn from Baudelaire's theoretical statements to his poetic works. The most astute of the poet's admirers (Paul Valéry, Jacques Rivière, and Walter Benjamin, in particular) have noticed what they call "weaknesses" in *Les Fleurs du mal*. Rivière gives some examples, which are emphatically appropriated by Benjamin: "Le mystique aliment qui *ferait* leur vigueur" (The mystical nutrient that *might* make them strong), "La servante au grand coeur dont vous étiez *jalouse*" (The big-hearted servant whom you were *jealous* of),[14] and so on. These weak spots could be dismissed merely as instances of bad writing, but they have a definable aesthetic effect which plays the poetic against the prosaic and is usually comical. The last line of "Le Cygne," "Aux captifs, aux vaincus! . . . à bien d'autres encor!" (To the captive, to the vanquished! . . . and to many others!) (1: 87), opens with a poetic evocation; but the rhythmic pattern of that evocation, which promises to build to a climax, is transformed into an empty numerical repetition with the prosaic "à bien d'autres encor!" An inverse moment can be detected in the opening of "Le Flacon" (The flask): "Il est de forts parfums pour qui toute matière/Est poreuse. On dirait qu'ils pénètrent le verre" (There are strong perfumes for which all matter/Is porous. One could say that they penetrate glass) (1: 47). Here the language sounds as though it might have been copied from a chemistry textbook, until we reach the *enjambement* "Est poreuse," at which point poetic stress coincides with the flattest of words—porous—to generate a sudden, comical energy.

If one is to develop a real taste for Baudelaire, these spots must be appreciated for their exquisite banality; that is, they represent something like an aesthetic of the everyday. For Bataille, such an aesthetic is not possible, since he has associated the everyday with nonaesthetic activity—"One could not better nor more precisely represent the distance between poetic and *everyday* vision. We forget ourselves when the arrow points to the road, or the bookmark to the page: but this vision . . . is subordinated to our search for the road (that we are going to take), or the page (that we are going to read)" (p. 44, my emphasis). Driving, reading, but not writing, comprise Bataille's notion of the everyday. If these activities are called "prosaic" they do not thereby acquire aesthetic proportions. Instead, the prosaic loses its aesthetic pretensions and becomes equivalent to any nonpoetic act. Baudelaire's everyday, on the other hand, does not consist of roads to be traveled but of speech, "common" speech; as such, the everyday is capable of infecting poetry, of insinuating itself into the aesthetic realm. It is only when we realize this that Sartre's criticism of Baudelaire begins to make sense. Contrary to Bataille's suppositions, Sartre does not find fault with Baudelaire for avoiding the political arena. As poet, Baudelaire would have met with Sartre's approval had he been like Rimbaud, "[who] does not put on an act, [but] really strives to produce extraordinary thoughts and feelings" (*Baudelaire*: 200). Baudelaire's poetry often turns to the commonplace in its style and in its themes at the same time that it presents itself as an extraordinary aesthetic accomplishment "tel que jamais mortel n'en vit" (such as no mortal has ever seen) ("Rêve parisien" 1: 101). Here is where the question of bad faith directly engages the poetry/prose distinction. We might compare this distinction to Sartre's description of "human reality" as being both "transcendence" and "facticity" (*L'Etre et le néant*: 92). The individual in bad faith can affirm these two dimensions as simultaneously equivalent to and different from one another. Likewise, Baudelaire's poetry can claim to transcend its common linguistic "facticity" while it reveals that same prosaic substance with disarming candor. The bad faith of this gesture is intimately tied to the idea of an everyday aesthetic: in order for common, everyday language to be aesthetic, it must be both itself and more than itself. While Bataille's definition of poetry originally excludes all prosaic elements and places a barrier between aesthetic and everyday activities, that definition is eventually modified under the pressure of Sartre's analysis and, I argue, in response to Baudelaire. After proclaiming the sovereign freedom of poetry, Bataille suddenly and surprisingly redefines his subject: "Poetry is always in a sense an opposite of poetry" (p. 50). Were we to ignore the content of this definition and consider its form alone, the expression "always in a sense" would already reveal bad faith working against the very process of definition. "Always in a sense" has the same modest tone that Sartre associates with statements of internal negation; it simultaneously poses and retracts the definition of poetry, leaving open the possibility of a definition that does not define:

With bad faith there appears a truth, a method of thinking, a type of being of objects; the world of bad faith, in which the subject suddenly enraps itself, has the following ontological characteristic—in this world, being is what it is not and is not what it is [*y est ce qu'il n'est pas et n'y est pas ce qu'il est*]. As a consequence, a singular type of fact appears: the *non-persuasive* fact. Bad faith seizes upon facts, but it is resigned from the beginning not to be convinced by them, not to be persuaded and transformed into good faith: it makes itself out to be humble and modest. . . . (*L'Etre et le néant*: 105, original emphasis)

Sartre's words enable us to see in Bataille's definition both the formal and the ontological characteristics of bad faith. The definition itself is not persuaded by its own processes, and this leads to the presentation of an object (poetry, in this case) which is its own opposite, "y est ce qu'il n'est pas et n'y est pas ce qu'il est." As Bataille explicates his definition, the Sartrean framework becomes even more pronounced: "There is an obligation inherent to poetry to make something fixed [*une chose figée*] out of a dissatisfaction. Poetry, in a first movement, destroys the objects that it apprehends, it renders them like the elusive fluidity of the poet's existence, and thus hopes to restore the identity between the world and man. But at the same time that it performs a dispossession, it attempts to *possess* that *dispossession*" (p. 50, original emphasis).

The passage has a distinct existential flavor: "une chose figée," "l'existence du poète," "l'identité du monde et de l'homme," are all rather Sartrean expressions. But even more than this, Bataille has borrowed, feature for feature, the definition of poetry that Sartre offers in *Baudelaire*: "All poets pursue in their own way the impossible synthesis between existence and being. Their quest leads them to select certain objects in the world that strike them as the most eloquent symbols of that reality in which existence and being would be identical; then they attempt to appropriate those objects through contemplation. The appropriation, as we have shown elsewhere, is an attempt at identification" (p. 219).

"Faire une chose figée d'une insatisfaction" (to make something fixed out of a dissatisfaction) describes succinctly the Sartrean synthesis of existence and being. Although Sartre does not speak of destruction in this passage, the investment of certain objects with properties of consciousness or "existence" implies the violation of their ontological opacity; only thus can they take on "the elusive fluidity of the poet's existence," to quote Bataille. What Sartre calls the "metaphysical lightness" of Baudelaire's poetry, his love of perfumes and other volatile essences, describes the dissipation of being that Bataille reads as violence. This first movement of poetry is followed in both Bataille and Sartre by a gesture of appropriation which would aim at recovering "the identity between the world and man." Such an "attempt at identification" is an impossible task, dividing the poetic enterprise against itself: "at the same time that it performs a dispossession it attempts to *possess* that *dispossession*." Poetry recognizes its own impossibility and resigns itself to remaining in the realm of unfulfillable hopes: "Thus it *hopes* [my emphasis] to recover the identity between the world and man."

It should be noted that by advancing this definition Bataille is jeopardizing his original attribution of a free essence to poetry. Suddenly poetry, much like prose, is "obliged" to engage in a continuous commerce with the world. True, Bataille places this commerce under the sign of destruction, but the destruction is not gratuitous; instead it is a "dessaisissement," an (il)legal dispossession which is constantly directed toward the law whereby the world possesses and repossesses itself. I argue that it is Bataille's need to account for the prosaic moment of *Les Fleurs du mal* within a generalized poetics that leads him to redefine poetry as a self-contradiction. Poetic identity is stretched to cover what would not be itself and the prosaic threat to poetic integrity is thereby concealed. The powers of bad faith are solicited so that difference may be retrieved for identity with a characteristic lack of conceptual rigor.

Since I have suggested that this redefinition of poetry is a kind of distant response to Baudelaire (distant, because Bataille never cites *Les Fleurs du mal* and undertakes his "defense of poetry" [p. 46] in very general terms), it would be appropriate to examine the question of poetic integrity more specifically by considering the poems of *Les Fleurs du mal* themselves. A first observation might be that, alongside the tradition of seeing Baudelaire's masterpiece as "a poetic work of the strictest unity,"[15] there exists another, equally well-established tradition of reading the work in terms of a radical internal opposition. Baudelaire himself contributed to this second tradition, by entitling the longest subsection of his poetry "Spleen et Idéal" and by a number of explicit declarations—"A un blasphème, j'opposerai des élancements vers le Ciel, à une obscénité, des fleurs platoniques" (Next to a blasphemy I will place heavenly transports; next to an obscenity, platonic flowers) (1: 195). It is possible to reconcile these two traditions by arguing that the first concerns an aesthetic evaluation of the poetry, while the second engages ethical issues and is more thematic in nature. While this argument is, on one level, quite true, it does not account for the odd ways in which the two traditions interfere with each other. There is, for example, the fact that the affirmations of aesthetic integrity were given, at the time of the trial of *Les Fleurs du mal*, as evidence of the poetry's ethical value: "[*Les Fleurs du mal*] are less a collection of poems than a poetic work *of the strictest unity* [*de la plus forte unité*]. From the standpoint of Art and aesthetic sensation they lose much if they are not read *in the order* in which the poet, who knows what he is doing, has placed them. But they lose even more *from the standpoint of the moral impact* that we pointed out at the beginning of this article if they are not read in order" (OC, 1: 1196, Barbey's emphasis). There is, in addition, the fact that certain descriptions of the poetry's duality (Benjamin divides it between *correspondances* and *spleen*) seem to engage aesthetic characteristics. Moreover, aesthetic success and failure are treated thematically in *Les Fleurs du mal*, and might be seen as dominating the high/low movements. Although the poet most often proclaims his aesthetic failure—"La Cloche fêlée" (The cracked bell), (1: 72)—

> Moi, mon âme est fêlée, et lorsqu'en ses ennuis
> Elle veut de ses chants peupler l'air froid des nuits,
> Il arrive souvent que sa voix affaiblie
> Semble le râle épais d'un blessé qu'on oublie . . .
>
> As for me, my soul is cracked, and when, laden with care
> It seeks to people the cold night air with its songs,
> Often its feeble voice
> Seems like the thick death-rattle of a forgotten, wounded man . . .

he sometimes affirms his aesthetic prowess—"Le Balcon" (The balcony), (1: 37)—

> Je sais l'art d'évoquer les minutes heureuses,
> Et revis mon passé blotti dans tes genoux.
> Car à quoi bon chercher tes beautés langoureuses
> Ailleurs qu'en ton cher corps et qu'en ton coeur si doux?
> Je sais l'art d'évoquer les minutes heureuses!
>
> I know the art of evoking the happy minutes,
> And relive my past curled up in your lap.
> For what sense is it to seek your langorous beauties
> Elsewhere than in your dear body and in your gentle heart?
> I know the art of evoking the happy minutes!

This interference of aesthetic and ethical components is of critical importance. It belies many of the post-Kantian prejudices that surround *Les Fleurs du mal*—that they are an instance of pure poetry, that they are flowers of evil because their beauty is indifferent to ethical or thematic considerations, that the aesthetic here constitutes a beautiful totality. It also raises problems for Bataille's critique of Sartre: To what extent is Bataille justified in suspending the ethical register of Sartre's analysis? Can the judgment of bad faith be dismissed in defense of poetry, while poetry takes on the formal characteristics of bad faith? Should bad faith be understood only in ethical terms, or does it describe the interference of aesthetic and ethical concerns? How does such an interference affect the issue of poetic specificity? I propose to consider these questions by looking in detail at two of Baudelaire's poems—"La Musique," which treats the problem of aesthetic indifference, and "La Muse malade" (The sick muse), in which a wish in bad faith furnishes the key to the poem's aesthetic character.

> La musique souvent me prend comme une mer!
>   Vers ma pâle étoile,
> Sous un plafond de brume ou dans un vaste éther,
>   Je mets à la voile;
>
> La poitrine en avant et les poumons gonflés
>   Comme de la toile,
> J'escalade le dos des flots amoncelés
>   Que la nuit me voile;
>
> Je sens vibrer en moi toutes les passions
>   D'un vaisseau qui souffre;
> Le bon vent, la tempête et ses convulsions
>   Sur l'immense gouffre
> Me bercent. D'autres fois, calme plat, grand miroir
>   De mon désespoir!

> Music often takes hold of me like a tide!
>   Towards my pale star,
> Beneath a ceiling of haze or in a vast ether,
>   I set sail;
>
> My chest thrust out and my lungs filled
>   Like sail-cloth,
> I scale the back of the heaped-up waves
>   That the night veils from me;

> I feel vibrating within me all the passions
> Of a suffering ship;
> The favorable wind, the tempest and its convulsions
> On the immense abyss
> Cradle me. At other times, a flat calm, great mirror
> Of my despair!

The first stanza of "La Musique" makes a claim for aesthetic indifference that seems to surmount the thematic duality of *Les Fleurs du mal*: "Sous un plafond de brume *ou* dans un vaste éther," Baudelaire writes, "Je mets à la voile" (Beneath a ceiling of haze *or* in a vast ether, / I set sail). It is not stretching matters to see in the opposition between foggy and clear weather a kind of climatic shorthand for "Spleen et Idéal." In most of Baudelaire's "Spleen" poems it is raining and the expanse of the sky has shut down—"le ciel bas et lourd pèse comme un couvercle" (the low, heavy sky weighs down like a lid) ("Spleen" 1: 74). The experience of the ideal, on the other hand, involves a beatific expansiveness, the opening out of a "vaste éther" ("Elévation" 1: 10)[16]:

> Au-dessus des étangs, au-dessus des vallées,
> Des montagnes, des bois, des nuages, des mers,
> Par-delà le soleil, par-dela les éthers,
> Par-dela les confins des sphères étoilées,
>
> Mon esprit, tu te meus avec agilité . . .
>
> Above the swamps, above the valleys
> Mountains, woods, clouds, seas,
> Beyond the sun, beyond the ethers,
> Beyond the confines of the starry spheres,
>
> My spirit, you move nimbly . . .

The aesthetic power of music is apparently such that it need not be determined by either of these experiences. One could argue that this marks the difference between music and poetry, that the former is not bound by thematic determinations and is free from the traces of lived experience that continue to haunt poetry. If this were the case, then poetry could no longer lay claim to the highest aesthetic privileges and music would realize Bataille's program for aesthetic sovereignty. While I find this line of argument intriguing, it moves rather too quickly toward the critique of Bataille and leaves unexamined the issue of aesthetic sovereignty itself. So, for the moment, we will treat the poem's claim to aesthetic indifference in general terms.

Interestingly, the poem, like Bataille, describes aesthetic indifference as a kind of tension—the extended sail or "les poumons gonflés / Comme de la toile" is pulled so taut that it may pass with equal ease through fair and foul weather—"Le bon vent, la tempête et ses convulsions." Similarly, Bataille affiliates Baudelaire's sovereign poetic stance with a relentless spiritual tension: "But since, by Sartre's own admission an 'unequalled tension' armed him, [Baudelaire] exploited his erroneous position to the maximum: a perfect movement of ecstasy and horror mingled give his poetry a plenitude that is sustained without weakness *at the very limits* of a free sensibility" (p. 53, original emphasis). As long as that tension is maintained, the climate of the external world can have no impact on the free aesthetic sensibility. What happens in "La Musique," however, is that tension is lost, leading to a division in the aesthetic. This occurs most obviously in the final stanza, where the poetic irregularity—the *rejet* of the second line is marked by being the end of the poem's first sentence ("Me bercent. D'autres fois, calme plat, grand miroir. . . .")—underscores a critical distinction between two types of aesthetic experience. "La musique *souvent* me prend comme une mer!" (Music *often* takes hold of me like a tide!); this first type of experience involves the communication of emotion—"Je sens vibrer en moi toutes les passions" (I feel vibrating within me all the passions)—but is missing a visual or representational component—"J'escalade le dos des flots amoncelés / *Que la nuit me voile* . . ." (I scale the back of the heaped-up waves / *That the night veils from me* . . .). I argue that the high tension of this experience is already threatened by the repetition of the word "voile" at the end of the first two stanzas. The repetition turns "sail" into "veil," and, in so doing, transforms the relationship of the subject "je" to the external world. The tense relationship that is mediated by the figure of the sail (even if, as Bataille would contend, it is primarily a tension *within* the subject) is lost once the limit between subject and world is described as a veil. The loss introduces, if only negatively, the element of vision and thereby prepares the second aesthetic moment of the poem. This second moment is as exclusive of the first as are the two properties of the sea: it may be either turbulent or reflecting, but not both simultaneously. Thus, the particular temporal structure that Baudelaire gives his poem: "La musique *souvent* me prend comme une mer!", "*D'autres fois*, calme plat, grand miroir/De mon désespoir!" The two aesthetic moments are separated by the distance that divides "often" from "at other times." In the second instance, a "flat calm" takes the place of turbulent emotion and the aesthetic experience becomes one of pure reflection.

It is peculiar that Baudelaire should associate music, even occasionally, with an aesthetics of representation; this seems to indicate that the aesthetic question of the poem does not involve generic distinctions, that is, between poetry and music or between representational and nonrepresentational art, and is, therefore, best approached in general terms. What the general perspective reveals, then, is that the declaration of aesthetic indifference cannot be sustained, that aesthetic indifference to the everyday world becomes aesthetic difference, a difference that is marked by an everyday temporality—"often" like this, "at other times" like that.

For both Sartre and Bataille, the subordination of the aesthetic to the everyday, or of poetry to the prosaic world, implies an ethical challenge to the sovereign claims of the aesthetic. Although the ethical dimension seems to have been elided from a poem like "La Musique" (much as Bataille seeks to elide the ethical from his defense of poetry), the challenge to the aesthetic persists: it persists on an ontological level, in the inability to define poetry or to unify aesthetic experience. In the prose poem "Le Thyrse," which has often been interpreted as a figure for Baudelaire's poetry in general,[17] the ontological question is directly linked to the problem of aesthetic difference: "Qu'est-ce qu'un thyrse?" (What is a thyrsus?) Baudelaire asks at the beginning of the poem. The question never receives a stable answer because the answer is always two-fold—a thyrsus is this and that, "ligne droite et ligne arabesque, intention et expression, . . . unité du but, variété des moyens, . . . (straight line and arabesque, intention and expression, . . . unity of ends, variety of means, . . .) (1: 336). What is produced by the line of questioning is a world whose ontological characteristics correspond to the ontology of bad faith. From the beginning, we have a question that must be posed but that cannot be completely answered; thus, the answer only returns us to the question and, suspended between question and answer, we have a strange object, a thyrsus, which is what it is not and is not what it is.

At this point I must appeal to Sartre's authority and to the coherence of his philosophical system to make the claim that such an ontology of the aesthetic implies a specifically ethical challenge (at the end of *L'Etre et le néant*, Sartre promises to follow his ontological treatise with an ethics, arguing that the discussion of being has made the latter both possible and necessary). In more intuitive terms, the ethical challenge can be seen as contained within the concept of bad faith: bad faith introduces the issue of judgment into the discussion of being. The description of being in bad faith becomes what Sartre calls "a moral description" (*L'Etre et le néant*: 690), inevitably tending toward judgments of value. In the following discussion of "La Muse malade," an early poem by Baudelaire, I propose to study the ways in which bad faith intervenes and coordinates the aesthetic and ethical implications of the poem.

> Ma pauvre muse, hélas! qu'as-tu donc ce matin?
> Tes yeux creux sont peuplés de visions nocturnes,
> Et je vois tour à tour réfléchis sur ton teint
> La folie et l'horreur, froides et taciturnes.
>
> Le succube verdâtre et le rose lutin
> T'ont-ils versé la peur et l'amour de leurs urnes?
> Le cauchemar, d'un poing despotique et mutin,
> T'a-t-il noyée au fond d'un fabuleux Minturnes?
>
> Je voudrais qu'exhalant l'odeur de la santé
> Ton sein de pensers fort fût toujours fréquenté,
> Et que ton sang chrétien coulât à flots rythmiques,

> Comme les sons nombreux des syllabes antiques,
> Où règnent tour à tour le père des chansons,
> Phoebus, et le grand Pan, le seigneur des moissons.

> My poor muse, alas! what is wrong with you this morning?
> Your haggard eyes are peopled with nocturnal visions,
> And I see by turns reflected in your complexion
> Madness and horror, cold and taciturn.

> The greenish succubus and the rose-colored elf
> Have they given you fear and love to drink from their urns?
> Has nightmare, with a despotic and unruly fist,
> Drowned you in the depths of a fabulous Minturn?

> I could wish that, exuding the odor of health
> Your breast were always frequented with forceful thoughts,
> And that your Christian blood would flow with rhythmic beats,

> Like the many sounds of antique syllables
> Where reign by turns the father of songs,
> Phoebus, and Great Pan, the lord of harvests.

At first reading, the poem lends itself to the simplest of oppositional structures. It casts aesthetic difference in historical terms, as the difference between the antique and the Christian worlds. The muse of antiquity is healthy and strong, while the Christian muse, the muse of the title, is sickly. By attaching the aesthetic in this manner to questions of sickness and health, Baudelaire invites a value judgment: simply put, it is bad for a muse to be sick, and this judgment seems to be confirmed by the poet's wish in the closing tercets—"Je voudrais qu'exhalant l'odeur de la santé . . ." Thus far, the aesthetic and ethical elements of the poem appear to be identical and we could end our interpretation here. The only problem is that such an interpretation conflicts with most of the established ideas about Baudelaire's aesthetics: whatever else one might say about the beautiful, one would not say that, for Baudelaire, it is simply equivalent to the good. Claude Pichois, in his notes to the Pléiade edition of *Les Fleurs du mal*, explains the anomalous features of "La Muse malade" by suggesting that the poem predates Baudelaire's 1852 essay, *L'Ecole païenne* (The pagan school), in which he attacks the antique aesthetic ideal. Although this dating is probably correct, I maintain that more is at stake in the poem's aesthetic peculiarities (or lack of peculiarities, because it is precisely the uncomplicated notion of aesthetic difference that is troublingly un-Baudelairean).

One way to complicate the preceding interpretation is to question the sincerity of the poet's wish: how could the author of *Les Fleurs du mal*, even in a moment of youthful inconsistency, really have preferred an antique muse? "Nous avons, il est vrai, nations corrompues,/ Aux peuples anciens des beautés inconnues" (We corrupted nations have, it is true,/ Beauties unknown to ancient peoples) (1: 12): in these verses, apparently contemporaneous with "La Muse malade," Baudelaire announces his allegiance to a modern aesthetic. Despite its origins in corruption, such an aesthetic is not presented here in a completely negative light: it possesses its own specificity, which cannot be placed on the same scale with the antique ideal. The weight of Baudelaire's later statements, along with an entrenched Romantic tradition which clearly influences his early writing, actually privilege the modern over the antique aesthetic. The latter is less beautiful for pursuing beauty exclusively, as Baudelaire argues in *L'Ecole païenne*: "An immoderate taste for form leads to monstrous and strange disorders. Ideas of the just and the true disappear, absorbed by the ferocious passion for the beautiful, the droll, the pretty, the picturesque, etc. (because there are different stages). The frenzied passion for art is a canker that devours everything else; and, since the absence of the just and the true in art equals the absence of art, man as a whole vanishes . . ." (*OC*, 2: 48–49).

With this argument in mind, we can reinterpret what is involved in the oppositional structure of "La Muse malade": rather than equating aesthetic and ethical judgments in both antique and Christian worlds, we can see those judgments as diverging in particular ways. Ethical determinations, ideas of "the just and the true," play no role in antique assessments of the beautiful; it is only in the Christian world that the aesthetic and the ethical begin to interfere with each other, although no longer in a symmetrical manner.

These are Baudelaire's suppositions in *L'Ecole païenne* and elsewhere. The burden now is to find textual evidence for this reinterpretation in "La Muse malade" itself.

A first clue that something is amiss in the apparent identification of aesthetic and ethical judgments lies in the poem's frank historicization of the aesthetic. If beauty were really truth and truth beauty, there would be no grounds for subjecting beauty to historical difference. As I argue in Chapters 1 and 4, the pattern of historical difference that characterizes many poems of *Les Fleurs du mal* is actually grounded in aesthetic difference: the inability of beauty and truth to coincide is presented as a history that recounts the loss of that coincidence. If this argument is also valid for "La Muse malade," then the wish to return to an antique aesthetic can never be fulfilled; aesthetic difference is an original premise that cannot be erased. The wish to "return" to a past condition that never existed can only be in bad faith: it recognizes from the beginning its own impossibility, it is resigned to its own powerlessness, and this gives it its particular nostalgic beauty. In this sense, the wish in bad faith provides "La Muse malade" with an aesthetic character that is neither antique nor Christian since it is not, in fact, determined by historical pressures.

A second line of evidence in support of the preceding remarks can be gleaned from a stylistic analysis of "La Muse malade." If Baudelaire's desire for a healthy muse were unequivocal, it stands to reason that the poem would reflect this on a stylistic level, perhaps by imitating the qualities of symmetry and balance that are often associated with the antique aesthetic ideal.[18] Now, this may seem to be the case because "La Muse malade" finds its stylistic focus in an expression of equilibrium: "tour à tour" (by turns). When "tour à tour" is used to coordinate the feverish alternation of madness and horror in the sick muse, one could argue that Baudelaire's wish has been fulfilled and that antique harmony has been restored to a condemned world. "Et je vois tour à tour réfléchis sur ton teint / La folie et l'horreur, froides et taciturnes." The symmetry of these lines is reinforced by the comma marking the caesura of the second alexandrine, and by the fact that the adjectives "froides" and "taciturnes" apply equally to "la folie" and to "l'horreur," thus minimizing the sense of alternation. However, the second time "tour à tour" appears—in the closing lines of "La Muse malade"— the expression does not give stylistic reinforcement to a symmetry implied by the evocation of antiquity. Instead, it creates a stylistic asymmetry which gives the poem its distinctly Baudelairean charm. "Où règnent tour à tour le père des chansons, / Phoebus, et le grand Pan, le seigneur des moissons." The final alexandrine develops a new rhythm with the emphasis on "Phoebus," which is separated from "Pan" by a comma, unlike "la folie et l'horreur" of the earlier lines. Moreover, the two gods are given separate epithets: one is "le père des chansons," the other "le seigneur des moissons," and this separation is accentuated by the placement of the epithets on different lines. These distinct epithets contrast with the adjectival couple, "froides et taciturnes." Thus the second "tour à tour" of the poem takes the elements that were massed symmetrically by the first "tour à tour" and unlinks them. This means that the evocation of the antique ideal occurs at the moment when "La Muse malade" departs, at least on the stylistic level, from that ideal. In other words, the historical and stylistic features of the poem diverge, underscoring aesthetic difference in the very process of wishing it away.

The stylistic departure from antique equilibrium points to even greater irregularities involving the thematic opposition between Christian and pagan worlds. Although we would expect the epithets that characterize Phoebus and Pan to emphasize an antique idiom, this is not entirely the case. First of all, the titles "père" and "seigneur" are more Christian than pagan in flavor. This is not too troublesome where Phoebus is concerned, since he *is* the god of music and "père des chansons" may pass for an appropriately classical attribution. But Pan is most notably a god of herds and flocks and associated, not with cultivated nature and the harvest, but with "mountains, caves, and lonely places."[19] It is true that Baudelaire might have chosen to evoke the harvest because he needed a word to rhyme with "chansons," but one may then ask why he did not pick the appropriate deity to rule over "les moissons." Rather than view this as mere solecism, I suggest that there is an intended irony in the designation of Pan as "le seigneur des moissons." When we pass from the Greek to the Christian tradition, the harvest gains in figurative connotations: it still represents fertility and prosperity, but it also stands for judgment. On the day of judgment, evil is separated from good, just as the tares are cut from wheat in the time of harvest. The "seigneur des moissons," the one who presides over judgment, is Jesus Christ. Thus, a Christian figure appears like a persistent shadow behind the antique images.[20]

Given these stylistic and thematic observations, it is possible to argue that bad faith coincides with the poem's aesthetic character via the expression "tour à tour." The return to antiquity is described as the alternating reign of two antique gods. As we have seen, within this alternation, which at first appears harmonious, there exists a possible conflict: if Pan casts a Christian shadow then his reign is not so easily reconciled with that of Phoebus. Although this simultaneity of reconciliation and conflict is easily expressed in thematic terms, that is, as the relationship between the Greek and the Christian worlds, it is actually determined by the logical possibilities of the alternation "tour à tour." The logic of "tour à tour" touches on the prose/poetry question of our previous discussion. If "tour à tour" were to serve the cause of poetry, the alternation of two terms would have to hint at a higher or deeper reconciliation. Such is the case, for example, in "Correspondances," where night and light or mind and senses are harmonized "dans une ténébreuse et profonde unité" (into a somber and deep unity). But "tour à tour," if it succeeds in reconciling opposing terms, does so on a superficial level. When children "take turns" at play, a parent is usually behind their cooperation; the reconciliation thereby achieved is determined, not internally, but externally. This is why it is easy to imagine childlike cooperation veering toward more hostile modes of alternation—"often" it is my turn, "at other times" yours, and so on—which are fundamentally *prosaic*. Similarly, "tour à tour" offers superficial prospects of harmony but maintains the incongruity of the terms it would coordinate.

It is in identical terms that Sartre describes the coordinating powers of bad faith. Incommensurable elements, whether they be human facticity versus human transcendence or the Greek versus the Christian world, are played against each other in such a way that we can neither synthesize nor separate them. All we can do is to refigure their relationship repeatedly. For "La Muse malade," beauty and judgment are brought into the game of refiguration, first through their emblems—the Greek "chansons" and the Christian "moissons." But as we consider the activity of figuration itself, it should become clear that beauty and judgment are implicated both by their emblems and by the functioning of "tour à tour." When opposing elements are figured together, they are harmonized in an aesthetic moment, which we can imagine as the rule of "le père des chansons"; this moment, however, is not of indefinite duration (in this it resembles the occasional mirror, the aesthetic moment of "La Musique"), but is constantly interrupted. The interruption does not leave us with the absence of a figure, as might be the case for a Mallarmé poem; instead, we are compelled to *re*figure the relationship between opposing terms. Thus, the principle of division, which can be pictured in the harvest sickle, does not put an end to harmony. Because this is so, it is only possible to assess indirectly the dividing powers of judgment, as the constant threat to any given aesthetic configuration. One could say, of course, that "tour à tour" provides us with a stable and accurate figure for the relationship between beauty and judgment. This would be a kind of aestheticist position in that it ultimately rests its faith upon a figure. But if we see in "tour à tour" a key to the aesthetic character of Baudelaire's poetry in general, we will have to acknowledge that this figural key consistently distances itself from beauty as such. Beauty is thus only partially fulfilled by the aesthetic character of the poetry. Any "aestheticism" based on this partial fulfillment of the beautiful would have to be qualified; it could not be a post-Kantian aestheticism that suspends indefinitely the disruptive occurrences of judgment.

By the foregoing analysis I hope to have shown that the notion of bad faith can contribute to the discussion of Baudelaire's aesthetics. Bataille's efforts to bracket bad faith as an ethical concept merely lead to its reproduction in aesthetic terms, as it lends its features to the definition of poetry. This results in a curious defense of poetry that can only betray its own intentions: the affirmation of poetic specificity that Bataille makes in separating poetry from prose, or the aesthetic from the ethical realm, produces an unintended generalization of the poetic. Suddenly, poetry is what it is not and is not what it is; consequently, poetry is most often to be found where it is not. This is why Bataille finds it necessary to pursue his defense of Baudelaire by referring to "a project *outside the limits* of poetic form" (p. 57, my emphasis), namely, the sketch of a play that Baudelaire recounts in a letter to Hippolyte Tisserand.[21] The play tells the story of a drunken sawyer who murders his wife and who expresses his strange passions in nonsense songs. In Bataille's analysis, these meaningless jingles mark a culminating moment of poetic excess: although Baudelaire never succeeded in writing the play, "at least . . . with such a project he went as far as he could go" (p. 58).

It is intriguing that the same paradoxical dynamic can be detected in the original defense of Baudelaire's poetry in 1857. In his statement of support for *Les Fleurs du mal*, Barbey d'Aurevilly justified what might otherwise have been considered a feeble tactic with the following declaration:

> We neither can nor will cite anything from the collection of poems in question, and here is why: a cited poem can only be appreciated for its individual merit, and we must not be mistaken, in M. Baudelaire's book each poem, along with its specific details and turn of thought, has *a very important value stemming from its situation in the whole volume* [*une valeur très importante d'ensemble et de situation*], a value we must not take away from it. (1: 1196, original emphasis)

Once again, the defense of poetry involves a displacement of the poetic: Baudelaire's poetry is not where it is and, for this reason, cannot be cited. The bad faith of such a defensive strategy is easy to identify, and doubtless contributed to the condemnation of *Les Fleurs du mal* in the nineteenth century. I maintain, however, that the bad faith of Barbey's defense is perfectly consonant with its aesthetic acumen: it is this connection between bad faith and the aesthetic that the twentieth-century controversy over Baudelaire reveals.

CHAPTER THREE

The Caricatural Mechanism in Baudelaire's Poetry

Georges Blin gives a succinct explanation for what he perceives as the average reader's resistance to Sartre's *Baudelaire*: "It is a fact that despite its great mastery this study does not win the reader to its cause . . . This is because the demonstration of existential psychoanalysis is naturally converted into an unwarranted indictment. One feels constantly deported from the neutral ground of explanation towards that of reproach or accusation" (*Le Sadisme de Baudelaire*: 123). Although Blin senses that there is something "natural" about this conversion of analysis into accusation, he is at a loss to explain it: "One cannot explain how J.-P. Sartre was able to brood at such length over this distressed soul [*cette intimité douloureuse*] without feeling even that ounce of sympathy that enables understanding" (p. 124). With this second statement, Blin, perhaps unwittingly, acknowledges the difficulty of sustaining an objective analysis of Baudelaire's "intimité douloureuse." Were one to avoid drifting into accusation, one would need a minimum dose of human sympathy. Such sympathy serves the ends, not of analysis, but of understanding, and we once more find ourselves confronted with issues of an ethical nature. In other words, the choice is not, as Blin would have it, one which runs between neutral explanation and tendentious judgment. Our explanation will always manifest an ethical tendency, and thus it remains for us to choose between two unavoidably ethical modes.

Sartre's reproaches derive from an application of the *lex talionis* to the moral domain: "every man has the life that he deserves," or the more familiar "you reap what you sow," becomes the axiom of this ethical discourse. Far from being the expression of a cranky and idiosyncratic subjectivity, Sartre's judgment of Baudelaire is based upon an objective ethics, one which takes no account of elusive, subjective qualifications, such as intention. Blin's alternative reading of Baudelaire does not elide the problem of judgment, but introduces a subjective (or better yet, intersubjective) element into the proportion; hence Blin's insistence that sympathy is necessary to understanding recalls another well-known, ethical axiom: "Judge not, that ye be not judged. For with what judgment ye judge, ye shall be judged: and with what measure ye mete, it shall be measured to you again" (Matt. 7: 1, 2). The sympathetic understanding Blin advocates involves, of course, a suspension of judgment, but it does not do away with the ethical category as thoroughly as an aestheticist might wish. The *lex talionis* still functions perfectly, only now what is exchanged, measure for measure, is judgment itself: "By what judgment ye judge, ye shall be judged." This explains to a large extent the reaction against Sartre, since his own application of a strict rule was returned to him, and he was *judged* a poor poet.

It does not matter that Blin can locate "veritable prose poems" (p. 122) in Sartre's discussion of Baudelaire, because the verdict of "poor poet" has nothing to do with Sartre's objective capabilities as a writer. "Poor poet" instead passes judgment on Sartre's judgment, and is thus equivalent to a verdict of "narrow" or "literal minded." Such a verdict in no way exceeds the ethical domain, and the fact that "poetry" comes to figure the large measure or the broad mind does not take us "beyond" the ethical and into the aesthetic domain. Furthermore, the judgment against Sartre does not invalidate the claims to objectivity of his original analysis; that is, we are not now in a position to say that Baudelaire positively did not reap what he sowed in the course of his life. In other words, the content of an objective ethical analysis is not brought into question when we find it an injustice that one sows "poetry" (the large measure) and reaps condemnation.

This latter point has been obscured in the judgments of Sartre's *Baudelaire*, and not without reason. The key to the problem lies in Blin's observation that "the demonstration of existential psychoanalysis is naturally converted into an unwarranted indictment" (p. 123). Had the *content* of Sartre's analysis been different, had he demonstrated, for example, that Baudelaire fit the psychic profile of a liar or a thief, we would not find ourselves so wary of acquiescing to the facts and thereby drifting into abusiveness. French letters have often accommodated themselves to authors of dubious moral fiber, and few literati feel that the mention of François Villon's criminal antics constitutes an abuse of his poetic genius. However, Sartre did not uncover murder or thievery when he subjected Baudelaire to an ethical analysis—instead, he uncovered bad faith. In some respects, this judgment must appear rather mild, since Sartre detects only the ruse of bad faith where others might see a confession of serious crimes.[1] But this is precisely the difficulty, because it is possible to grant an objective status to, say, thievery, while bad faith resists objective classification; as a consequence, bad faith wreaks havoc with judgment itself. One may prove a thief a thief and then choose to grant forgiveness, thus keeping distinct the large and small measures of judgment; but, once bad faith has been proved, there appears to be no recourse to the large measure and condemnation is inevitable. Thus, the one who would judge is left in a peculiar situation: if he acknowledges the crime, he cannot forgive it, and if he wishes to forgive he must deny the crime all objective existence. We know from Sartre's example that, in the first instance, when the judge chooses to acknowledge the crime and condemn, he simultaneously risks being caught in his own condemnation. Because this is an unappealing prospect, we might suppose that there really is no choice for a judge but to forgive and forget. However, when we realize that the task here is not in fact to forget, but to deny what one sees, this option appears as much as the other to deprive the judge of the freedom of a good conscience.

In the second instance, there is an equal risk of contamination, only now what spreads is not condemnation but bad faith. At the very moment when the judge chooses to overlook the objective existence of bad faith, his own judgment is infected with the conduct: he forgives what he pretends is not there, or sees without seeing, which is the definitive characteristic of bad faith. Such forgiveness, therefore, does not count bad faith as negligible; instead, it spells the displacement of bad faith from an *object* of judgment to the *subjective figure* of judgment. This "conversion" is as natural as the one that leads Sartre from analysis into abuse, and both reveal the enslavement of judgment once the problem of bad faith has been posed. The question now remains, Was it Sartre who first posed the problem of bad faith or can we locate that problem more specifically in Baudelaire's poetry? If we may be guided by our reading of "La Muse malade," even the poetry's purely aesthetic self-presentation is undermined by a slippage toward the subjective figure: the poetry exists, no longer in and of itself, but as a desire for poetry, and a qualified desire at that.[2] To use Sartrean terminology, Baudelaire's poetry does not exist *en-soi*, and this slippage outside the realm of being *en-soi* is accompanied by "a permanent risk of bad faith" (*L'Etre et le néant*: 107). We saw that permanent risk of bad faith in the aesthetic expression "tour à tour," but we should now examine whether a more general application of this analysis may be made to Baudelaire's poetry.

Critics have frequently recognized Baudelaire's concern with the "extra-poetic." In fact, Paul Valéry attributed Baudelaire's phenomenal success to extra-poetic factors: "This great posthumous favor, this spiritual fertility . . . must depend not only upon his intrinsic merit as a poet, but also upon exceptional circumstances" ("Situation de Baudelaire," 1: 599). Among these circumstances is Baudelaire's position in the history of French letters, his "situation," as Valéry calls it. Before he could begin the exercise of his poetic faculty, Baudelaire was constrained to a specifically *critical* activity: he had to mark his difference from overwhelmingly illustrious predecessors—Lamartine, Hugo, and Musset. Valéry cites the *Projets de préface* in which Baudelaire declares that, after a process of elimination, he chose as his poetic task "to extract *beauty* from Evil" [*extraire la beauté du Mal*]. In the same preface, Baudelaire mentions another of his extra-poetic concerns: "Ce n'est pas pour mes femmes, mes filles ou mes soeurs que ce livre a été écrit; non plus que pour les femmes, les filles ou les soeurs de mon voisin" (It is not for my wives, my daughters or my sisters that this book was written; not any more than for the wives, daughters or sisters of my neighbor) (*OC*, 1: 181). Thus, not only is *Les Fleurs du mal* to be explained and supported by a historical situation, it also requires a specific reading public. Like Baudelaire's poetic task, this public is chosen through a process of elimination—"pas pour mes femmes," and so on. By these negative gestures, Baudelaire simultaneously defends his poetry and establishes its fundamental *dependency*. If *Les Fleurs du mal* attains to the success of a more universal poetry, this is because it has hopped on the crutches of history and an idiosyncratic readership. It is useful here to remember the lines from "Le Soleil": "C'est lui qui rajeunit les porteurs de béquilles / Et les rend gais et doux comme des jeunes filles" (It is he who rejuvenates those who carry crutches / And makes them merry and gentle as young girls) (1: 83). The sun in this poem, "ainsi qu'un poète" (like a poet), is capable of investing all objects, noble and ignoble, with its glittering prestige: "Et il s'introduit en roi, sans bruits et sans valets, / Dans tous les hôpitaux et dans tous les palais" (And he enters like a king, without noise and without menservants / Into all hospitals and all palaces). True, this prestige seems to equalize the crippled hospital inmate and the presumably well-favored palace dweller; but it does not permit the cripple to leave his crutches and stand on his own power. Similarly, *Les Fleurs du mal* may bask in the sun of "[a] great posthumous favor," but it does not thereby transcend its dependent condition.

The concerns expressed in Baudelaire's *Projets de préface* are evident, too, in his prefatory poems. Although the selection of a specific reading public is not explicit in "Au lecteur" (To the reader), the opening lines, much like those of a sermon, orient the reader in a particular direction: "La sottise, l'erreur, le péché, la lésine, / Occupent nos esprits et travaillent nos corps" (Foolishness, error, sin, stinginess, / Inhabit our minds and torment our bodies). Baudelaire's cagey use of the pronouns "our" and "we" eliminates all those readers who cannot, or who absolutely will not, admit such lethal qualities into their intimacy. Walter Benjamin concludes from the declaration, "Et le riche métal de notre volonté / Est tout vaporisé" (and the rich metal of our will / Is all vaporized), that Baudelaire sought out *poor* readers, ones who would be lacking the will power to concentrate. Benjamin takes Valéry's notion of a "situational" poetry one step further, outside what may still be called the history of literature and into the history of human experience. If Baudelaire wrote for poor readers, Benjamin argues, this was because he foresaw a change in "the climate for lyric poetry," that traditional lyricism would soon have nothing to do with the "structure" of everyday experience ("Motifs": 155–56). Baudelaire's poetry thus becomes a kind of historical wager, aimed at a readership that did not yet exist in 1857, but that would come into full-fledged being by the turn of the century. With this analysis, Benjamin concludes that "[Baudelaire's] work cannot merely be categorized as historical, like anyone else's, but it intended to be so and understood itself as such" (p. 162).

The distinction Benjamin makes here is crucial, and confirms the dependent status of *Les Fleurs du mal*: a poetry that may be categorized as historical should not be confused with a poetry whose constitutive category is historicity. This latter poetry cannot be conceived of as a beautiful totality; it cannot be taken either in or out of context, depending upon the mood or the temperament of its exegete. That is why we should pay particular attention to Valéry's choice of the word "situation," because it means more than the context, either literary or social, in which Baudelaire found himself. A good comparison on this point is Hugo's poetry, which frequently stands as a counterpoint to Baudelaire's.[3] Hugo was far from oblivious to the historical upheavals of his century, and wanted his poetry to be deeply implicated in these. In the opening poem of *Les Feuilles d'automne* (Autumn leaves), "Ce siècle avait deux ans . . ." (This century was two years old . . .), Hugo insists upon the simultaneous appearance of himself (he was born in 1802) and of the imperialist ambitions of Napoléon ("Déja Napoléon perçait sous Bonaparte") (Already Napoleon was showing beneath Bonaparte). As Hugo's poetry evolves, it traces the story of the author's growing republicanism, his relationship to Louis Napoléon, and his long, political exile. Consistently, Hugo saw himself and his poetry at the center of historical agitations: "Tout souffle, tout rayon, ou propice ou fatal, / Fait reluire et vibrer mon âme de cristal, / Mon âme aux mille voix, que le Dieu que j'adore / Mit au centre de tout comme un écho sonore!" (Every breath, every beam, whether propitious or fatal / Makes my soul of crystal shine and vibrate, / My soul of a thousand voices, which the God that I worship / Placed at the center of all things as a sonorous echo!).

It is, however, precisely the centrality of this poetry that precludes its historical "situation." Hugo's sonorous soul, no matter where it strayed, was always "au centre de tout." Even in exile it spoke, not of a single eccentric destiny, but of the destiny of everyman. "Ah! insensé qui crois que je ne suis pas toi" (Oh! senseless one who thinks that I am not you), Hugo wrote to the French public from his isolation in Guernsey.[4] We may therefore assume that Hugo's poetry would have remained essentially what it is—a vibratory echo—had the author found himself in different historical circumstances. In other words, this poetry may invite a contextual reading without depending in any critical way upon extra-poetic considerations. Such is not the case with Baudelaire's poetry and Valéry's reading of its situation. Without a series of extra-poetic accidents, Valéry contends, Baudelaire might have become "an emulator of Gautier" or "an excellent artist of the Parnassian school" ("Situation de Baudelaire": 599), but he would not have been the poet we now know. Thus, when we speak of his poetry's situation, we imply its determination by *external* factors.

In the question of determination it is useful to supplement Valéry's notion of situation with Sartre's later treatment of the word. We are familiar with the ethical import Sartre gives to his study of man *en situation*: to be *en situation* implies both that one must accept the determining power of external circumstances and that one is under ethical obligation to act. If one yields entirely to the force of circumstance and refuses responsibility for one's own agency, then there is ethical failure and "the risk . . . of bad faith" (*L'Etre et le néant*: 107). If, on the other hand, one claims absolute agency, one risks bad faith from another direction, by failing to acknowledge the merely reactive element of one's conduct. Therefore, a properly ethical understanding of one's situation involves recognition of what Sartre calls "[a] double and inverse determination" (p. 306). The example he gives to illustrate this determination is of a fictive self peering through a keyhole: "Let us imagine that I have been reduced, out of jealousy, self-interest, or vice, to sticking my ear against a door, to peeping through a key-hole" (p. 305). On one side of the door there is presumably a spectacle, and on the other side, a jealous man. It is the relationship between the spectacle and the jealousy that interests Sartre, because this relationship reveals the complex determination that he associates with the word "situation": "there is only a spectacle to be *seen* behind the door because I am jealous, but my jealousy is nothing more than the simple, objective fact that *there is a spectacle to be seen* behind the door.... This situation reflects simultaneously my facticity and my freedom" (p. 306, original emphasis). Now, this double reflection ("simultaneously my facticity and my freedom") merely repeats what Sartre has called the double and inverse determination: the self is revealed as both actively passive and passively active. We should not be surprised, therefore, to find a similar double image in Baudelaire's depiction of the poet *en situation*. His portrait, once more from "Le Soleil," has all the furtive characteristics of Sartre's jealous man:[5]

> Le long du vieux faubourg, où pendent aux masures
> Les persiennes, abri des secrètes luxures,
> Quand le soleil cruel frappe à traits redoublés
> Sur la ville et les champs, sur les toits et les blés,
>
> Je vais m'exercer seul à ma fantasque escrime,
> Flairant dans tous les coins les hasards de la rime,
> Trébuchant sur les mots comme sur les pavés,
> Heurtant parfois des vers depuis longtemps rêvés.
>
> Along the old suburbs, where there hang from hovels
> Shutters, harboring hidden lewd desires,
> When the cruel sun strikes with redoubled force
> On city and fields, on roofs and crops of grain,

I go alone to practice my fantastic fencing game,
Sniffing in every cranny for the accidents of rhyme,
Stumbling upon words as upon paving stones,
Sometimes bumping into long-dreamed-of verses.

The key to the poet's situation lies in the last two lines: "Trébuchant sur les mots comme sur les pavés, / Heurtant parfois des vers depuis longtemps rêvés." Just as Sartre's jealous man is determined in his jealousy by the contingent existence of "a spectacle to be seen behind the door," so Baudelaire's poet becomes such by virtue of the words and rhymes that lie strewn, apparently haphazardly, in his path. The verbs "trébuchant" and "heurtant" emphasize the accidental element of poetic activity. But this does not explain the situation in its entirety, because the poet must collaborate with chance and dream at length of the verses he will later stumble upon. The "double and inverse determination," which is necessary for the situation to be defined in ethical terms, lies in the balance between chance discovery and dream. If poetic activity were simply equivalent to dreaming, there would be no "situation" in the Sartrean sense; this in turn would deprive poetic activity of any ethical implications. "If it is enough merely to conceive of something in order to realize it, here I am plunged into a world similar to the world of dreams, in which what is possible can in no way be distinguished from what is real . . . The distinction between a mere *wish*, the *representation* that I might choose and *choice* itself being abolished, freedom disappears as well" (*L'Etre et le néant*: 539, original emphasis). In a world where "what is possible can in no way be distinguished from what is real," choice and freedom, two necessary features of the ethical realm, drop away. Although Baudelaire might display momentary disgust with "un monde où l'action n'est pas la soeur du rêve" (a world where action is not the sister of dream) ("Le Reniement de Saint Pierre": 1: 122), his fundamental sense of the aesthetic requires a disjunction between action and dream, the real and the possible, the project and its realization. Thus Baudelaire could write disparagingly of Musset's "utter incapacity to understand the work through which a reverie becomes a work of art."[6] This criticism approaches "Le Soleil" in the definition it gives of the work of art. Reverie produces verse only through effort ("Je vais m'*exercer* seul") and time ("des vers depuis *longtemps* rêvés"), and so the original momentum of the dream is broken. Hence, when the dream coincides with reality and the poet discovers his long-cherished verses, he stumbles, indicating the disjunction we have outlined between realization and project, and so on.

Such stumbling marks the ethical moment of poetic activity and should not be interpreted in a fortuitous sense: that is, the Baudelairean poet is not a surrealist who stumbles upon poetic combinations *within* a magically unified universe. As Sartre has amply demonstrated, the surrealist universe resembles "a world in which what is possible can in no way be distinguished from what is real," in which there is no "passage from potentiality to action," but instead "the rising up *ex nihilo*, the sudden appearance of a fully constituted object,"[7] which object will stand as the work of art. When one stumbles upon the surrealist object, this is no way disturbs the magical unity of the surrealist universe and certainly marks no radical disjunction between reality and dream. Furthermore, surrealist stumbling is effortless and involves no choice on the part of the one who stumbles; nor can it be said that the stumbling artist is exercising a freedom of any kind since the artist as subject has been bracketed and "*there is no one* to free" (Sartre, "Situation de l'écrivain" [The writer's situation]: 367, my emphasis). In other words, the ethical criteria of choice and freedom are missing from the surrealist scenario. This is not true in the case of the poet of "Le Soleil," whose stumbling reflects his complex ethical situation, "simultaneously [his] facticity and [his] freedom." The guilty tone of the first stanza indicates that the poet has not been able to rid himself of his responsibility as subject, that even the shutters reflect back his intentions. Thus we are given to understand that his stumbling is not an "innocent" accident, that he has, to some degree, freely chosen his happenstance.

"Le Soleil" contains an elegant figure for this double ethical reflection in the mirror relationship between poet and sun. At first, the two are presented in a simple, natural relationship: when the sun begins to shine, the poet starts working. These two incidental activities become analogous, however, when the sun's light is described in terms of its "traits redoublés," and the poet's pen works out a "fantasque escrime." It is tempting to see each activity as perfectly reflected in the other, were it not for several asymmetries in their depiction. The sun's attack upon the sleeping suburb is qualified as "cruel," perhaps because it is carried out with such economy of effort: only one verb is necessary—"le soleil cruel *frappe*"—for "la ville et les champs, . . . les toits et les blés," all to fall to the sun's superior power. The poet, by comparison, is less cruel and more quixotic in his aggression: he sniffs and stumbles and bumps about repeatedly, and never quite makes himself master of "the accidents of rhyme." For this reason, his activity is only an imperfect reflection of the sun's light, and much more constrained by the poet's "facticity."

The imperfection of the poet/sun analogy thus opens the possibility for a third interpretation of their relationship: the poet may be seen as attempting, with lesser forces, to emulate the sun. To a certain extent this third interpretation returns to a natural or realistic order of things, but one which admits of ethical determinations. The first interpretation presents a natural order which lacks ethical significance, because poet and sun remain mutually exterior phenomena—no double, inverse determination is possible where only exteriority exists. This double determination is absent from the second interpretation as well: when the poet is seen as an analogue of the sun, any real exteriority of one to the other is obscured in favor of their resemblances; these resemblances would allow no residue of facticity to remain with either poet or sun and, therefore, the activity of each would involve no ethical engagement with reality. Since the poet/sun analogy is imperfect, however, an element of mutual exteriority is guaranteed, and the poet's efforts become "realistic"; in other words, he imitates the sun, not because an analogy between the two is given, but because he has *chosen* the sun as an object for emulation and now strives with predictable awkwardness to realize his project. Although he may thereby invent analogies between his conduct and that of the sun—for example, "Quand *ainsi qu'un poète*, il [le soleil] descend dans les villes, / Il ennoblit le sort des choses les plus viles" (When, like a poet, [the sun] descends into the cities, / He ennobles the lot of the lowliest things)—these analogies are partial and require his continuous energies to sustain them.

We can sense this ethical effort behind the comparisons of "Le Soleil" in the curious analogical structure of the lines: "Ce père nourricier, ennemi des chloroses, / Éveille dans les champs les vers comme les roses" (This foster father, enemy of anemias, / Awakens in the fields verses / worms as well as roses). Here the double meaning of *vers*—verses and worms—is exploited, although not in a traditional way, to underline the contrast between the immortal art of the poet and mortal things, such as a woman's beauty. The traditional pun has a kind of morbid dignity, which is not true of these lines, because the worms in question are not evocative of death and the tomb. Instead they are lively creatures who come out to bask in the sun. If the lines are to be read in this naturalist sense, the "comme" of "les vers comme les roses" must be given an additive meaning—worms *as well as* roses are awakened in the fields. In other words, if we take *vers* to be worms, there is no analogy at all, only a vaguely grotesque little scene which is, moreover, inaccurate from a naturalist viewpoint (worms come out principally when it rains). There are also no grounds for comparison here between poet and sun. However, perhaps because the words *vers* and *roses* are so charged with poetic connotations, the reader very quickly skips over the naturalist scene and imagines instead poetry springing from the earth, "comme les roses," *like* roses. The sun thereby becomes *like* a poet, and the fundamental analogy of "Le Soleil" is thus reaffirmed. But this analogy has been bought at a price, the price of the naturalist scene, which puts a strain on our senses of good taste and of verisimilitude. To use a common stylistic expression, one could say that Baudelaire's analogy is "forced"; this *aesthetic* judgment reveals the willful or *ethical* character I have attributed to the poem's analogical structure.

We can describe this ethical character of the analogies most succinctly by analyzing the possible figural relationships of the terms *vers* and *roses*. Either Baudelaire's *comme* is additive, and there are "worms as well as roses," or it engenders analogy, giving "verses like roses."[8] *Vers* and *roses* are thus imperfectly analogous, their given resemblances always threatened by the pure exteriority of the additive. This, as I have shown, is the kind of imperfect analogy that exists between poet and sun in the poem; when the poet and his activity are involved, such imperfection of resemblance allows for the possibility of emulation, that is, an ethically oriented activity. When it is a case of *vers* and *roses*, however, the ethical intention is not so easily retrievable. True, one may feel that when "verses like roses" becomes "worms as well as roses," a step toward the ethical has been made; this is so, not only because the ethical must break with the beautiful interiority of analogy,[9] but also because worms in and of themselves seem more "ethical" than poetry. If we wish, though, to keep the worms and roses in a strictly natural setting, we will never rigorously locate an ethical intention; it is not by intention that the worm appears to us as homely and, hence, as an apt vehicle for ethical meanings. Only if we leave the realm of nature, not to return to that of analogy, but to explore the emblematic values of worms and roses, will we recover an ethical intention. Michael Riffaterre has expounded at length, in his discussion of Blakes's poem "The Sick Rose," upon the emblematic potential of the worm/rose opposition. As an opposition, Riffaterre argues, worm versus rose "generates when pushed to its paradigmatic extreme a polarization of the worst evil, Death, and of the greatest good, Love" ("The Self-sufficient Text": 43). In other words, at stake in the various contrasts between beauty and ugliness, purity and decay, and so on, that come to mind when we compare roses with worms, is the specifically ethical opposition between good and evil. Something of this emblematic use of rose and worm may be intended in "Le Soleil," particularly because the two terms are not fully motivated by the naturalist setting. Once the ethical emblem has been posed, moreover, it becomes possible to integrate other features of the poem into the ethical intention: the "porteurs de béquilles" (those who carry crutches) and the "jeunes filles" (young girls) take on the colors of age versus youth, the "hôpitaux" and the "palais" become the two extremes of the wheel of fortune. It is true that Baudelaire does much to lighten the emblematic touch, for example, by making *vers* and *roses* plural, which diminishes the sense of their opposition. Because the sun, too, functions as a reconciling force in the poem, we are discouraged from taking opposing figures to their "paradigmatic extreme" and giving them a stark, ethical interpretation. But even the sun cannot bring to *vers* and *roses* an ultimate reconciliation, which would be to transform "worms as well as roses" into "verses like roses," thereby swallowing up all emblematic opposition in perfect analogy. Only the poet could do this, and here at last the complete figure of the double reflection between poet and sun may be seen. Whereas "Le Soleil" opened with the poet's emulation of the sun, it ends with the sun's emulation of the poet: "ainsi qu'un poète, . . . Il ennoblit le sort des choses les plus viles" (Like a poet . . . he ennobles the fate of the basest things). Of course, the ennobling powers of the sun do not extend so far as to make roses of worms, so in these matters the sun could never replace the poet. This situation thus reflects the poet's peculiar freedom. At the same time, however, the poet is confronted with the limits of his facticity: in the natural world he could never compete with the sun so as to awaken worms and roses in the fields. Thus sun and poet are engaged in a double inverse determination, which cannot be reduced so that one or the other finally triumphs, and which may be traced, as I have done, in the figural permutations of the expression "les vers comme les roses."

My analysis may seem to have digressed from the question of bad faith, so it would be useful to take stock of what has been established by examining the "situational" nature of Baudelaire's poetry. First, as a situated poetry, *Les Fleurs du mal* is not self-determining. This is not to say that the poems are unoriginal or that Baudelaire failed to develop his own idiom; rather, as Valéry stresses, what is most idiomatic about this poetry is determined by factors external to poetry as such. Both history and ethics may enter into the explication of the poetry's "situation," because both offer ways of accounting for its (the poetry's) lack of self-sufficiency; thus, when we contrast the originality of *Les Fleurs du mal* with that of Hugo or of the Surrealists, the latter may appear as lying outside history and ethics. This qualification only holds, however, if we affirm Benjamin's distinction between poetry that may be categorized historically (or ethically) and one which adopts history as a constitutive category. In the second case, which is the case of *Les*

Fleurs du mal, history (or ethics) remains simultaneously *external* and *essential* to the poetry. For this reason, history and ethics present the poetry with a specific ontological threat. I have already shown how this threat is generated by Sartre's ethical reading of *Les Fleurs du mal*: the judgment which seems to be called for by an intimate intelligence of Baudelaire's verse is also experienced as an alien pronouncement, hostile to the very essence of poetry. In Benjamin's reading of Baudelaire, history similarly functions as an intimate alien, both endowing *Les Fleurs du mal* with a mark of absolute distinction—"his work cannot merely be categorized as historical, *like anyone else's*" ("Motifs": 162, my emphasis)—and undermining the conditions of possibility of poetry. Although there is not the space here to examine the historical threat in all its nuances, we can focus on the figure that Benjamin privileges—Baudelaire's "hypocrite lecteur."[10] This "least rewarding type of audience" is, in many respects, the personification of the intimate alien; as the poet's hypocritical brother, the reader both embraces and disowns Baudelaire's poetic offering. For Benjamin, the reader becomes, by virtue of this dual status, the prime repository of historical meanings: Baudelaire's historical insight is confirmed by the fact that "he was eventually to find the reader at whom his work was aimed."[11] It must be emphasized that the reader's ambivalent relationship to *Les Fleurs du mal* is not one which may be explained by flightiness of character or unsteadiness of taste—such explanations, by locating all ontological instability in the personality of the reader, leave the work of art intact. But the reader of *Les Fleurs du mal* poses a threat to the poetry, not merely because he may choose to dislike it: he is a threat because, to quote Benjamin, he is the one at whom the work is *aimed*; in other words, the reader, having been constituted as the *end* of the poetry, is essential to it. We can justifiably toy here with the two meanings of the word "end": the reader, as the aim or goal of the work, gives the latter its essential orientation; but, by the same token, the reader may do away with the work, putting an end to it. Thus, when Benjamin alludes to the reader's inhospitability toward poetry, this should be understood in an absolutely critical sense: what is at stake is not just the reception of a work, *Les Fleurs du mal*; the question is, rather, will there be a work at all?

It is within the context of this ontological question that the problem of bad faith resurfaces. My purpose was to leave Sartre's analysis temporarily aside and, if possible, to trace the figure of bad faith directly from *Les Fleurs du mal* itself. Of course, this is not a simple undertaking, because *Les Fleurs du mal* itself contains a self-alienating moment. It may therefore seem difficult to decide whether the judgment of bad faith has been produced by the poetry's own self-alienating mechanism, or whether Sartre brought an alien interpretation to the poetry. If we recall, however, that bad faith *is* a self-alienating mechanism, the decision becomes easier to make. Here is how Sartre describes that mechanism in *L'Etre et le néant*: "The first act of bad faith is to flee what one cannot flee, to flee what one is. Now, the very project of flight reveals to bad faith an intimate disintegration at the heart of being, and bad faith wishes to be this disintegration" (p. 107). The self-alienating impulse of bad faith reveals "an intimate disintegration at the heart of being," and it is this ontological ambiguity that is most pertinent to my analysis. To sustain the comparison with *Les Fleurs du mal*, this is the doubtful poetic being that Jacques Rivière compares to "a weariness of the voice" or "a sudden modesty" when he cites the lines:[12]

> Et qui sait si les fleurs nouvelles que je rêve
> Trouveront dans ce sol lavé comme une grève
> Le mystique aliment qui *ferait* leur vigueur.
>
> And who knows whether the new flowers I am dreaming
> Will find in this soil washed like a sandy beach
> The mystical nutrient that *might* make them strong.

The ambiguity of such being lies in the fact that it is not a simple flight from being toward nothingness, or toward the Surrealist "Impossible," which haunts Bataille's reading of Baudelaire. It is not a flight from being because it "wishes *to be* this disintegration [of being]." The alienating moment returns to determine bad faith in its *being*, the flight from self becomes an attempt at self-recovery.

This same movement appears in Baudelaire's evocation of his "hypocrite lecteur,—mon semblable,—mon frère!" (hypocritical reader,—my kin,—my brother!). In one and the same gesture Baudelaire repulses his reader with the charge of hypocrisy, and claims him as another self; thus the poet seeks, not to play the hypocrite, but *to be* one. Since hypocrisy itself reveals an ontological split between being and appearance, the desire to *be* a hypocrite is a desire to be this "disintegration at the heart of being." Thus, we find the figure of bad faith governing the relationship to the reader, that relationship which Benjamin has interpreted in historical, that is, in ethically neutral terms. Here, in other words, bad faith does not enter into the interpretation as an object of judgment, but it does describe the shape of the interpretation itself: history, in the guise of the reader, becomes the site of the poetry's flight from and retrieval of self. I analyzed something similar at the outset of this chapter in the slippage of bad faith from an objective content of *Les Fleurs du mal*, to the subjective figure of the charitable judgment on the work. It is not enough to say that we do not "see" the bad faith, in order to conclude that it is not there or that it must originate "outside" the poetry.

Of course, the efforts to determine whether bad faith originates "inside" or "outside" *Les Fleurs du mal* are complicated by the fact that bad faith has, in the most rigorous sense, neither origin nor outside. Sartre demonstrates this when he distinguishes between bad faith and a Machiavellian project of self-persuasion, which would have a definite point of departure: "It should in fact be noted that the project of bad faith must itself be in bad faith: I am not only in bad faith at the end of my efforts, when I have constructed amphibological concepts for myself and when I have persuaded myself.[13] To tell the truth, I have not persuaded myself: to the extent that I could be persuaded, I always have been. And, at the very moment when I prepared myself to be in bad faith, I had to be in bad faith with respect to those very preparations" (*L'Etre et le néant*: 104). The consciousness that engages in a project of bad faith is always already in bad faith; any attempt to step "outside" the project of consciousness is therefore bound to fail, because the step outside only realigns consciousness within the project of bad faith.

This may explain the observation that bad faith "slips" back and forth from the order of the object to that of the subject. The reflexive activity of consciousness, by which consciousness participates in the subjective order, contaminates and is contaminated by the prereflexive consciousness that it takes as its object—hence, the impossibility of deciding whether bad faith has passed from object to subject or vice versa.

Although the undecidable origin of bad faith seems to invalidate the thesis that bad faith "begins" with *Les Fleurs du mal* and not with Sartre's reading of the work, in favor of that thesis one may still make the following remarks: even before Sartre's *Baudelaire*, the defenders of *Les Fleurs du mal* exhibited the "undefinable tone of smiling protectiveness" (*Baudelaire*: 108) that Sartre maintains is called for by the poetry, and which involves a certain reluctance to examine the poetic object too closely; after Sartre's essay, this particular defense is repeated, with the same tone and the same blind spot, by those who would protect the poetry from Sartrean philistinism. Even if it cannot be claimed for a certainty that the bad faith of both critical defenses originates with the poetry, it is clear at least that Sartre's essay does not bring bad faith from the "outside" to disturb an intimate critical relation: that relation, like the self-relation of the contaminated consciousness I have just considered, is always already disposed to bad faith. If it is impossible to determine the origin of bad faith in one or the other terms of the relation, it is nevertheless possible to locate bad faith inside, as opposed to outside, that relation. And when one remembers that *Les Fleurs du mal* offers itself, not as a beautiful totality, but as fundamentally dependent upon its relationship to the reader, then it is not surprising that the weight of the evidence points to the relational essence of the poetry as an original locus of bad faith.

The evidence in question is of two kinds. There is the empirical evidence I have accumulated by examining various critical reactions to Baudelaire's poetry; and there is the evidence, supplied principally by Benjamin's reading of the poem "Au lecteur," which reveals the bad faith of the critical relation as a *prescription* of the poetry. This prescription is more or less implicit in "Au lecteur": the reader is persuaded to adopt the tremulous, hypocritical being offered to Baudelaire's "brother," without knowing in any precise way what the consequences of refusal might be. This ignorance is accompanied by the vague suspicion that refusal is impossible, that were one to refuse the prescribed reader's role, one would only be conforming more perfectly to it.[14] These undefined aspects of the prescription become more clear, however, if we turn from "Au lecteur" to its "architectural" double, the later "Épigraphe pour un livre condamné." The exact date of composition of "Épigraphe" is unknown, but it was probably intended as the prefatory poem to the second edition of *Les Fleurs du mal*. Although Baudelaire by no means relinquished the persuasive mode in "Épigraphe," his persuasiveness is laid bare, so to speak, and shown to be the handmaiden of an openly imperative mode of discourse. Hence the poet addresses potential readers with a series of commands: "Jette ce livre saturnien" (Throw away this saturnine book), "Lis-moi, pour apprendre à m'aimer" (Read me, and learn to love me), "Plains-moi! . . . Sinon, je te maudis!" (Pity me! . . . If you don't, I'll curse you!). Along with these overt imperatives, the consequences of disobedience or nonconformity to the poet's prescriptions are clearly spelled out:

> Lecteur paisible et bucolique,
> Sobre et naïf homme de bien,
> Jette ce livre saturnien,
> Orgiaque et mélancolique.
>
> Si tu n'as fait ta rhétorique
> Chez Satan, le rusé doyen,
> Jette! tu n'y comprendrais rien
> Ou tu me croirais hystérique.
>
> Peaceful and bucolic reader,
> Sober and naive man of good will,
> Throw away this saturnine,
> Orgiastic and melancholic book.
>
> If you have not studied rhetoric
> With Satan, the artful dean,
> Throw it away! either you won't understand a thing
> Or you'll think me hysterical.

Here we have the portrait of the reader who in no way corresponds to the specifications given in "Au lecteur." The "sobre et naïf homme de bien" is not a nonconformist out of spite, however, but out of native incapacity. Even if he felt enough spite in him to disobey the command to throw away "ce livre saturnien," his native incapacity would assert itself: "tu n'y comprendrais rien / Ou tu me croirais hystérique." In the most rigorous sense, then, the "lecteur paisible et bucolique" is not a reader: whether he obeys or disobeys the poet's injunction, whether he tosses out the poetry or runs his eyes over it, he is not reading. This is because the naïf is invulnerable to the ruses of rhetoric and cannot comply with the command intended for those who read: "Lis-moi, pour apprendre à m'aimer." Since the naïf cannot help but be equivalent to his native self, he cannot help but fulfill the task assigned to him—*not* to read *Les Fleurs du mal*. In Sartrean terms, the good faith of such a person is guaranteed: both his invulnerability to persuasion and his inability to transgress the moral imperative directed at him assure his authenticity. Of course, from a Baudelairean perspective, such a person is all the more comical because of his sober dignity, and thereby demonstrates his affinity with subhuman forms of life: "The most comical animals are the most serious," Baudelaire writes in *De l'essence du rire* (On the essence of laughter): "for example, monkeys and parrots" (*OC*, 2: 532). The paradox of authenticity, which both describes the perfection of human moral character and resembles the *en-soi*, the mode of being of animals and things, is apparent in the figure of the "lecteur paisible et bucolique." Given Sartre's unqualified privileging of authenticity, we might imagine that he was unaware of the concept's paradoxical potential, and attribute this blind spot to his own position as a naive nonreader of Baudelaire. Surely much of the reaction against Sartre's *Baudelaire* could be summed up in terms similar to those of "Épigraphe": Sartre understood nothing of the poetry, he accused Baudelaire of a hysterical self-indulgence, and displayed the philosopher's ignorance of the fine art of rhetoric. If this judgment were unequivocally true, however, it would not have occurred as a *scandalized* judgment. Sartre's ignorance and incomprehension would have provoked laughter, perhaps, or simple condescension, had he written *Baudelaire* in a moment of artless good faith; but the scandal of his reading, because it *is* a reading, lies in the fact that he could have done it differently. In this, Sartre must be distinguished from the "sober and naive man of good will" who, like "monkeys and parrots," can be true only to his native limitations. There is no native truth to Sartre's position with respect to Baudelaire, and this is because, in perfectly Baudelairean fashion, Sartre is "et la victime, et le bourreau" (both the victim and the executioner)[15] of his own analysis. Even though the dominant tone of the study is that of the executioner or judge, this tone constantly borders on its opposite, denunciation verges on confession. The account of Baudelaire's fatherless childhood and resentment of his mother's second marriage could easily be a page from Sartre's autobiography.[16] Baudelaire's effeminate characteristics and passive tendencies are visible in Sartre's description of an early photograph of himself: "I am pink and blond, with curls; I have plump cheeks and, in my eyes, an affable deference towards the established order" (*Les Mots*: 26). The scandal of Sartre's reading is as much a function of his complicity with his subject as it is of his hostility. Thus, when a contemporary critic can quote Valéry—"All blame of another amounts to saying: *I am not you* . . . It is impossible to understand and to punish at the same time"—apropos of Sartre's *Baudelaire*, there is a fundamental misunderstanding of the bad faith animating this critical relation (Sartre/Baudelaire), as well as any of the others I have examined.[17]

If, in fact, Sartre could have written a different book, if the tone of confession could have dominated that of denunciation, then we must suppose that Sartre was *capable* of carrying out the prescription: "Lis-moi, pour apprendre à m'aimer." His failure to do so indicates, therefore, not native inability, but a kind of choice. Once more, we may look to "Épigraphe" to illuminate this choice and its consequences:

> Mais si, sans se laisser charmer,
> Ton oeil sait plonger dans les gouffres,
> Lis-moi, pour apprendre à m'aimer;

Ame curieuse qui souffres
Et vas cherchant ton paradis,
Plains-moi! . . . Sinon, je te maudis!

But if, without becoming bewitched,
Your eye knows how to plumb the depths
Read me, and learn to love me;

Curious soul, who suffers
And goes seeking your paradise,
Pity me! . . . If you don't, I'll curse you!

These stanzas leave aside the self-equivalent nonreader and turn to the real reader. The real reader is not self-equivalent, but exists as a perpetual self-transcendence, which Baudelaire in *Mon coeur mis à nu* calls a double simultaneous postulation: "Il y a dans tout homme, à toute heure, deux postulations simultanées, l'une vers Dieu, l'autre vers Satan" (There are in every man, at every hour, two simultaneous postulations, one towards God, the other towards Satan) (OC, 1: 682). We should not be misled by Baudelaire's affirmation that the double postulation is present in "every man," because the human, for Baudelaire, is not defined in biological terms; "every man" is, rather, "Every man worthy of the name" (Tout homme digne de ce nom),[18] while "the sober and naive man of good will" ranks among "monkeys and parrots." In "Épigraphe," the two poles of the double postulation are given in "les gouffres" and "ton paradis." Furthermore, the double transcendence is experienced through the two modalities of knowledge and suffering: knowledge opens onto the depths of the abyss—"Ton oeil *sait* plonger dans les gouffres"—and suffering is equivalent to the aspiration toward paradise—"Ame curieuse qui *souffres* / Et vas cherchant ton paradis." Baudelaire's double simultaneous postulation seems to fall within the moralist tradition that is summed up by Blaise Pascal's reflections on "the disproportion of man": "Let us thus understand that the condition of man is double. Let us thus understand that man exceeds man infinitely . . ." For Pascal, however, this disproportion is inherent to the human condition, understood as a *universal* condition of human beings. This is why the solution to that disproportion—"[man] was inconceivable to himself without the aid of faith" (*Les Pensées* 131–434, OC: 515)—may be posited with a cool, mathematical precision, that is, without false, insinuating eloquence. The double simultaneous postulation, as it appears in "Épigraphe," lacks both a universal character and a mathematical solution. We can appreciate this if we consider that the self-transcending soul in "Épigraphe" does not leave behind all that is particular to itself in order to accede to a universal nature; instead its self-transcendence exacerbates its particularity, it becomes *more* idiosyncratic. Each pole of transcendence marks a difference from the universal: the negative pole, "*les* gouffres," in multiplicity; the positive pole, "*ton* paradis," in the use of the possessive. The self-transcending soul thus comes to figure, not the human condition, but a *curious* condition, one which departs from the norm. This would pose no problem if it were not for the fact that the curious soul is put in the place of the universal soul, that the idiosyncratic transcendence is offered as the only transcendence.

We can read this usurpation in the final imperative of the poem—"Plains-moi! . . . Sinon je te maudis!"—which brings us back to Sartre's choice not to respond to the poetry's pathos. The fate of Sartre's *Baudelaire* indicates clearly enough that the poet's threat is not an idle one. The dilemma that was noted at the beginning of this chapter—the critic of Baudelaire succumbs either to an epidemic of bad faith or to an epidemic of condemnation—is described in the option the poet gives his reader, to pity or be cursed. Of course, it is easier to accept this description in the case of Sartre than it is in the case of the pitying critic: the ends of justice may be served when the one who curses is paid back with a curse, but it does not seem right when the one who pities receives the infection of bad faith as recompense. The injustice, however, is not a truism—pity does not necessarily lead to bad faith—but occurs as a result of the curious soul's usurpation of universality. This will become plain if we compare the configuration of pity and transcendence in "Épigraphe" with Rousseau's well-known treatment of pity.[19] Rousseau's pity also requires the self-transcendence of the pitying subject, but unlike the double simultaneous postulation,

Rousseau's transcendence has only one modality—that of knowledge. Suffering, far from directing the self beyond the self, fixes it upon itself. In other words, suffering, for Rousseau, is not a modality of human transcendence but of human facticity: "When one suffers," he writes in *Émile*, "one pities only oneself." True pity, on the other hand, only takes place once the self is no longer suffering and can accede to knowledge: "In order to pity another's pain, one must doubtless *know* what it feels like, but one must not *feel* it" (p. 270, my emphasis). Now, the knowledge of the pitying subject must be more than a recollection of past aches and pains, and more than an acquaintance with the particular misfortune of the object of pity. The knowledge that accompanies Rousseau's pity is the knowledge of a transcendent concept: that of humankind, "le genre humain." The object of pity, then, must actually be this transcendent concept, or pity risks corruption of the kind we have seen with Baudelaire's benevolent critics: "In order to keep pity from degenerating into weakness, it must be generalized and extended to all of humankind" (*Émile*: 303–4). In this way if the object of pity is universal, the pitying subject, too, will transcend its own particularity and participate in the concept of humankind. Obviously, this is not what takes place with the reader of "Épigraphe" who yields to the imperative "Plains-moi!" It is true that the yielding reader transcends himself to a certain degree, but only to identify with another idiosyncratic subject; where true pity would have ended in a concept of the universal human, this false pity cannot transcend the image of the poet as a *caricature* of the human. It is almost as though Baudelaire no longer has the patience to persuade and to develop the pathos he displays in "Au lecteur": that pathos can speak convincingly of "us" and, at several points in the poem, rises above the emphatic tone and self-conscious eloquence of the rest.[20] There are no similar moments in "Épigraphe," and here is where one may feel that pathos has been replaced by caricature. The poet no longer appears to us in brief but realistic glimpses—crying out of spite and disappointment, clinging to a dessicated object of pleasure, or trembling before his own criminal thoughts. Instead, he is nothing but the double simultaneous postulation, and we are not persuaded but commanded to respond to this summary outline with pity. Because it derives from the false transcendence of caricature and not from the transcendent concept of the human, the imperative "Plains-moi! . . . Sinon, je te maudis!" only mimics a true moral imperative. To return once more to Pascal, this kind of mimicry is the hallmark of tyranny and abusive eloquence: "Thus, this kind of talk is false, and tyrannical: I am beautiful, so I must be feared; I am strong, so I must be loved" or, in Baudelaire's case, "I am spiteful, so I must be pitied." The tyrant's discourse lacks the mathematical coolness of Pascal's "he was inconceivable to himself without the aid of faith," because the tyrant speaks "out of place": "Tyranny consists of the universal and *out of place* desire for domination" (*Les Pensées* 58–332, pp. 506–7, my emphasis). The caricature is in this respect simply another figure for the tyrant, who would usurp the place of humankind; such usurpation, or false transcendence, generates a falsely transcendent discourse, one which we have already associated with the maxims of bad faith. These maxims—"je suis trop grand pour moi" ("I am too great for myself), "l'amour, c'est beaucoup plus que l'amour" (love is much more than love)—point to a universal human transcendence, but have the effect of making this the property of a single individual, of imprisoning transcendence in facticity. Although Baudelaire speaks of "ton paradis" in "Épigraphe," the final command indicates that only the poet has the keys to paradise, that to suffer his malediction is actually to be excluded from (false) transcendence, and that "your" paradise is really "my" paradise.

Against the background of the foregoing analysis, it is finally possible to assess the implications of Sartre's choice *not* to obey the mock imperative, "Plains-moi!" It would be incorrect to argue that Sartre's disobedience spells the authenticity of his position with respect to Baudelaire; as we have noted, Sartre's reading as much as any other is caught in the tropological instability of bad faith ("I am, I am not you"). Of course, the fact that bad faith is indifferent to its own imperatives, that obedience and disobedience come down to the same thing, is only one more indication that there is bad faith. If we were dealing with a transcendent moral imperative, this would not be the case. The interest of Sartre's disobedience is not, therefore, that it allows him to escape from bad faith, but that it reveals bad faith at the heart of Baudelaire's poetry. While those who are compelled by the pathos of the poetry persist in seeing it as an essential manifestation of beauty,[21] Sartre's identification of bad faith allows him to see an intersubjective relation, the poet's contract with his reader, at the very moment of beauty. Thus, Sartre can express his admiration for the lines from "Le Guignon":

> Mainte fleur épanche à regret
> Son parfum doux comme un secret
> Dans les solitudes profondes.
>
> Many a flower regretfully gives off
> Its perfume, sweet as a secret
> In deep solitudes.

and still see in these the false transcendence of bad faith, the "metaphysical lightness" of the curious soul who desires its own solitude to stand in the place of a universal human solitude.[22]

True to Baudelaire's threat that the pitiless would be excluded from his poetry's promise of transcendence, Sartre's reading has been qualified as *reductive*; in other words, the judgment of bad faith is said to take no account of truth that might exceed the sphere of facticity: "*Baudelaire* has those positive and negative features native to the art of caricature. The poet is relentlessly reduced to a portrait that at once enlightens because it exaggerates the importance of certain basic features and misrepresents for it is willfully ignorant of complexities that might stand in the way of the simplification";[23] "It must nevertheless be admitted that the doctrine in whose name Sartre interrogates Baudelaire's 'project' is here willfully simplified in the sense that one *simplifies* algebraic formulae . . .";[24] "[Sartre's] language, through the automatic association of certain images with certain themes, distorts his argument and his portrait of Baudelaire: he reduces Baudelaire to an abstraction."[25] We should note that in these criticisms Sartre's reduction is perceived as both chosen—"*willfully* ignorant," "*willfully* simplified"—and unreflexive, insofar as it proceeds through "automatic

120   The Caricatural Mechanism

association." There is a clue here to the status of that reduction, since Sartre cannot be held fully responsible for its mechanics: the choice between pathos and caricature has been *given* by the poetry, and the rejection of one leads automatically to the other. Although we may see this option most clearly in the two "contractual" poems, "Au lecteur" and "Épigraphe," *Les Fleurs du mal* is filled with self-caricature. Take, for example, the incantatory grandeur of Baudelaire's "Invitation au voyage" (Invitation to travel) (1: 53):

> Les soleils mouillés
> De ces ciels brouillés
> Pour mon esprit ont les charmes
> Si mystérieux
> De tes traîtres yeux,
> Brillant à travers leurs larmes.

> The drenched suns
> Of these hazy skies
> To my mind have the charms
> So mysterious
> Of your treacherous eyes,
> Shining through their tears.

The spell of this beautiful poem seems to be parodied in the abbreviated images of another piece, "Madrigal triste" (Sad madrigal) (1: 137):

> Que m'importe que tu sois sage?
> Sois belle! et sois triste! Les pleurs
> Ajoutent un charme au visage,
> Comme le fleuve au paysage;
> L'orage rajeunit les fleurs.

> What do I care if you are chaste?
> Be beautiful! and be sad! Tears
> Add a charm to the face,
> Like a river to the landscape;
> Storms rejuvenate the flowers.

As in "Épigraphe," suffering and pathos are deprived of transcendent dimensions by a mock imperative: "Plains-moi!" or "Sois triste!" What follows in "Madrigal" is a caricature of the sorrowing soul, whose charm is no longer mysterious but merely ornamental: "Les pleurs / Ajoutent un charme au visage, / Comme le fleuve au paysage." Of course we could go back and argue that the "charmes / Si mystérieux" of "Invitation" are just as transparently ornamental, and that the mystery in question is a false one (the woman's tears, for example, are no real mystery to the poet if he himself is tormenting her). But our ability to establish an equivalence between the transcendent portrait and its reduction does not invalidate the observation that pathos and caricature are played off against one another. Instead, the reduction functions as a kind of touchstone to reveal the false quality of the pathos, mystery, transcendence, and so on, to which it is opposed.

This is how we must understand Sartre's reductive portrait of Baudelaire: such a caricature, as I have shown in the reading of "Épigraphe," cannot pretend to transcend idiosyncracy in the way that a concept like humankind can; that is why caricature must be seen in terms of *distortion*, as an imprisoned transcendence which itself is caught in falsehood; at the same time, however, the explicitly reductive tendency of caricature, by uncovering falsehood in heights of pathos, depths of character, and other transcendences, upholds an absolute distinction between the false and the true. This distinction is not to be found "within" caricature, then, but stands as the transcendent criterion to which caricature, in its relationship to pathos, points. From this perspective we may see Sartre's charge of bad faith not only as the caricatural reduction of Baudelaire's poetry and as its condemnation to falsehood; to the extent that the poetry is impelled toward its own caricature, to that extent it is engaged, not in a mock imperative, but in an ethical imperative which maintains truthfulness behind the indifferent differences of bad faith. At the very moment when the poet cries "Plains-moi! . . . Sinon je te maudis!", pathos itself is caricatured, thus revealing the indifference of obedience to the command. But we may only perceive this indifference *as* indifference if, like Sartre, we are willing to read without pity, to run the risk of the poetry's malediction, and to find our reading after the fact "more truly and more strange," to quote Wallace Stevens ("Tea at the Palaz of Hoon"). That is to say, our intelligence of the poetry becomes closer and more canny when we subject ourselves to its self-estranging mechanism. Sartre's example, as maddening as it is, and because it is maddening, is a case in point.

CHAPTER FOUR

The Allegorical Architecture of 'Les Fleurs du mal'

These lines, from Baudelaire's "Danse macabre," were written in 1858, presumably during a voyage from Paris to Alençon:

> Aucuns t'appelleront une caricature,
> Qui ne comprennent pas, amants ivres de chair,
> L'élégance sans nom de l'humaine armature.
> Tu réponds, grand squelette, à mon goût le plus cher!

> Some people will call you a caricature,
> Those drunken lovers of flesh who do not understand
> The nameless elegance of the human frame.
> You answer, great skeleton, my dearest desire!

The subject of the poem was a small statue Baudelaire had seen earlier that year in the atelier of Ernest Christophe, and which represented the skeleton of a young woman dressed in a voluminous gown and bedecked with flowers. The work had appealed to Baudelaire both because it reproduced "the shrill irony of the early *danses macabres*" (C, 1: 535), and because it constituted a real aesthetic novelty: "It is generally believed, perhaps because the ancient world was not acquainted with the skeleton, that it ought to be excluded from the domain of sculpture."[1] This peculiar coincidence of the old and the new is repeated in the circumstances under which Baudelaire composed his poetic "explanation" of the statuette: as Claude Pichois has commented, "In the compartment of a train,

[Baudelaire] dreams of *danses macabres* and the Middle Ages" (*OC*, 1: 1030). The composition of "Danse macabre" may thus be seen as emblematic, if not of *Les Fleurs du mal* as a whole, at least of the section entitled *Tableaux parisiens* in which the poem is found. The *Tableaux* are intended to represent modern Paris in its multiple nuances, but this intention is realized by means of allegory—"one of the *primitive* forms . . . of poetry," to quote Baudelaire himself in *Le Poème du hachisch* (*OC*, 1: 430, my emphasis).

It is worthy of note that Baudelaire describes the aesthetic effect of Christophe's statue—its antique novelty—in terms of caricature. If it is correct to assume an emblematic status for "Danse macabre," then the general question of caricature in Baudelaire's poetry ought to find a particularly complete elucidation in this case.[2] And, indeed, if we examine the cited stanza of "Danse macabre" with some care, we will discover the caricatural mechanism of *Les Fleurs du mal* in its most general instance. Before we can arrive at this discovery, however, we should notice that, in the tradition of the memento mori, the poem's meaning is organized around an opposition between life and death. In order for the poem to have its full impact (both aesthetic and ethical), this opposition must be minimized without being abolished, so that the trappings of life adhere to death—"O charme d'un néant follement attifé" (O charm of a nothingness, extravagantly decked out)—while the figure of death becomes visible beneath life's fleshly profusion:

> Pourtant, qui n'a serré dans ses bras un squelette,
> Et qui ne s'est nourri des choses du tombeau?
> Qu'importe le parfum, l'habit ou la toilette?
> Qui fait le dégoûté montre qu'il se croit beau.
>
> Nevertheless, who has not held a skeleton in his arms,
> And who has not eaten of the things of the tomb?
> What do perfume, garment or grooming matter?
> He who acts disgusted shows that he fancies himself beautiful.

We are already familiar with the way in which Baudelaire's poetry involves a playful figuration and refiguration of opposing terms (e.g., antiquity and Christianity in "La Muse malade"); at times these appear starkly antithetical, at other times they seem to approach a kind of reconciliation. We have also seen how this process of figuration is identical to the rhetorical operation that, for Sartre, indicates the presence of bad faith. It should not be surprising, then, if the odor of bad faith can be detected in "Danse macabre," thereby distinguishing the poem from its medieval models. Of course "the shrill irony" of the latter seems to be at work in the Baudelaire, in lines like "Vit-on jamais au bal une taille plus mince?" (Has a slimmer waist ever been seen at a ball?) for example. But something more (or less) is at stake here. The "shrill" edge of Baudelaire's irony is softened by a curious sincerity, which presents the macabre in a touching light: "*Pour dire vrai*, je crains que ta coquetterie / Ne trouve pas un prix digne de ses efforts" (*To tell the truth*, I fear that your coquetry / Might not find a prize worthy of its efforts) (my emphasis). The sincere tone is audible even behind the question "Vit-on jamais au bal une taille plus mince?," which can linger in the ear as an enthusiastic appraisal of the skeleton's legitimate charms. It is this sincerity which makes the poem seem more "modern" than "medieval," by giving it precious overtones: the life/death opposition is trivialized in a recurring question of *taste*—"Tu réponds, grand squelette, à mon goût le plus cher!," "Les charmes de l'horreur n'enivrent que les forts," and so on.[3] The trivializing tendency of the poem's sincerity is shared by the operation of bad faith, in ways that Sartre has fully demonstrated in *L'Etre et le néant*: "In the end, the goal of sincerity and that of bad faith are not so different," he writes in summation of his argument.[4] For our purposes, however, we need only note that, in "Danse macabre," sincerity serves the rhetorical ends of bad faith, by minimizing the life/death opposition and its sharply ironic potential.

The foregoing analysis should help us to pinpoint the role of caricature in the cited stanza. Here the life/death opposition occurs in the form of a difference of taste between the "drunken lovers of flesh" and the poet, whose aesthetic desires are met by the "great skeleton." In other words, life and death oppose one another as flesh opposes bone, and the gravity of the memento mori is consequently lightened; this is so both because flesh and bone together participate in the living organism and because the choice between the two is, as we have seen, presented as a matter of taste. On first reading the fifth stanza of "Danse macabre," we might suppose that the caricature in question plays only an incidental role in the central opposition: "Aucuns t'appelleront une caricature / Qui ne comprennent pas / . . . l'élégance de l'humaine armature." Caricature thus appears to be a simple misnomer for what is properly called the "human frame," and we are encouraged to dismiss the misdesignation. What becomes apparent, though, when we try to imagine the stanza without "caricature," is that the word refuses to be dismissed. This is not only because the word is strikingly peculiar in itself (as far as conventional poetic vocabulary is concerned), but also because it answers to the peculiarity of other words ("armature," and "squelette") that share its unconventional quality and its sonorities. A specific tension involving "caricature" is achieved in that these same words, "armature" and "squelette," repulse "caricature" as an improper synonym while they attract the word as a stylistic equivalent: hence "caricature" is and is not the human frame or skeleton, that is, does and does not occupy the second position in the life/death opposition. In a simpler fashion, "caricature" approaches and recoils from the first term of that opposition, life, by offering to the minds of the "amants ivres de chair" a parodic representation of flesh. The sum of these observations can be given as follows: the caricature of "Danse macabre," far from being incidental to the play of life and death in the poem, designates that play with remarkable precision. Neither flesh nor bone, yet approximating both, caricature coincides with the poem's rhetoric of bad faith, as described in the preceding paragraph.

At this point, some general conclusions may be drawn from the reading of "Danse macabre." Because caricature is uncovered at the rhetorical heart of this emblematic poem, we may assume that the caricatural mechanism occupies a similarly critical position for Baudelaire's poetry as a whole. Moreover, because the mechanism corresponds to what I have identified as the rhetoric of bad faith, the examples I have considered thus far of bad faith or caricature in *Les Fleurs du mal* should acquire a more completely exemplary status. Now the question becomes, How are such conclusions to be viewed in terms of a general description of Baudelaire's poetics? Is it possible to read a poetics into the stanza under consideration and thereby to acquire a clearer picture of Baudelaire's poetry in general?

The answer to the second part of the question should lead logically back to the first. Yes, a poetics is at stake in "Danse macabre," and one which represents *Les Fleurs du mal* more generally than the canonical poetics of "Correspondances." This will become evident once the extended significance of flesh versus bone in the former poem is examined. That this opposition presented a problem of poetics for Baudelaire may be seen in his discussion of the skeleton in the *Salon de 1859*: "The sculptor quickly understood what mysterious and abstract beauty lay in this thin carcass, which is clothed in flesh, and which is like the blueprint of the human poem. And this caressing, biting, almost scientific Grace took its place, clear and cleansed of the stains of humus, among the innumerable Graces that Art had already extracted from an ignorant Nature" (OC, 2: 678). This is one of the rare organic analogies (a poem is like the human form) to be found in Baudelaire's corpus, and he is careful to "cleanse" the analogy of most of its organic aspect. Flesh first appears, not as a synecdoche for the living organism, but as an article of clothing—"this thin carcass, which is *clothed in flesh*" ("à qui la chair sert d'habit")—thus losing its natural connotations; furthermore, if there is some analogy implied between "the stains of humus" and human flesh, both of which adhere to the skeleton, then these figures for "ignorant Nature" are rather excluded from Baudelaire's aesthetic insight; that is to say, the insight that compares poem to human form is itself presented as an "extract," "purified" of organic substances. Thus, we are left with the skeleton, that blueprint of the human poem, which comes to figure poetry proper insofar as poetry *is* the blueprint, the extract or abstract that Art draws from Nature.[5]

The skeleton of poetry, which is poetry, corresponds to what Baudelaire called the secret architecture of his own work. We need only reflect on a qualification like "mysterious and abstract beauty" in order to see the correspondence quite plainly. The skeleton is mysterious, just as the architecture is secret, in a highly unusual manner. Of course, when the human form is contemplated, the skeleton is hidden, and when *Les Fleurs du mal* is read, presumably the sensual surface of the poetry conceals its architectural structure. There is nothing overly peculiar in this state of affairs. But the mystery and the secret in question are not actually properties of the skeleton or the architecture: once uncovered, the latter should strike us as perfectly accessible phenomena, capable of elucidation by an architectural or anatomic vocabulary, which is scarcely mysterious. The peculiarity of Baudelaire's poetics, however, lies in the fact that the skeleton of poetry remains mysterious even when it is fully exposed. This may explain why the grace of the skeleton in the passage above is described as "biting" and "almost scientific." It is not a thoroughly scientific grace, because it falls just short of explicability, and hence the ironic "bite" that points to a mystery beyond explanation. As previously noted, the significance of the Baudelairean skeleton is hereby displaced: it begins as the hidden design of the human poem, which poem includes a covering of flesh; but as the flesh is peeled away, the hidden design recedes, and the skeleton comes to stand for the poetic mystery in its totality. The process of unpeeling thus takes on an indefinite dimension so that the flesh is never quite dispensed with and the bone is never quite reached. This indefinition is no doubt what prompts those who would pinpoint the architecture of *Les Fleurs du mal* to take one of two tones: either they move rapidly to the bone of the matter—"In the beginning there are ... for Baudelaire 'two simultaneous postulations'"[6]—and leave skeptics to point out all the rich poetic surfaces that are not accounted for by such a schematization; or else they leave the poetic skeleton behind a partial veil, and, in the name of prudence, give only a vague designation: "If there really is a secret architecture in this book—and many speculations have been devoted to it—the cycle of poems that opens the volume probably is devoted to something irretrievably lost."[7]

It should now be possible to articulate the role of caricature in a general consideration of Baudelaire's poetics. In "Danse macabre," it was caricature that occupied the indeterminate position between flesh and bone. In the preceding discussion, this position appears to be held, not by any poetic entity, but by the process of reading that moves between the surface of the poetry and its architecture. Now it must be determined in what way caricature corresponds to the process of reading *Les Fleurs du mal*. On the abstract level of the analogy I have just established, caricature and reading share an epiphenomenal quality: in the same way that the caricature of "Danse macabre" could be dismissed as a misnomer for the "human frame," so the reading of *Les Fleurs du mal* as I have described it may pass as an inadequate substitute for the poetry's architecture. In other words, the ideal reading would be nothing but the purely adequate revelation of the architecture, and anything short of this would be mere "caricature." Of course, in the poetics Baudelaire has given us, an ideal reading of the sort is not possible: the moment we designate an architecture, it recedes, and our reading thus acquires the status of a perpetual approximation. It is by dint of the perpetual necessity to repeat the designation that the reading simultaneously loses much of its epiphenomenal quality and becomes intimately associated with the poetic object as such. This should not surprise us, in view of what I have termed the "relational essence" of Baudelaire's poetry ("relational essence" being an amphibological concept of the kind generated by bad faith). The movement of the reading toward an essential coincidence with the poetry may thus be called caricatural.

If the poetics derived from "Danse macabre," is indeed more generally representative of Baudelaire's poetry than the poetics of "Correspondances," then this ought to be demonstrable on an empirical as well as on an abstract level. It is easy to accumulate empirical instances of *correspondances* in *Les Fleurs du mal*, a fact which has contributed, even more perhaps than the explicit presentation of the poem as an ars poetica, to the popular conviction that herein lies the key to Baudelaire's aesthetics.[8] And it is true that much of what we consider most inimitable in Baudelaire seems to realize the synesthetic "transports de l'esprit et des sens" (transports of the mind and senses) with a masterful, almost mathematical precision: ("La Chevelure") (The head of hair) (1: 26)—

> Un port retentissant où mon âme peut boire
> A grand flots le parfum, le son, et la couleur;
> Où les vaisseaux, glissant dans l'or et dans la moire,
> Ouvrent leurs vastes bras, pour embrasser la gloire
> D'un ciel pur où frémit l'éternelle chaleur.
>
> An echoing harbor where my soul can drink
> Long draughts of perfume, sound and color;
> Where the ships, sliding in watered gold,
> Open their vast arms, to embrace the glory
> Of a pure sky where eternal heat trembles.

However, as Baudelaire mentions in the poem "Correspondances," this symbolic synesthesia occurs only sometimes and thus cannot be generalized. Although this would appear to strengthen the case for an emblematic interpretation of "Danse macabre," it actually makes the case more difficult. Because Baudelaire's *correspondances* stand for the possibility of symbolic generalization, that is, because they describe the passage from any particular odor, sound, or color to the totality of "une ténébreuse et profonde unité" (a somber and deep unity), when these *correspondances* fail to be generalizable the process of generalization is itself brought into question. On what grounds, therefore, can one claim an emblematic status for "Danse macabre"? Obviously, there is a kind of double bind at work if we argue that "Danse macabre" may be an emblem of *Les Fleurs du mal* because the breakdown of symbolic generalization that occurs in the poetry as a whole occurs in this particular poem as well. Such an argument, which restores the symbolic passage from part to whole at the moment that its content describes the breakdown of this passage, should remind us once more of a rhetoric of bad faith. If, however, we do not dismiss this rhetoric as rigorously invalid, we may be able to advance in our progressively approximative reading of Baudelaire's poetry. A first observation is that the caricature of "Danse macabre" does in fact figure the failed totalization of the human poem: caricature describes the obstructed passage from flesh to bone, which passage, had it been possible, would have permitted the human poem to be a beautiful totality. As a kind of would-be symbol, caricature takes the place of the failed totality by standing as an inadequate substitute for flesh and bone together, that is, as a dummy totality. Now the question becomes, How systematically can we trace the empirical occurrence of this failed totalization?

To answer this question we might begin by examining *Les Fleurs du mal*, not for an architecture per se, but for the approximation of an architecture.[9] This procedure is indicated because, as I have shown, the dummy totality of caricature is nothing if not such an approximation. A useful point of departure for this examination might be Benjamin's previously cited statement that "the cycle of poems that opens the volume probably is devoted to something irretrievably lost." The statement has the advantage of imprecision, which, in this instance, extends its general applicability. And, indeed, when we consider the cycle of poems that Baudelaire entitled *Spleen et Idéal*, the dominant tone is one of an undefined nostalgia. At times it appears to be nostalgia for a squandered youth—"Ma jeunesse ne fut qu'un ténébreux orage" (My youth was nothing but a sombre storm) (1: 16)—at other times for a bygone era—"Du temps que la Nature en sa verve puissante / Concevait chaque jour des enfants monstrueux" (In the days when Nature in her prime of power / Each day conceived colossal children) (1: 22)—and yet again for the unfulfilled promise of an artistic career—"Bien qu'on ait du coeur à l'ouvrage, / L'Art est long et le Temps est court" (Although our heart is in the task, / Art is long and Time is short) (1: 17). The two final poems of this section, "L'Irrémédiable" and "L'Horloge" (The clock) make explicit that the loss of any ideal—"Une Idée, une Forme, un Etre / Parti de l'azur et tombé" (An Idea, a Form, a Being / Fallen from the blue sky) (1: 79)—is related to the more general question of the passage of time ("L'Horloge" 1: 81):

> Tantôt sonnera l'heure où le divin Hasard,
> Où l'auguste Vertu, ton épouse encor vierge,
> Où le Repentir même (oh! la dernière auberge!),
> Où tout te dira: Meurs, vieux lâche! il est trop tard!

> Soon the hour will come when divine Chance,
> When august Virtue, your virgin spouse,
> When Repentance itself (oh! the final inn!),
> When all will say to you: Die, old coward! it is too late!

Time, then, gives loss a generalized figure—"*tout* te dira: . . . il est trop tard!"—and in this way, "L'Horloge" serves to encapsulate the preceding poems.

If the "something lost" has something to do with time itself (and here I am in agreement with Proust, who claimed to find in Baudelaire a precedent for his own search for time lost), then the reading of the *Spleen et Idéal* cycle need not be bound by the activity of identification—that is, what was lost, when was it lost, and where should we start looking for it. This positive activity has its place in *Les Fleurs du mal*, and Baudelaire does not refrain from supplying answers to the preceding questions: youth and beauty, among other things, have been lost, and the place to look for them is at times unambiguously indicated ("Le Balcon" 1: 37):

> Je sais l'art d'évoquer les minutes heureuses,
> Et revis mon passé blotti dans tes genoux.
> Car à quoi bon chercher tes beautés langoureuses
> Ailleurs qu'en ton cher corps et qu'en ton coeur si doux?

> I know the art of evoking the happy minutes,
> And relive my past curled up in your lap.
> For what sense is it to seek your langorous beauties
> Elsewhere than in your dear body and in your gentle heart?

But this kind of identification is caught up in a movement that exceeds it, in the same way that the limits provided by Jeanne's body designate simultaneously a circumscribed and a limitless space. This may be plainly seen in the lines of another poem (1: 27):

> Je t'adore à l'égal de la voûte nocturne,
> O vase de tristesse, ô grande taciturne,
> Et t'aime d'autant plus, belle, que tu me fuis,
> Et que tu me parais, ornement de mes nuits,
> Plus ironiquement accumuler les lieues
> Qui séparent mes bras des immensités bleues.

> I adore you like the vault of the nocturnal sky,
> O vase of sadness, O great taciturn one,
> And love you all the more, my beauty, in that you flee me,
> And that you seem, ornament of my nights,
> To multiply ironically the leagues
> That separate my arms from the blue immensities.

By embracing the "vase de tristesse," which, despite its tremendous capacity, remains a container and provides the limits of an enclosed space, the poet experiences the ironic transformation of limit into limitlessness, as the expanse of the "voûte nocturne" accumulates between his outstretched arms.[10] In tracing the figure of time lost throughout the first part of *Les Fleurs du mal*, our task similarly involves following the periodic identifications beyond themselves, and beyond our own schematizing powers.

The first time that time itself is given a prominent figure in *Spleen et Idéal* is in the fifth poem, "J'aime le souvenir de ces époques nues" (I love the memory of those naked epochs). Here the figure is so schematized that one cannot help but notice it. The poem opens with a portrait of antiquity, which Baudelaire paints in paradisical colors. The inhabitants of a pagan world are coddled by their gods, Phoebus and Cybele, who provide an abundance of sun and fertile seasons and generally guarantee an existence "sans mensonge et sans anxiété" (without lies and without anxiety). Time is experienced as the loss of this pagan world, or rather as the disjunction between this and a modern world (1: 12):

> Le Poète aujourd'hui, quand il veut concevoir
> Ces natives grandeurs, aux lieux où se font voir
> La nudité de l'homme et celle de la femme,
> Sent un froid ténébreux envelopper son âme . . .
>
> The Poet today, when he wishes to understand
> These native grandeurs, in the places where one sees
> The nakedness of man and that of woman,
> Feels a shadowy cold envelop his soul . . .

Thus far the features of time appear to have a positive character— even if time is not a positive entity, but the disjunction between yesterday and today, still these two remain stable terms. The past and the present in and of themselves have a specific content, which is underscored by the critical distinction between a naked and a clothed condition. As long as past and present keep such stable physionomies, we cannot say that "J'aime le souvenir" describes the loss of time, but only the loss of paradise. Time, which marks that primitive loss, is itself a trickier thing to lose.

If we move to the final stanza of the poem, however, we should quickly become aware that the stakes have changed. Critics have registered this shift by wondering whether the final stanza might not originally have belonged to another poem. Although there is not enough evidence to prove or disprove such a speculation, we do know that Baudelaire allowed "J'aime le souvenir" to go untouched through several publications. Presumably, then, he intended the poem to remain as we now know it. Our burden thus becomes to find another means of accounting for the apparent shift. This is not a simple task, since the shift seems to involve both content and style and, in each case, to tend in a different direction. We should therefore proceed cautiously, with a description of the various changes.

On the level of content the final stanza begins predictably enough with an allusion to the "corrupted nations" of the modern world. These are, for the first time, presented in a positive light, as having their own sickly kind of beauty: "Des visages rongés par les chancres du coeur,/Et comme qui dirait des beautés de langueur . . ." (Faces eaten up by the cankers of the heart,/And what could be called languishing beauties . . .). Although this optimistic note is new in the poem, it does not constitute a shift in content, but rather a development of the original thematics. What strikes us as peculiarly inappropriate occurs instead in the following lines: "Mais ces inventions de nos muses tardives/N'empêcheront jamais les races maladives/De rendre à la jeunesse un hommage profond" (But these inventions of our belated muses/Will never keep the sickly races/From offering a profound homage to youth). The peculiarity here has something to do with a rerouting of the redemptive impulse. We were expecting more reasons to find consolation in an aesthetics of modernity, perhaps a word of praise of the sort Baudelaire gives in "De l'héroïsme de la vie moderne" (The heroism of modern life) for the nineteenth-century frock-coat.[11] The consolation we are offered, however, is more deeply rooted in resignation. The merit of the present time is not linked to any of its intrinsic properties, but to the generosity of its backward glance: it acknowledges all that it is not and thereby acquires the game dignity of the very old who bestow blessing upon the very young. This brings us, of course, to the second surprising element of these lines, one which involves an evident shift in content. It is fair to describe the opening stanza of "J'aime le souvenir" as a salute to antiquity, and we expect the backward glance of the present to take in the antique prospect and return in some sense to the poem's beginning. When we find instead a salute to youth, despite the fact that this is consistent with the redemptive tone of the last stanza, we are within our rights to feel that an "unauthorized" substitution has been made. Baudelaire even precedes the salute to youth with a dash, thus marking the separation of this passage from the rest of the poem. The only way that it is possible to reconcile this change of content with the expectations of a return to the opening stanza is if we argue that Baudelaire is following a logic of ontogeny recapitulating phylogeny—in other words, the aging process of the individual corresponds to that of humankind, and therefore antiquity may be retrieved in youth. This is not a far-fetched hypothesis, and Baudelaire did not disdain to use such a logic explicitly, for example, in the forty-seventh fragment of *Mon coeur mis à nu* (OC, 1: 707). We should note, however, that this means of retrieving the original content of the poem actually undermines what at first seemed to be the stable physionomies of past and present. If the physionomy of the present includes youth as the symbolic recapitulation of antiquity, then the disjunction between past and present must be less decisive than we had thought. Moreover, time, which was nothing if not that disjunction, the "froid ténébreux" that enveloped the soul of the modern poet and prevented him from imagining anything but the present, has become something less negative, interior to the present and detectable within its features. Thus, time becomes the potential object of an experience—in other words, time may occur within the limits of a given experience, an individual may "grow old," for example, and this may take place as a continuing process and not as a series of disjunctions between multiple selves.[12] This interiorization of the figure of time may, in part, explain the curiosity of the poem's opening line—"J'aime *le souvenir* de ces époques nues." Realistically there is no place within the modern poet's experience for the memory of antiquity but, once the symbolic equivalence of individual and species has been established, such an occurrence becomes no less curious than the individual's memory of childhood in old age. In sum, then, the content of "J'aime le souvenir" reveals simultaneously the interiorization of the temporal figure and the symbolic totalization of individual experience.

On the level of style, however, the final stanza of the poem reveals a different kind of movement. Rather than recapitulating the somewhat stiff and symmetrical style of the first stanza, the salute to youth "discovers" a new style (at least within the limits of this poem): we are suddenly treated to an instance of Baudelairean *correspondances* with the metrical accent being shifted from units of two or four to units of three:

> —A la sainte jeunesse, à l'air simple, au doux front,
> A l'oeil limpide et clair ainsi qu'une eau courante,
> Et qui va répandant sur tout, insouciante
> Comme l'azur du ciel, les oiseaux et les fleurs,
> Ses parfums, ses chansons et ses douces chaleurs!

> —To holy youth, with simple air and gentle brow,
> With eyes limpid and clear like running water,
> Who goes, free from care, scattering everywhere
> Like the blue of the sky, birds and flowers,
> Its perfumes, its songs, and its sweet warmth.

The sense of beatitude that is evoked in these lines is largely due to their stylistic nuances: the triple meter seems, at first hesitatingly, then with more confidence, to step out from its symmetrical background like any figure of life being born from stasis.[13] It is no accident that perfumes begin to circulate in this atmosphere, in place of the "statues," "machines," and "fruits purs" of the first stanza.

The Allegorical Architecture of 'Les Fleurs' 137

Not only does this involve a change toward more mobile images, it also accompanies a difference in rhetorical structure. The statues and fruit of the opening are both stable images and stable vehicles in the metaphorical representation of humankind. In other words, the metaphorical transaction between, say, the fruit and the women at the end of the first stanza, is of a very limited nature: "Fruits purs de tout outrage et vierges de gerçures, / Dont la chair lisse et ferme appelait les morsures" (Fruits, unravaged and flawless, / Whose smooth and firm flesh called out to be bitten).[14] Here, the fruit transports its firm flesh to the women, a transaction which enables us to endow fleshiness with ethical qualities (purity, virginity). But, perhaps because we did not need the fruit to give to women fleshy connotations, or else because women and fruit are a canonical couple (not always metaphorically, but sometimes metonymically; for example, Eve and the fruit tree in Eden), the transaction appears redundant. Consequently, the metaphor may strike us as dull, since the exchange of qualities between its two terms has done little to transform our perception or understanding of either term.

In contrast to this stable metaphorical system, the *correspondances* of the final stanza are so extensive as to confuse a clear identification of the metaphor's terms. True, it may seem as though "youth" at least is a stable term, the object of the homage and, hence, the tenor of its metaphorical representation. This semblance of stability, however, cannot withstand close analysis. First, it should be noted that the syntax of the homage is less straightforward than it may appear. There is no problem with the basic components of the sentence—"A la sainte jeunesse . . . qui va répandant . . . ses parfums"—but a difficulty arises with the very clause that gives us the principal metaphor of the passage—"Comme l'azur du ciel, les oiseaux et les fleurs . . ." The straightforward reading of the clause would have "comme" modify "répandant"; thus, youth would spread its perfumes like the sky, birds, and flowers spread theirs, and so this final trio would constitute the metaphorical vehicle. The problem with this reading is that it does not account for another syntactical feature of the poem, the commas of the last two lines: "Comme l'azur du ciel, les oiseaux et les fleurs, / Ses parfums, ses chansons et ses douces chaleurs!" With no other syntactical mark than a comma to separate these lines, the tendency is to read "ses parfums, ses chansons" as a continuation of the preceding enumeration. The consequences of this tendency are twofold: first, "comme" would no longer link the sky to youth, but to youth's perfumes and songs, and these latter would replace youth as the metaphorical tenor. This uncertainty concerning the tenor of the metaphor is directly related to the use of the word "comme," a word noticeably absent from the first stanza of "J'aime le souvenir," and whose destabilizing potential in Baudelaire's poetics should now be familiar to us. Second, if we tend to read the last two lines of the poem as the continuation of a single list, then we simultaneously minimize the distinction between tenor and vehicle. Even though there is a metaphysical as well as a metaphorical hierarchy at work (flowers give off perfume, birds sing songs), this, too, is minimized by the closing syntax. It thus is no longer possible to speak of an exchange of qualities between two terms, because the terms in themselves are uncertain and because the distinction between a substance and its qualities is no longer operative. If a flower and its perfume are reduced to the same metaphysical plane, then a flower could not give away its perfume and still remain a flower. Put in other terms, the metaphorical exchange that takes place in the salute to youth also constitutes a threat to metaphysical categories, in particular to the concept of essence. It is, of course, remarkable that in Baudelaire the perfume (synonymous with "essence" even in English) becomes the privileged figure for the undoing of essences; but this is to be expected from what we have called the rhetoric of bad faith—an attempt to seize for being the disintegration of being itself.[15] We should therefore note with interest, and possibly with some suspicion, that this rhetoric so frequently coincides with the effect of novelty, with what in *Les Fleurs du mal* has come to be considered the "modern" style.

Now it ought to be possible to give an overall assessment of the critical rupture in "J'aime le souvenir." Evidently my analysis of the poem's two styles works against the symbolic totalization that was implied by my reading of the poem's content. To return to the figure of time, which has been the focal point of my investigation, at the very moment when the past is recovered on the level of content, something new is produced on the level of style. I have already located a similar, although less critical occurrence of this phenomenon in the last two stanzas of "La Muse malade." The question now becomes, Is it possible to make sense of this contradictory movement? Can we repeat for the poem as a whole the kind of symbolic reconciliation we were able to perform with respect to the content alone? A tentative answer is yes—tentative because we should now be aware that any symbolic formulation of Baudelaire's poetry is only a pause in the *danse macabre*, that is, a moment of equilibrium in the process of reading. For the moment, then, time becomes the answer to the riddle, which is all the more comforting in that we had supposed time to be part of the question. In the course of "J'aime le souvenir," however, the figure of time undergoes a transformation, one I have already alluded to and which permits time to fulfill a dual function. As was stated earlier, the original figure of time as the difference between yesterday and today is subject neither to loss nor to recovery—that difference may require the loss of something else, but this is nearly the opposite of losing the difference. To lose the difference we would have to retrieve what was lost, and thus the pure loss of time would require the perfect restoration of all things. To call this a *loss* of time, however, seems to be a misnomer, because it corresponds more exactly to an elimination of time as a meaningful concept. Similarly, the recovery of time in this instance is a conceptual absurdity—to recover time, we would have to lose something permanently, even beyond recollection, in which case we would have no means of judging what had been lost or found. It is only when the figure of time becomes interior to the individual subject that loss or recovery may be applied to that figure. This is because, as I have argued, only interiorized time can be experienced, and loss and recovery rigorously understood are experiences. In this way, the simultaneous loss and recovery of time need not be seen as a pure contradiction, because the condition of possibility of each experience is the same. In fact, one could go so far as to define time, in a sphinx-like manner, as the thing that can only be found by losing it, or vice versa.[16] With this definition in mind, the contradictions of the homage to youth begin to make perfect sense—the interior experience of time is epitomized in these five lines by a loss ("Et qui va répandant sur tout, insouciante . . .") which spells a recovery (of youth, of the good old days, and so on). The metrical interest of the homage, which distinguishes it from the rest of the poem, adds to the plausibility of this reading by drawing attention to the temporal dimension. It is as though an inner clock were set off in this passage, very close to the clock that begins to vibrate more explicitly at the beginning of "Harmonie du soir" (Evening harmony): "Voici venir les temps où vibrant sur sa tige / Chaque fleur s'évapore ainsi qu'un encensoir . . ." (Now has come the time when, vibrating on its stem / Each flower evaporates like a censer . . .) (1: 47). The "melancholic waltz" that ensues in the latter poem is, from a metrical standpoint, more perfectly executed in "J'aime le souvenir."

The success of our efforts to restore a symbolic unity to "J'aime le souvenir" should not obscure the fact that we are primarily concerned with the architecture of the poetry as a whole, rather than with individual poems. If it is true that the loss of time has something to do with the *Spleen et Idéal* cycle in general, then what we have discovered in "J'aime le souvenir" ought to point beyond this poem to the series of poems that follow it. And, indeed, this is the case, at least on a limited scale. In fact, the series that runs from "La Muse malade" (7) through "Le Guignon" (11) and possibly "La Vie antérieure" (12) seems to be governed by the same figurative pattern as "J'aime le souvenir," and indicates an ulterior development. First, there is a repetition of the primitive temporal difference—in "La Muse malade" this is the familiar difference between antiquity and a Christian modernity; in "Le Mauvais moine" (The bad monk), the Christian world is divided into an early pious era and a later period of idleness: "O moine fainéant! quand saurai-je donc faire / Du spectacle vivant de ma triste misère / Le travail de mes mains et l'amour de mes yeux?" (O idle monk! when will I learn to make / From the living spectacle of my dreary misery / Work for my hands and my eyes' passion?) (1: 16). This historical difference becomes more personalized in the following poem, "L'Ennemi," where the distinguishing features are "ma jeunesse" (my youth) and "l'automne des idées" (the autumn of ideas) (1: 16). It should be clear that with each repetition of the temporal difference an interiorization of the figure is performed, in such a way that the symbolic correspondence between individual and species is implied. We would expect, therefore, from our study of "J'aime le souvenir," that the interiorization of the temporal figure would bring with it the lyric voice of the homage to youth, that by the time we reached "L'Ennemi," the atmosphere would be charged with perfumes and the other indices of Baudelaire's *correspondances*.

In point of fact, however, the stylistic movement of these poems appears to be the reverse. The closest thing we get to *correspondances* occurs in the last two stanzas of "La Muse malade" (I refrain from citing these—they have been sufficiently analyzed); here, as in "J'aime le souvenir," there is the simultaneous "nostalgic newness," but what underwrites this movement is no longer a sturdy symbolic relationship: instead, the individual *wishes* its connection to the species—"Je *voudrais* qu'exhalant l'odeur de la santé" (I could wish that, exuding the odor of health) and so on. The location of meaning within the individual subject, rather than consummating a symbolic union as it does in the traditional lyric (the lyric voice is thought to constitute a universal "I"), actually weakens the likelihood of such a union. This weakened possibility is expressed by one of Rivière's "word[s] full of weakness,"[17] "Je *voudrais*" (I *would like*), which contrasts remarkably with other expressions of will in Baudelaire, for example, "Je *la veux* agiter dans l'air comme un mouchoir" (I *want* to shake it in the air like a handkerchief), which the poet says of the head of hair in "La Chevelure." What is thus begun in "La Muse malade" is a movement which, while it concentrates meaning progressively within the individual, at the same time isolates the subject more and more from the realm of meaning. Even the slight possibility of meaning that is afforded by the weak will is lost to "Le Mauvais moine," whose problem is that he cannot bring himself to do anything. Were he able to rouse himself to action, presumably he could inscribe himself within the tradition of "Plus d'un illustre moine, aujourd'hui peu cité" (More than one illustrious monk, today rarely cited) and thereby recover history for experience.

This particular recovery is what I have attributed to the homage to youth in "J'aime le souvenir," but its sustained possibility is brought seriously into question by the later poem. The question is raised, not for reasons of pathos—that is, this poor monk shows no promise of shouldering the historical burden—but for reasons involving the ulterior development of the temporal figure. Along with the first interiorization of time (within the Christian era), there is the separation of the "modern" monk from temporal experience altogether—"Mon âme est un tombeau que, mauvais cénobite / Depuis l'éternité je parcours et j'habite" (My soul is a tomb where, as a bad cenobite / I have traveled and dwelled for all eternity). This is the first instance in *Les Fleurs du mal* of an empty eternity, one which appears to be characterized by the absence of time, either as a mark of difference or as the object of a simultaneous loss and recovery.[18] The obstacle to the monk's working is, therefore, more than the collapse of his will—he lacks the necessary temporal dimension to bring any work to fruition. His situation becomes all the more curious when we realize that he stands outside both history and experience. The interiorization of the temporal figure, which we have deemed to be the condition of possibility of experience, actually lies outside the individual subject, somewhere within the history that is set against eternity and its emptiness. In other words, interior experience and its lyrical expression have been displaced so that they no longer occur within the individual subject. This displacement is registered in the poem by a breakdown of the inside/outside distinction. "Mon âme est un tombeau" makes a certain amount of metaphoric sense, and does not seem too unusual as a depiction of sorrow or despair; but, once the figure develops and the tomb is exploited, not for its emotive connotations, but for its function as a container analogous to the cloister of the first stanza, then simple representational categories begin to be violated—How can one dwell *within* one's own soul, or examine one's experiences as though they were paintings on a wall?

The figure Baudelaire gives us of the monk traversing the tomb of his soul is not a figure of introspection in any normal sense. The inner self has been completely exteriorized as a "spectacle vivant," leaving nothing to the subject but a mobile eye. Because the subject cannot interiorize or experience the self, the latter becomes strangely reified—although the spectacle of the self is a *living* one, the life in question does not suggest a fully developed subjectivity. This kind of reduced self is common in Baudelaire's *Spleen* poems —the singing sphinx, the stunned king, and the snow-engulfed corpse of "Le Goût du néant" (The taste of nothingness) are similar figures. What interests me here, however, is less the emotive potential of the figure (this following the cue given by the figuration in "Le Mauvais moine"), than the fact that it represents the pure exteriorization of inner experience. As we have seen, this exteriorization is produced by the same movement that tended to interiorize time and experience within the individual subject. The symbolic totality of that subject, at the very moment of its affirmation, is revealed to be a dummy totality as subject and self are isolated. Once again, we are confronted with the comedy or self-caricature of Baudelaire's verse, which treats the claims of the inner self in a manner similar to Gustave Flaubert's treatment of Charles Bovary's cadaver: "[The doctor] cut it open and found nothing." The joke, of course, requires that the claims of the self be made in bad faith, that they follow the model of Sartre's "I am too great for myself" rather than the symbolic model of the lyric "I."

Although the preceding development, which has been identified as an ulterior development of the temporal figure, may be somewhat hidden in "Le Mauvais moine," it becomes explicit in the following poem, "L'Ennemi." This is the first poem in the series to present history as a personal phenomenon, and yet the lyricism we might consequently expect is missing. In place of the lyric "I," we are confronted with a scrupulously, almost painfully, allegorical subject. Before this point in the *Spleen et Idéal* cycle, Baudelaire had offered a smattering of allegorical figures—the pagan gods and antique localities, as well as the representation of seasons in "Quand Janvier lâchera ses Borées" (When January unleashes its north wind) (1: 15), fall into this category—but these remain decorative and often escape notice in the overwhelming pathos of the opening section. In contrast, the allegory of "L'Ennemi" becomes an implacable machine, interfering with the poem's very evident pathetic intention:

> Ma jeunesse ne fut qu'un ténébreux orage,
> Traversé çà et là par de brillants soleils;
> Le tonnerre et la pluie ont fait un tel ravage,
> Qu'il reste en mon jardin bien peu de fruits vermeils.
>
> My youth was nothing but a somber storm,
> Traversed here and there by brilliant suns;
> The thunder and rain have worked such havoc,
> That but few ripe fruit remain in my garden.

Although it is not fully apparent, the allegorical machine is already at work in these beginning lines. To appreciate this fact it might be useful to compare this representation of youth with the one I have discussed in "J'aime le souvenir." While "J'aime le souvenir" treated the subject of youth in general, it did so idiomatically, with Baudelairean vocabulary and style. Here, however, even with the possessive presentation of "ma jeunesse," the vocabulary and the images are borrowed from a stock of sentimental clichés. Claude Pichois' notes on the poem draw attention to efforts at finding a certain originality in the use of the word "ténébreux," which presumably livens the cliché "the storm of youth";[19] but "fruits vermeils" is beyond this kind of redemption, and concludes the stanza on a purely conventional note. Furthermore, the most striking consequence of the use of the adjective "ténébreux" is to permit a mechanical extension of the cliché rather than its renewal: in other words, the storm begins to acquire specific predicates—gloom, thunder, rain, and ravages—but these are conventional accompaniments, and add nothing to the imagery of storminess.

> Voilà que j'ai touché l'automne des idées,
> Et qu'il faut employer la pelle et les râteaux
> Pour rassembler à neuf les terres inondées,
> Où l'eau creuse des trous grands comme des tombeaux.
>
> Now I have reached the autumn of ideas,
> And must use spade and rake

To collect anew the flooded soil,
Where the water carves out holes as big as tombs.

It is in this second stanza that the allegorical mechanism of "L'Ennemi" becomes apparent as a representational absurdity. The expression "l'automne des idées" develops the cliché "the storm of youth" in two directions: narratively, because we thereby assume youth's storm to be a Spring which is followed by this autumnal condition; and rhetorically, because we now suppose the poem to be functioning as an allegory of the seasons of life. But far from heightening the poem's opening imagery, this development interferes with our ability to "picture" what is happening. Take, for example, the "fruits vermeils": the allegory of the seasons actually makes this image more difficult to interpret, because ripe fruit should be associated with autumn and the harvest rather than with spring. These should be the fruits of the poet's labor, but they seem to occupy his garden from the beginning, before any activity on his part; and, curiously, they do not ripen with the passage of the seasons, but simply diminish in number—"il *reste* en mon jardin bien peu de fruits vermeils" (but few ripe fruit *remain*). Similarly, the spade and rakes, which are instruments of cultivation, seem out of place in the harvest season; they indicate an activity which should have preceded autumn and the presence of ripe fruit. The "natural" relationship between labor and its fruits, a development which we could have imagined without difficulty, has been suspended in favor of the mechanical development of the allegory. The spade and rakes of the second stanza, as well as the activity of regathering the dispersed soil, all constitute an *automatic* and *literal* response to the cliché of devastation given in the first stanza. This kind of response is the hallmark of allegory *per se*, whose mechanical, literalizing tendency occurs at the expense of representation.[20] The allegory here, rather than serving a decorative function, actually describes the rhetorical character of "L'Ennemi."

This allegorical character is not without significance for the figure of time, which remains of primary interest to my analysis. As I have noted, the decorative allegories of *Les Fleurs du mal* often engage the temporal dimension, either as figures of months and seasons, or as representatives of antiquity. But this spells a merely incidental relationship between allegory and time, since other subjects (boredom, love, etc.) could be similarly allegorized. Furthermore, these allegories leave the temporal dimension "intact": the succession of the seasons remains fully natural and thus subject to nonallegorical representation (the most exemplary instance being a calendar of seasonal photographs). What occurs in "L'Ennemi," however, is the more critical interference of allegory and time. With the mechanical extension of the allegory and the disruption of the natural development of the seasons, another kind of temporality, one which is rhetorical as opposed to natural, is generated. Youth and maturity, or spring and fall, become subordinated to the figures of dispersion and regathering, which have no necessary organic relationship to one another. There is no simultaneity between these two figures, as there was in the last stanza of "J'aime le souvenir," which allowed us to posit the existence of an inner experience. The absence of simultaneity in "L'Ennemi" is consistent with the allegorization of the self: the self that lies outside itself among the objects of an allegorical garden can never coincide completely with itself. This may explain the difficulties posed for interpretation by the Enemy of the final stanza: the Enemy seems to be located within the most intimate recesses of the self ("[il] nous ronge le coeur") ([he] gnaws at our hearts), and yet can never be recovered *for* the self, is always alien and resistant to symbolic recuperation, as attempts to assimilate the Enemy to Time, or Death, or Boredom have proven.

To return, however, to the temporal figures of dispersion and regathering, since these have no organic connection, they may occur in almost any order, or may alternate with one another in an open-ended movement. For "L'Ennemi" this would mean that the poet could slip back and forth from maturity to youth simply by gathering and then dispersing the elements of his garden. This slippery temporality should help us to understand (retrospectively, of course) the series of rebeginnings that mark the poems we have been considering since "J'aime le souvenir." In each instance the loss of a world requires a refounding of the world, so that a new beginning is as much a perpetual possibility as the attending loss. This perpetual possibility of renewal is made explicit in "L'Ennemi," with the first mention of the new in *Les Fleurs du mal*: "pour rassembler *à neuf* les terres inondées, / Où l'eau creuse des trous grands comme des tombeaux" (to collect *anew* the flooded soil, / Where the water carves out holes as big as tombs). Significantly, the new in its first occurrence is a recurrence, which once more underscores the allegorical temporality of the poem by freeing the figure of renewal from any organic necessity.[21] Something similar happens in the celebrated final lines of "Le Balcon," where the natural phenomenon of the rising sun is dislocated from a simple cyclical temporality. The sun is freed from a natural temporality by becoming multiple, so that with each rising it is not the same old sun that we see after a natural cycle has been accomplished, but something renewed, whose newness is not a function of time but of the figure of rising itself:

> Ces serments, ces parfums, ces baisers infinis,
> Renaîtront-ils d'un gouffre interdit à nos sondes,
> Comme montent au ciel les soleils *rajeunis*
> Après s'être lavés au fond des mers profonds? (my emphasis)
>
> These vows, these perfumes, these infinite kisses,
> Will they be reborn from an abyss we may not plumb,
> Like *rejuvenated* suns rising in the sky
> After bathing in the depths of deep seas?

If in this disclosure of an allegorical temporality we find what I have called the ulterior development of the temporal figure, then our efforts to approximate the architecture of *Les Fleurs du mal* come against a particularly difficult obstacle. Past this point there is no development possible, and the question must be asked, Does the rest of the poetry lie in a kind of unreadable suspension, beyond any attempts to organize the poems into a logical sequence? It is true that extremely thorough endeavors, like Albert Feuillerat's 1941 "L'Architecture des *Fleurs du Mal*," lose anything like an overall sense of sequence to localized, incomplete cycles—"Baudelaire's experience as a poet," "Baudelaire seeking Beauty in Love," "Baudelaire's meditations on the influence of Boredom," and so on. There is not the space here to examine these minor movements in the light of the allegorical temporality previously outlined. But it should be recognized that the repeated reinstitution of local cycles builds the allegorical case, as it were, while a larger development tends to undermine the temporal freedom we have associated with allegory.

An anecdotal piece of evidence, which should not be overlooked when the question of allegory is raised, involves Baudelaire's own reading of *Spleen et Idéal*. Between the first and second editions of *Les Fleurs du mal*, perhaps under pressure of the obscenity trial in which the poetry's architecture played a critical role in its defense, Baudelaire subjected his collection to a scrupulous reexamination and reorganization. It is generally accepted that the resulting edition of 1861 is the definitive one, L. F. Benedetto echoing the consensus that it is "from the standpoint of the disposition of the poems, the most perfect" (p. 62). Individual aspects of this reorganization, like the decision to end the *Spleen et Idéal* cycle with "L'Irrémédiable" and "L'Horloge" instead of "La Musique" and "La Pipe," are in themselves worthy of detailed treatment. But, for the moment, because we wish to approximate a global perspective in our reading, we should direct our attention to the most obvious feature of Baudelaire's rereading—the institution of the series of poems titled *Tableaux parisiens*.

As was stated at the outset of this chapter, *Tableaux parisiens* are characterized by allegory, a fact which doubtless explains Walter Benjamin's particular interest in them. It should not surprise us, then, that Baudelaire's efforts to totalize the architecture of *Les Fleurs du mal* should result in an openly allegorical subdivision of the poetry. Not that this subdivision can stand easily as a symbol for the poetry as a whole—if this were the case, Baudelaire would more likely have placed *Tableaux* at the end of the collection where they could have played the subsumptive role, instead of leaving the end to death, "La Mort," with its literal finality. But, as I have already shown with the reading of "Danse macabre," the totalization of allegory always leaves a residue; Baudelaire's organization of

Les Fleurs du mal thus reconfirms the earlier insight. Much could be said concerning the particulars of this reconfirmation but, again, my aim is to work out the totalizing potential of Baudelairean allegory as far as I am able. To this end I will move from the architecture of the poetry, for which Baudelaire functions as the reader of his own text, to his aesthetic writings, in which the allegoresis moves beyond Baudelaire's own productions and beyond the medium of poetry itself.

CHAPTER FIVE

Baudelaire Against Photography
An Allegory of Old Age

꧁

It is common critical practice to divide Baudelaire's life into two distinct phases: an optimistic youth and a premature, embittered old age. From a biographical standpoint it is difficult to determine the moment of transition from one phase to the next, and many of Baudelaire's declarations create the impression that he experienced life as a continual verging on decrepitude: "Je ne suis pas positivement vieux," he wrote at the age of thirty-four, "mais je puis le devenir prochainement."[1] For the critic who is strictly interested in Baudelaire's literary and critical production, however, an early and a late period can be easily distinguished. Between 1846 and 1857, Baudelaire developed his idiom and thoroughly revised certain of his attitudes towards antiquity, the bourgeois reader, and the fate of the poet. Whether this occurred circumstantially, or whether, as Paul Valéry suggests, because Baudelaire discovered Poe and adopted the American writer's fatalism, Baudelaire's later work is increasingly querulous and seems to reveal an aging and discouraged author.

Baudelaire's two major *salons*, written in 1846 and 1859, fit nicely into this schema. The *Salon de 1846* opens with a dedication "Au bourgeois," and ends with a praising of modern life and its particular beauties. In between, Baudelaire pursues a definition of Romanticism as aesthetic modernism, that is as "the most recent, the most current expression of the beautiful." Although others in 1846 might have considered Romanticism past its prime, Baudelaire thought differently: "If few Romantics have remained, it is because few among them found Romanticism; but all of them sought it sincerely and loyally" (OC, 2: 420). The scarcity of Romantics then, must not be confused with the decadence of the movement. Romanticism remains a kind of holy grail—perhaps aging those who seek it, but itself untouched by time. Eugène Delacroix is described as "the head of the *modern* school," that is, as Romantic par excellence, and his paintings merit this attention because they are "great, *naïvely* conceived poems" (my emphasis). Naiveté and Romanticism become the two major criteria by which Baudelaire will criticize the paintings of the Salon.

All this faith in youth and the potential of the times is lost to the *Salon de 1859*. The old tolerance of aesthetic failure—"few among them found Romanticism, but all sought it sincerely and loyally"— has become a condemnation: "It is beyond doubt that mediocrity has always held sway; but it is both true and distressing that it reigns more than ever, that it has become absolutely triumphant and cumbersome" (OC, 2: 610). The bourgeois consumer of art has been transformed from "the majority,—in number and intelligence" into a "Hyperborean beast from antiquity, eternal spectacle-wearing, or rather, scale-wearing Eskimo, whom all the visions of Damascus, all thunder and lightning could never enlighten!" (2: 655). Romanticism itself is no longer spoken of as a fresh and timely expression, but as a memory: "That period was so fine and so fertile," Baudelaire writes in 1859, "that the artists in those days forgot no need of the human spirit" (2: 645). In contrast, "L'Artiste moderne," to whom Baudelaire devotes a chapter, is mainly interested in technical effects and popular success; like his scaly-eyed patrons, he is unappreciative of the spiritual difficulties involved in imaginative creation. Baudelaire calls him an *enfant gâté* (spoiled child) who has profited from the noble reputation of his predecessors.

There is no doubt that the Salon of 1859 lent itself to Baudelaire's ill humor. For the most part, the paintings were of minimal interest—"No fireworks; no undiscovered geniuses," Baudelaire reported. But his complaints went even further. This was to be Delacroix's last Salon, and the public had had over thirty years to examine the latter's prodigious oeuvre; yet his *Christ Entombed* elicited the same scandalized criticisms as had his first Salon painting, *Dante and Virgil*, in 1822. Only the explanation for his faults had changed: in 1822 he drew badly and abused color because of a youthful and undisciplined temperament; in 1859 he did the same things, but because his hand had grown palsied with age. Maxime du Camp went so far as to wonder, "What are these ghost-paintings that are being shown under his name?" (2: n. 1, p. 1396). Baudelaire, of course, decried this as absurd, public injustice; but the image of a ghostly Delacroix seems to have lodged in his mind and reinforced the nostalgic tone of the *Salon*. Typically, Baudelaire even re-created himself in the image of his idol: "... [Delacroix] sometimes makes me want to live as long as a patriarch, or, despite all the courage it would require for a dead man to consent to live again . . . to be revived in time to see the delights and praises that he will inspire in the future" (2: 637). This self-casting as patriarch or as ghost was not a passing fancy on Baudelaire's part. He adopted the voice of a spectral old man throughout the *Salon de 1859*. Once again, it is difficult to decide how or why Baudelaire would adopt such a voice. Was it for personal reasons, because he was embittered by illness and the recent trial of his poetry? Did his defense of Delacroix simply disguise an immediate desire to avenge himself upon the bourgeois public? Or was there something impersonal in the persona of the old man and, if so, how can one interpret that persona's utterances?

Since the answer to these questions is not simple and cannot be uncovered through direct inquiry, I would like to focus my attention on an incidental (or seemingly so) feature of the *Salon de 1859*: Baudelaire's denunciation of photography. Given the general tenor of the *Salon*, the denunciation comes as no surprise: it is part of Baudelaire's criticism of current trends in art and of his contention that popular opinion is wielding a greater influence in the aesthetic domain. Moreover, the denunciation appears to "date" Baudelaire. His attitude may be characterized as reactionary, not only from a twentieth-century perspective, but according to the criteria Baudelaire himself established in the *Salon de 1846*. There he argued that reactionary artists, those who turn their backs on modern life, do so by confusing moral and aesthetic decadence. They pretend that painting cannot be renewed in a morally corrupt climate, and thus excuse their own lack of inventiveness and dependence upon past aesthetic models: "Many people attribute the decadence in painting to the decadence in morals. This preconception of the ateliers has reached the public at large, and is a poor excuse on the part of artists. They had a vested interest in painting nothing but the past; the task is easier, and it suited their laziness [*la paresse y trouvait son compte*] (2: 493). Baudelaire contended, against such prejudice, that moral and aesthetic decadence affect different spheres: "One concerns the public and its sentiments, and the other involves only the ateliers" (2: 493). In 1859, with "Le Public moderne et la photographie," Baudelaire seems to disregard his earlier contention and collapse aesthetic issues into questions of public morality. The 1859 Salon saw the first exhibition of photographs, not yet included among, but adjoining the exhibition of paintings. Instead of assessing this phenomenon in terms of "the ateliers," Baudelaire concentrates on "the public and its sentiments": "If photography is permitted to supplement art in a few of its functions, *it will soon have supplanted or corrupted it altogether, thanks to the natural alliance it will find in the foolishness of the multitude*. It must therefore be reminded of its true duty, which is to be the servant of the arts and sciences, but a very humble servant, like printing and stenography, which have neither created nor supplemented literature" (2: 618, my emphasis).

Permission, corruption, duty, humility: the language of this warning belongs, not to the aesthete, but to the moralist. Naturally, then, the warning is not limited to a small community of artists. "The multitude," the greater public, is involved, as it both contributes to and suffers from aesthetic corruption: "If [photography] is allowed to trample upon the domain of the impalpable and the imaginary . . . then woe be onto us!" (2: 618). The "woe" of aesthetic corruption is so extensive as to touch us all, and Baudelaire leaves little room to imagine that some might escape its disastrous effects. In sum, the denunciation of photography presents all the features of a reactionary diatribe.

If we wish, however, to "date" Baudelaire on the basis of his reaction, that is, to claim that he could no longer greet "the new" with enthusiasm or that his modernist tendency had found its limit at the photograph, we run into certain critical difficulties. First, we should realize that each interpretive option (that Baudelaire had become "old," or that "history" and its developments had simply outdistanced him) relies upon a particular notion of time. In the first instance, we may deem Baudelaire "aged" because of his moralist intonations and blatant use of categorical thinking. Presumably, a young Baudelaire would have readjusted his thoughts to entertain the aesthetic potential of photography. The Baudelaire of 1859 excludes photography from the aesthetic domain, "the domain of the impalpable and the imaginary," and consigns it to the domain of technology. Such a categorical exclusion is intimately tied to Baudelaire's moralist stance, as we may gather from the exhortation: "[Photography] must therefore be reminded of its true duty." The assignment of photography to a place, that is, the categorical gesture, is simultaneously a moral imperative, a "duty." Of course, this kind of imperative cannot be affected by historical contingencies; if photography happens to leave its proper place, that place is still its own, and the passage of time will not legitimize its pretensions to belonging elsewhere. In other words, Baudelaire's reaction to photography is thoroughly ahistorical. We may interpret his ahistorical moralizing as a sign of old age, but in doing so we eliminate our own possibilities of attaining to historical insight. This is because the view which sees moralizing as the portion of old age is itself firmly ensconced within the moralist tradition. That the elderly speak of duty because their charms have faded and their wits are slow is a classical topos. When we determine Baudelaire's age on the basis of his moralizing, we have not advanced beyond the wisdom of Célimène in Molière's *Misanthrope*: "Il est une saison pour la galanterie, / Il en est une aussi propre à la pruderie" (There is a season for love affairs, / There is also one for prudishness). Such wisdom is ahistorical in that it describes only a cyclical temporality, that of the seasons of life. One may assign a season to Baudelaire's reaction, but that assignment remains as categorical as the reaction itself. History, then, lies outside this kind of interpretation.

The second interpretive option, that Baudelaire's reaction to photography merely marks the limits of his modernism, seems to avoid the hermeneutic circle of the first interpretation. When we no longer appeal to Baudelaire's interior experience of time, an experience which is subsumed by the human life cycle, then a purely external, linear temporality becomes possible. The task of the critic becomes simply to locate Baudelaire and his views along a time line of aesthetic history. We may notice, for example, that Baudelaire advocates "modernism" in defense of the Romantic painters, but not with respect to the photographers; on these grounds we may conclude that Baudelaire's views are Romantic and that his "modernism" is meaningless outside the context of the Romantic movement. The difficulty with this method is that Baudelaire's views, both generally considered and in the *Salon de 1859*, defy linear periodization. True, the *Salon de 1859* is largely a discourse on the imagination, the most Romantic of shibboleths. But Baudelaire's imagination does not function like a canonic Romantic faculty. The Romantic imagination is typically set against classical conventions—rules of prosody, genre distinctions, and so on. In the *Salon de 1859*, however, Baudelaire uses his own notion of the imagination to support the classical hierarchy of genres in painting. History painting, he argues, is to be privileged above genre painting because the former requires "the most rigorous imagination and the most strenuous effort" (see "Religion, History, Fantasy," 2: 628–29). We are left, then, with a curious aesthetic anachronism—a Romantic classicism or a classical Romanticism—which resists location in a linear history of art. Since Baudelaire's reaction to photography partakes of this same anachronistic character (he uses a "classical," categorizing gesture to defend the "Romantic" imagination against photography), we must accept that our attempts to "date" that reaction inevitably raise questions as to the validity of our own historical suppositions.

In order to demonstrate this point in greater detail, I would like to examine Walter Benjamin's reading of Baudelaire's reaction to photography. Benjamin first cites the *Salon de 1859* in his 1931 essay, "Short History of Photography." He contrasts Baudelaire's denunciation with Antoine Wiertz's enthusiastic assertion that photography is "the extract of painting" and poses no threat to art or to the productions of genius. Neither Baudelaire nor Wiertz, at least in Benjamin's estimation, is sensitive to the "authenticity" of the photograph. Leaving aside the more cryptic connotations Benjamin attaches to the word "authentic," we can still grasp some of his meaning: both Baudelaire's condemnation and Wiertz's approval are largely formulaic; that is, neither takes the shape of a specific response to photography. Wiertz, no less than Baudelaire, is tied to an aesthetics that derives its value from painting alone. Benjamin maintains (in the "today" of 1931) that one can only give meaning to either reaction by "displacing the accent" and reading the two together. In so doing one will see that each reaction mirrors the other and that both are *premature*. This is as far as Benjamin takes the historical view of the *Salon de 1859* in "Short History"; but he will return to the *Salon* eight years later, with a considerable development of the historical perspective.

In "On Some Motifs in Baudelaire," Benjamin analyzes the same *Salon* passage he had quoted in "Short History," and which I have quoted in part. The complete citation is as follows:

In those dismal days, a new industry came into being which contributed not a little to confirming foolishness in its belief . . . that art is and can only be the exact reproduction of nature. . . . An avenging god granted the wish of that multitude. Daguerre was his messiah. . . . If photography is permitted to supplement art in a few of its functions, it will soon have supplanted or corrupted it altogether, thanks to the natural alliance it will find in the foolishness of the multitude. It must therefore be reminded of its true duty, which is to be the servant of the arts and sciences.

The second time Benjamin refers to this passage, he does not mention Baudelaire's failure to acknowledge an "authentic" character of photography. Instead, he commends the accuracy of the poet's instincts: "To Baudelaire there was something profoundly unnerving and terrifying about daguerreotypy; he speaks of the fascination it exerted as 'startling and cruel.' Thus he must have sensed, though he certainly did not see through them, the connections of which we have spoken" ("Motifs": 186). The connections Benjamin has in mind are those that link technological developments, such as photography, to a "society in which practice is in decline." Once these connections have been made, it becomes difficult to argue for the authenticity of the photograph. For Benjamin, an authentic object is one that bears the mark of the practiced hand that made it. This criterion is singularly lacking in the case of the photographic image, which remains untouched by the complex equipment that enters into its production.[2] Clearly Benjamin has shifted the center of gravity of his argument. What interests him now is the opposition between two societies, industrial and preindustrial, and the *analogue* of that opposition in two forms of memory, voluntary and involuntary—terms which he has borrowed from Proust. Photography aligns itself both with industrial society and with the workings of voluntary memory, because the range of the latter is *extended* by the photograph. More of the world may be kept in a kind of permanent record, to which anyone may have access at any time; no detail need be forgotten or subject to the vagaries of involuntary memory.

As Benjamin notes, Baudelaire's attempt to restore the distinction between "art" and "industry" confirms the connection between the photograph and voluntary memory: "If [photography] quickly enriches the traveler's album and restores his eyes to the precision that his memory lacks . . . nothing could be better. If it saves from oblivion . . . precious things whose form will disappear and which merit a place in the archives of our memory, it will be thanked and applauded" (2: 618–19). Thus we have evidence of the connections that Baudelaire "sensed"; what he did not "see through," however, and what Benjamin hopes to reveal, is that art and industry are involved, not in a categorical opposition, but in a dialectical one. The region of art or "the domain of the impalpable and the imaginary" (which Benjamin associates with involuntary memory) cannot remain distinct from the encroachments of industry. "The perpetual readiness of volitional, discursive memory, encouraged by the technique of mechanical reproduction, reduces the scope for the play of imagination" ("Motifs": 186). For Benjamin this dialectical necessity is mediated by the masses, and he finds his opinion seconded in Baudelaire's references to "the natural alliance that [photography] will find in the foolishness of the multitude." Of course Baudelaire did not credit the "natural alliance" between photography and the masses with any historical necessity, but in this he was showing "scarcely . . . Solomonian judgement." It is not possible to halt historical processes simply by claiming they are tasteless.

Benjamin's argument is compelling, and not only because time has validated the aesthetic ambitions of photography. Were we to forget the history of the photograph since 1859 and to remember only Baudelaire's denunciation, we might easily come to an identical conclusion. This is because Baudelaire, perhaps in his eagerness to sustain the case against photography, assigns not one but two limitations to its role. The first limitation is the categorical one: photography has its own domain, it preserves "the pendulous ruins, books, engravings and manuscripts that time devours . . ." (2: 618). The second limitation, which does not seem unrelated to the first, permits the transition from categorical to dialectical thinking: photography, like printing and stenography, is "the servant of the arts and sciences, but a very humble servant [*une très humble servante*] . . ." (2: 618). The compulsive repetition, "but a very humble servant," sounds a warning; there is no need for this servant to be humble, unless it is recognized that she may one day triumph over her master. Benjamin's dialectical reading seems to cut to the heart of "Le Public moderne et la photographie," even explaining the stylistic peculiarities of the chapter: the pressures of the master/slave dialectic cause Baudelaire's categorical logic to stutter, thus occasioning his repeated emphases and anathemas ("In vain, modern Complacency howls, belches up all the flatulence of its bluff personality, vomits out every indigestible sophism . . .") (2: 618). The historical forces that Benjamin will set in opposition to Baudelaire's denunciation are already inscribed within the latter's text.

These indications of a dialectical moment in Baudelaire's *Salon* do not, however, lend simple credence to Benjamin's reading. For one thing, they suggest that Baudelaire's assessment of photography and its possibilities may have been less naive than Benjamin imagined. For another, they require that greater emphasis be placed upon the *Salon* as text. Benjamin's reading is persuasive to the extent that it supplies the *Salon* with an "outside," an historical context. The dialectical interest of the reading occurs, not within the written work, but between the work and its context: to one side of the *Salon* we have the photograph as technological innovation; to the other, there is something more vague, which may correspond to history, or to the modern aesthetic sensibility, or to both. In any case, the *Salon* itself is seen as a moment of pure reaction, determined by its context, and not as a properly critical statement of its context. Once we notice an element of dialectical complexity within the *Salon*, however, the passage "outside" the work becomes less assured: if the text does not offer blind resistance to its context, then the distinction between inside and outside begins to break down; the negative gesture which should have returned us to the outside, may only implicate us further in the textual workings. This is, if one likes, the labyrinth of reading, and Benjamin does not avoid it despite his atextual treatment of the *Salon*. The inside/outside distinction becomes confused when Benjamin's effort to situate the *Salon* within a historical context becomes a self-reflexive one. In order to situate the *Salon*, Benjamin must claim to read the same photographic phenomenon as Baudelaire, only with the use of superior dialectical tools. These tools are superior because they coincide with historical processes; in other words, the dialectic is both a method of reading and the very subject of history. Thus, when Benjamin's reading situates Baudelaire's reaction, that reading doubles as history. This is why there is some confusion as to where the reading leads: if it finally points to what Benjamin calls "the open air of history," it only does so by means of a self-reflexive or aestheticizing moment. Once more we find all the ironies of the labyrinth: through self-reflexivity Benjamin hopes to reach the open air; through aesthetic activity he sets his sights on history. This "situation" has its own interest, but it does not guarantee the success of Benjamin's attempt to subordinate the *Salon* to an historical context. In fact, since his reading reduplicates so many of the terms and conceptual oppositions of the *Salon*, one might argue that the reading is largely situated by the *Salon*, and not vice versa. This is the possibility I consider by examining the *Salon* in some of its textual complexity.

A first observation should be that Baudelaire does not conceive of his criticism as a reaction against the things he sees. On the contrary, after noting the absence of vigorous and original painting he writes, "Do not be surprised that banality in the painter has engendered *commonplaces* [*le lieu commun*] in the writer" (2: 608–609, original emphasis). Criticism thus appears as the close offspring of its context, almost as its context's reproduction. Moreover, criticism seems to reflect the mode of its own generation by taking on the form of verbal repetition—the commonplace. Baudelaire does not simply imply that this need always be the case; he claims that a more innovative Salon "[would have] required new categories of critical language" (2: 608). But, under the circumstances, "old," classical categories will do. The textual project that Baudelaire undertakes is to repeat these categories in such a way as to reveal their "positively *stimulating* nature" (2: 609, original emphasis). Repetition, then, and not reaction, characterizes the *Salon*.

If we are to accept Baudelaire's description of his project, we must at least question how it accounts for photography. The 1859 Salon may have been nothing new as far as its paintings were concerned, but this cannot be said of the photography exhibit. Whether the photographs were of aesthetic interest or not, their very presence was a novelty. In Benjamin's eyes, and particularly from the materialist standpoint he takes here, such a novelty is of critical importance. For Baudelaire, however, the photography exhibit is only symptomatic of a perennial flaw in the French temperament: "[In France] the exclusive taste for the True (so noble when it is limited to its real applications) . . . crushes and chokes out the taste for the Beautiful . . . [The French public] is not artistic, naturally artistic; philosophical, perhaps, moralist, ingenious [*ingénieur*], enamored of instructive anecdotes, and what have you, but never spontaneously artistic" (2: 616). Baudelaire's categorical logic, which assigns photography to a limited domain, first creates distinctions in the area of taste. The opposition between art and industry must therefore be understood as a specific case of the *principal* opposition between the taste for the Beautiful and the taste for the True. When, as in the French temperament, the taste for the True becomes excessive and leaves its proper place, then one may deduce any number of consequences. It only follows that photography, with its power to produce a close likeness of its subject, may be hailed as more true and hence as aesthetically superior to painting. By the same token, the technical facility of a painter may be valued over any other talent. Although the invention of photography encourages an excessive taste for the True in matters of art, photography is not the condition of possibility of that taste. Instead, Baudelaire maintains that photography is the fulfillment of a misguided wish on the part of the French public. The public reasons, "Thus, the industry that would give us a product identical to nature would be the absolute art." And Baudelaire adds, "An avenging god granted the wish of this multitude. Daguerre was his messiah" (2: 617).

Next to Benjamin's materialist interpretation of the relationship between photography and aesthetic taste, Baudelaire's suggestion of wish fulfillment may seem like a piece of magical thinking. This is largely a function, however, of his categorical logic, which allows him to deduce a place for photography without having to offer a causal explanation for its genesis. Given the existence of an aesthetics of natural imitation, one may posit the possibility of a perfect embodiment of that ideal. I insist that this is a categorical deduction as well as a rhetorical tactic; in other words, Baudelaire does not give a proleptic presentation of photography (providing the terms of its condemnation before he even mentions the technique) merely to convince readers to heed his warning. There is also a critical necessity involved in maintaining the distinction between what Baudelaire has called "the phenomena of the physical and of the moral worlds" (*Exposition universelle de 1855*, 2: 580). By "previewing" the phenomenon of photography within the phenomenon of taste, Baudelaire is able to keep the moral world from collapsing into the physical world. This is a double imperative since the ability to make any kind of critical distinction is at stake in the effort to preserve the discrete character of the moral world. To use Baudelaire's terminology, critical distinctions number among moral phenomena. Although Baudelaire does not spell this out explicitly, it may be rapidly deduced from his statements on the nature of the physical world. As the public becomes increasingly occupied with physical phenomena, it loses the faculty of critical thinking: "Ask any good Frenchman who reads *his* newspaper every day in his pub, what he understands by progress: he will answer that it is steam, electricity and gas lighting, miracles unknown to the Romans, and that these discoveries testify fully to our superiority over the Ancients; how much darkness has gathered in that unfortunate brain, how bizarrely it confuses things of a material and a spiritual order!" (2: 580, original emphasis).

The notion of progress introduced in this passage implies at one and the same time a confusion of categories and the ascendency of a materialist viewpoint: "What I mean by progress is the progressive domination of matter," Baudelaire writes in the *Salon de 1859* (2: 616). It is here that we may best seize his difference from Benjamin. For Baudelaire, it is not possible to write a properly *critical* history from materialist premises. These premises can only exacerbate the confusion of categories, until we find ourselves in a situation where progress and decadence coincide. If belief in progress continues, Baudelaire warns, "the diminished races of humanity . . . will sleep upon the pillow of fate the senile sleep of decrepitude" (2: 580). Thus, both progress and decadence, which we meant to use as historical concepts, become the dreams we dream on "the pillow of fate"; and such dreams can only give a false picture of history for the same reasons that, in Benjamin's words, fate is "temporal in a totally inauthentic way" ("Fate and Character": 308).

Curiously then, Baudelaire's position with respect to history seems to have come full circle; without leaving his original categories—because he promised he would only repeat himself—he now appears to argue in the name of true historical understanding. The condemnation of photography is no exception to his general argument: Baudelaire maintains that the photograph has contributed to a weakening of the historical imagination. On this point he invites us to consider that the new technique was immediately put, not to a thoroughly novel use, but to the fabrication of historical "scenes": "By collecting and grouping rogues and hussies, decked out like butchers and washerwomen at Carnival, by asking these *heros* to please hold their perfunctory grins [*leur grimace de circonstance*] for the time necessary to the operation, one could be sure to render the tragic or idyllic scenes from ancient history" (2: 617, original emphasis). It is hard to say whether this fashion did greater disservice to the ancients or the moderns but, in either case, historical understanding suffered. In Baudelaire's view, such understanding characterizes "the sublime art of the actor," an art that is disgraced and parodied by the fabrication of historical scenes. Although Baudelaire does not expound upon this opinion, the "grimace de circonstance" that he attributes to the costumed public gives us a clue to his meaning: the grimace is dictated by no other necessity than that of the moment and consequently bears only an accidental relationship to the costume, decor, and so on, that surround it. It contains no temporal dimension and thus differs from the consummate theatrical gesture, which may resume an entire sequence of historical or fictional events. The historical photograph provides instead a neutral medium for the confused coexistence of old and new; hence Baudelaire's detection of a carnival-like atmosphere, in which his rogues and hussies stand time on its head.[3]

Photography is not, however, the only medium in which the effects of a weakened historical understanding may be felt. Baudelaire criticizes on identical grounds what he calls "l'école des pointus"[4] in painting (2: 637). This school involves "the transposition of everyday life into an antique setting" (2: 637), as well as the calculated use of scumbling to give a time-worn appearance to canvases. Baudelaire suggests that painters aspiring to the school consult a newly released book by Edouard Fournier—*Le Vieux-*

Neuf: Histoire ancienne des inventions et découvertes modernes (The old-new: The ancient history of modern inventions and discoveries)—and himself adopts "le vieux-neuf" as an apt epithet for the paintings in question.

Although Baudelaire is well aware of the comic potential, both of historical photographs and of the "vieux-neuf" trend in painting, he refuses to grant either the full aesthetic dignity of the caricature. He says of "l'école des pointus": "By its mania for dressing the trivia of modern life in antique clothing, it constantly commits what I would call an inverse caricature" (2: 639). In order to understand what Baudelaire means by an inverse caricature, we should first examine the qualities he attributes to caricature itself. The aesthetic value of caricature is intimately tied to history, and most spectacularly to revolution. As Baudelaire writes in *Quelques caricaturistes français*: "The revolution of 1830, like all revolutions, brought on a caricatural fever . . . in this heated war against the government, and particularly against the king, [the combatants] were full of courage and ardor [*on était tout coeur, tout feu*]" (2: 549). Thus caricature, through its critical power, constitutes a revolutionary force. This force, however, must be conceived primarily in aesthetic terms; that is, if the caricatural war of 1830 was led "particularly against the king," this was not because the political hierarchy made Louis Philippe the prime target of artists, but because his caricature by Charles Philipon was a surpassing aesthetic success: "This fantastic epic is dominated, crowned by the pyramidal and olympian *Pear* of litigious memory" (7: 549).[5] We may learn, too, from the exemplary pear-king that the critical or revolutionary potential of caricature resides in the power to sustain *likeness*. As Philipon demonstrated in "Le Charivari," his caricature of Louis Philippe could be linked by a series of images to a "natural" portrait of the king. Were this not the case, the artist might have been charged with a lack of talent rather than lèse-majesté. Once again we come against the conundrum of Baudelaire's thoughts on history: the caricature partakes of the revolution, not by bringing into being something radically new, but by reproducing likenesses.

Given that "le vieux-neuf," either in painting or in photography, also involves the reproduction of likeness, how can it be said that such reproduction *inverts* caricature? We might be more tempted to say that it simulates caricature or caricatural effects. And yet Baudelaire is clear that in some way the work of caricature is undone by "l'école des pointus." This may best be appreciated if we consider that the historicity of the caricature is not *given* to the caricaturist; that is, he does not copy a revolutionary moment, but produces that moment as he copies. Otherwise his activity would not be an aesthetic one. In the case of "le vieux-neuf," however, "history" is presented to the painter or photographer as the jumble of old and new elements; this jumble need only be reproduced. Something, then, in the simple reproduction of "le vieux-neuf" undoes history as Baudelaire understands it. It should first be apparent that any dialectical tension is lost when old and new are immediately juxtaposed; and when a supposedly aesthetic activity does nothing to generate that tension, then even Benjamin would agree that history has been suspended.

Benjamin could only quibble, therefore, with a second contention that may be derived from Baudelaire's remarks on caricature and history. As we have observed, caricature is aesthetic, and hence historical in Baudelaire's sense, only if it is not fully dependent upon a limited moment in history; with the Pear, of course, this limited dependency may be difficult to discern, since the king of France is captured by the king of caricatures, and history and art seem to coincide. Baudelaire delights in this kind of coincidence, which he often gives as the figure of a Golden Age. Thus he says, in reference to Carle Vernet's engravings of fashionable folk at the end of the eighteenth century, under the Directory: "As it was with fashion, so it was with human beings: men resembled paintings; the world had modelled itself upon art" (2: 544). Such a coincidence, however, implies no absolute determination, because sometimes history will do the work of caricature—"Often caricatures themselves . . . become more caricatural as they become more out of date" (2: 545)— and sometimes a caricature, like Gavarni's *Lorette*, will create history by spawning a generation in its image.[6] In their mutual determination, neither history nor the caricature is grounded in real chronology. When Baudelaire attempts to organize recent French caricature into a history, he therefore claims that one must look to the style of the work and not to the date of its execution: "the word 'modern'," he writes, "applies to style and not to time" (2: 545). The modernity of caricature thus has little to do with the modernity of historical photographs and "l'école des pointus." The latter depend entirely upon real chronology; although the photographer who dresses his models in antique togas seems to enjoy freedom from chronology, his photograph is absolutely tied to the moment of its production. This is true of the "vieux-neuf" paintings as well, since Baudelaire views them as thoroughly *topical*: they belong to France in the midnineteenth century, and to no other time or place. For Benjamin such topicality should be the basis for a materialist dialectic; for Baudelaire it marks the end of dialectical possibilities, and hence, history.[7]

When we take stock of the preceding alignments between caricature and photography, it becomes apparent that any attempt to read the two dialectically will run aground. Either we follow Baudelaire's lead and see photography as suspending the dialectic of caricature, or we consider photography as the caricature of caricature. Upon reflection, however, the second option proves to be no option at all: since caricature always already involves the production of difference through the reproduction of likeness, photography can only reproduce the caricatural process without making it differ from itself. In other words, photography either *is* caricature or suspends caricature; and this option remains categorical. That is, either photography may be classified as a kind of caricature, or it disrupts the category of caricature without opening a way to the latter's dialectical recovery. Baudelaire subscribes to the second possibility, which means that, for him, the dialectic can only function if categorical logic remains intact. As we have already seen, this makes it impossible to write the sort of materialist history Benjamin has in mind. The materialist moment and the dialectic cannot be made to fit together; one suspends the other, and vice versa, indefinitely.

Baudelaire Against Photography

The incompatibility of the materialist moment and the dialectic can be traced in Benjamin's two essays, despite the historical materialism propounded in "On Some Motifs in Baudelaire." This becomes apparent when we consider how the "authenticity" of photography changes from one essay to the next. In "Short History," that authenticity is opposed to the *inauthentic* reactions of Baudelaire and Wiertz, which fail to reach the "open air of history." These latter, then, are doomed to topicality. Benjamin underlines their historical inauthenticity by eliminating the difference between Wiertz's *progressive* attitude and Baudelaire's *reactionary* one: it does not matter that Wiertz projects his vision forward and Baudelaire backward, since neither attains to dialectical understanding. This analysis approaches Baudelaire's commentary on materialist ideology and "the pillow of fate." When such an ideology holds sway, progress and decadence become mirror images of one another, false projections of temporality within the closed circle of fate. The *fatum* which presides over both Baudelaire and Wiertz is that of the homogeneous moment, the only temporality available to a materialist ideology.

Somewhere beyond this enclosure, Benjamin posits the "authenticity" of the photograph, which gives the promise of history. The photograph's authenticity is tied to no specific moment, a fact we may deduce from Benjamin's assertion that "it will not always be possible to link this authenticity with reportage . . ." ("Short History": 51); in other words, reportage is only a moment in the dialectic of authenticity. Thus, in "Short History," the dialectic and the materialist moment are held apart by the distance that separates authenticity from inauthenticity. With this in mind, we should not be surprised by what transpires in "On Some Motifs in Baudelaire": Benjamin attempts to bring the materialist moment into a dialectical arena, and the authenticity of the photograph evaporates. When he associates photography with voluntary memory, Benjamin actually reinforces the link between the photograph's authenticity and reportage, and thereby short-circuits the dialectical possibilities he had earlier envisioned. If the photograph is only authentic by virtue of its ability to preserve positive information, and if the materialist dialectic is riveted to this moment of pure positivity, then sooner or later the materialist dialectic will be revealed as an *inauthentic* temporality, perhaps even as fate in a progressive-seeming mask. This is why the distinction between authentic and inauthentic appears to vanish in the later essay, why the photograph's authenticity is bound up in its inauthenticity, and why its fruits seem more fatal than epoch-making. Not only does Benjamin claim that photography banishes beauty from its reproducible sphere, he also maintains that it seals off "the womb of time" from which beauty had been drawn and puts an end to the hope for something new, which might have compensated beauty's loss. In view of such comments, Benjamin must have "seen through" the dialectic he proposed in the name of photography; a true dialectic would have freed beauty and time from the rule of fate.[8]

The difference in Benjamin's treatment of photographic authenticity from one essay to the next should be sufficient to invalidate the historical materialist thesis that photography determines our perception of it. Moreover, photography appears in the second essay, not only as a technological fact, but also as a metaphor. That is, not only is the photograph an object upon which Benjamin may construct a history; photography also becomes the figure for that history. Although I do not examine that figuration thoroughly here, some details may be noted. Take Benjamin's contention that "The perpetual readiness of volitional, discursive memory, encouraged by the technique of mechanical reproduction, reduces the scope for the play of the imagination" ("Motifs": 186). If we compare Proust's and Baudelaire's remarks on voluntary memory with this statement, the metaphorical twist of the latter should become evident. For Proust, the voluntary memory is not necessarily "perpetually ready"; the willful attempt to remember does not always yield results. And when Baudelaire speaks of the photograph as an archival memory, this is because voluntary memory is not ready enough with information and stands in need of supplementation. From this perspective it seems as though voluntary, not involuntary memory would be most threatened by photography. Benjamin avoids this threat by changing the supplemental relationship between photography and voluntary memory into a metaphorical one: he makes voluntary memory *like* the camera, by transferring the latter's "perpetual readiness" to the former; this means that the camera no longer supplements a lack of memory, but "encourages" memory in one of its positive qualities. The transference of the quality of "readiness" is simultaneous with the photograph's encouragement of memory to reduce the scope for the play of imagination; in other words, the metaphorical process is simultaneous with the historical process Benjamin here describes. Thus, despite Benjamin's intentions, photography enters into history as metaphor and not as technological fact.

The photograph as metaphor should bring us back to Baudelaire's text, which, as I have argued, allows us to situate Benjamin's. If it is a metaphorical moment that inaugurates Benjamin's history, then that history confirms the "classical" categories of the *Salon de 1859* and, in particular, the priority of the moral over the material world. One could say that Benjamin's history is governed by the imagination, which Baudelaire calls "La Reine des facultés" (The queen of faculties): "It is imagination that has taught man the moral meaning of color, contour, sound and scent. It created, at the beginning of the world, analogy and metaphor" (2: 621). Here, metaphor is given its ontological priority as the first creation of the imagination and hence as the beginning of a history; this priority is moral, not material, since it is only their "moral meaning" that allows color, contour, and sound to participate in the metaphorical first moment. If it is true that Benjamin's history of the photograph fits the metaphorical model and thus presents a "classically" Romantic physiognomy, how may its features be distinguished from those of Baudelaire's *Salon*? If the latter is in some sense to provide a reading of Benjamin's history, those features cannot be simply identical. We might begin to consider their differences by examining the metaphorical status of the photograph in Baudelaire's text.

Interestingly enough, despite Baudelaire's championing of the metaphor, his metaphorization of photography is limited. Even when he appears to give photography a persona, that of "the servant of the arts and sciences," he does not thereby transfer subjective qualities to the technique. Although we are justifiably afraid for the future of the arts, this is not because photography is "encouraging" their demise: "the foolishness of the multitude" continues to be the agent of any aesthetic decadence.[9] This is why Baudelaire, unlike Benjamin, does not make of photography's "perpetual readiness" a figure of historical necessity. We would be wrong to assume, however, that Baudelaire is not interested in the metaphorical possibilities of the photograph. When, for example, he describes Delacroix's clean and rapid execution of paintings, he evokes something like the photographic process: "If a very clean execution is necessary, it is so the language of dreams may be clearly translated; if it must be very rapid, it is so nothing may be lost of the extraordinary impression that accompanied the conception . . ." (2: 625). The notion of high fidelity developed here is one which belongs to techniques of mechanical reproduction and seems out of place next to the Romantic "language of dreams." But it is precisely in this juxtaposition of the mechanical and the metaphorical that photography acquires a "moral meaning" for the *Salon de 1859*. When this "moral meaning" is applied to Delacroix, we are left with an unsettling image of the artist as machine: part of his subjective self, which presumably gave rise to the quality sui generis of his paintings, is subordinated to an impersonal, reproducing capacity. This may explain Baudelaire's description of his first encounter with Delacroix: "He evidently wanted to be full of indulgence and obligingness, for we chatted right away about commonplaces, that is, about the broadest and deepest questions" (2: 624). The breadth and depth of Delacroix's wisdom are contained within the most reproducible of verbal forms, the commonplace: "'Nature is only a dictionary,' he would often repeat." Thus Baudelaire underlines the mechanical quality of Delacroix's instruction and recalls the project of his own *Salon*—to repeat the commonplaces of Romanticism.

Perhaps we are now in a position to appreciate the difference between such repetition and a truly reactionary attitude. Baudelaire has no illusions about the possibility of returning simply to Romanticism: that he chooses to present the movement as everyone's possession, "what everyone ought to know," indicates his understanding that the cliché can never coincide with what it repeats. Although the term "cliché" was not yet in use, either for the photographic negative or as a synonym for the commonplace, Baudelaire's metaphorical allying of technique and verbal form seems to prefigure the word's current double meaning.[10] In this sense one could argue that Baudelaire's insight is fundamentally historical, while Benjamin's is reactionary insofar as it seeks to coincide fully with an originary, metaphorical moment. It does not matter that Benjamin locates this moment in modern times, with the invention of photography; the origin is equivalent to itself no matter where it occurs in real chronology, and Benjamin's purely metaphorical treatment of the photograph does nothing to disturb that equivalence. Once the metaphor is subject to repetition, however, once it becomes a cliché, then the temporal dimension is opened out and history becomes possible.

It is noteworthy that Baudelaire's metaphorization of photography engages the cliché as a *departure* from metaphor and thus responds to the specificity of the photographic technique much more than does Benjamin's metaphorization. One might even attribute a materialist insight to Baudelaire, because the cliché/photography relationship is not only metaphorical, but literal: that is, the photograph is not only *like* a verbal cliché, it *is* a visual cliché. This slippage toward the literal determination of meaning seems consistent with Benjamin's case that photography "reduces the scope" ("Motifs": 186) for metaphorical determinations. But it does not imply that meaning is thereby determined *materially*. If we find a metaphorical-literal tension in the term "cliché," this is not because of the material invention of photography, but because the photograph and the commonplace existed in a metaphorical relationship prior to the term's coinage. The *literal* occurrence of the term "cliché," which permits simultaneously a literalization of the metaphorical relationship, is thus an *immaterial* occurrence. The oppositional structure that gives Benjamin's second essay its ideological framework—on the one hand there is metaphor, on the other there is materiality—is thus rendered inoperative.

With this opposition no longer in effect, it becomes possible to reassess the question of Baudelaire's "age." If Baudelaire did not use his considerable metaphorical powers to create a new critical language in the *Salon de 1859*, this is not necessarily an indication that those powers had materially diminished. We should recall the over-readiness of critics to explain Delacroix's late paintings by invoking the artist's decrepitude. If we hesitate in dating Baudelaire on the basis of his chronological age, however, we should be equally wary of giving his "age" a purely metaphorical interpretation. Baudelaire does not become "like" an old man because of bitterness, shock, or horror; such an old age would consist solely of *affective* moments and lack any temporal dimension. Baudelaire's old age, on the contrary, involves nothing but acts of verbal repetition, which are grounded in the temporal and devoid of affect. This age, which lies in suspension between materiality and metaphoricity, is properly *allegorical*. Of course, it is Benjamin's accomplishment to have recognized the allegorical character of Baudelaire's aesthetics; if my analysis takes a somewhat different tack, it is only to question the alignment of allegory's literalizing tendency with the material. This alignment is not unique to Benjamin, but frequently underwrites the appearance of history in literary discourse as such.

Conclusion

༄

Revisionism can be a pleasure in and of itself, and it is perhaps the most consistent impulse behind the preceding essays. The ideology of Modernism has grown old, and critical discourse is still struggling to carry on its spirit while admitting that Modernism is a dead letter. My own work can be situated within such a struggle, although I have given myself a more limited objective: to examine Modernism, not as a fait accompli, but as a historical process in the case of one crucial figure. This involves questioning the portrait of Baudelaire as it has been given us by Modernism, finding the impurities in pure poetry and the moments of reaction in an otherwise progressive aesthetics. The opening chapters of my book are designed to show the literary-historical implications of this rereading of Baudelaire. Baudelaire once claimed that his interest in Delacroix had to do with questions of historical intelligibility—"If you take away Delacroix, the great chain of history is broken and falls to the ground" (*Salon de 1846*, OC, 2: 441). The statement is frankly more true of Baudelaire than it is of Delacroix: the history of Modernism and the aesthetic assessment of Baudelaire are mutually dependent to an astonishing degree.

Given this fact, it is possible to wonder where the project of this book might lead. I would argue that very few literary figures, even highly innovative ones, could be subjected to a similar treatment. Although nineteenth- and twentieth-century writers are frequently described as innovative or even revolutionary, this does not imply the same deeply historical character I attribute to Baudelaire. Rousseau is an epochal figure of similar significance, but most writers of the avant-garde are not. This is because their novelty does not pose a fundamental threat to their intelligibility.[1] I suspect, on the other hand, that the critical concerns that have guided my work on Baudelaire could be fruitfully applied to a study of Paul Valéry. The epistemological break between the nineteenth and twentieth centuries, which poses a crucial challenge to the intelligibility of Baudelaire's poetry, has proved even more decisive for Valéry, making him almost unreadable. In the most radical sense there are two Valérys—the first, a Symbolist poet, disciple of Mallarmé, and child of the nineteenth century; the second, a twentieth-century critic whose work Adorno could read as contemporary with that of Sartre, and whose social and political analyses are still cited in books on urban planning and in French newspapers and magazines.

Under these circumstances, a biography of Valéry would not be a biography like any other—to find its own principle of cohesion, such a biography would have to set the claims of an individual life against received patterns of historical interpretation in the starkest of terms. What does it mean for a single individual to be a true contemporary both of Sartre and of Mallarmé? How does Valéry's role as the broker of Modernism relate to his own peculiar historical situation? A project like this would extend my own by giving a specific signature, Valéry's, to the rupture between the nineteenth and twentieth centuries that I have treated more anonymously as a fact of history. It may be that the reinterpretation of Modernism can only take place through biography, understood as a serious critical tool.[2] This state of affairs has its ironies, because Modernist ideology has gone far to discredit the critical pretensions of biography; but revisionism seems to thrive on such ironies.

On a more theoretical plane, if I have succeeded at all in demonstrating the possibility of something like an aesthetics of bad faith, then the antagonisms that have marked literary criticism during its "cold war" period may be put in a different perspective. The same literary-historical processes that entrenched the canonical portrait of Baudelaire during the first half of the twentieth century also laid the groundwork for the development of what is loosely called French theory. This, at least, is the term used in the United States. French theory in France began with an equally vague designation, *la nouvelle critique*, which gestured at the practitioners of psychocriticism, structuralism, semiology, and so on. In *Criticism and Truth* (1966), Roland Barthes argued that "la nouvelle critique" began with the Liberation and with a very natural desire to rethink "our classical authors" in light of "new philosophies." It was in this intellectual environment that the debate over Sartre's *Baudelaire* took place. One could summarize the long-term effects of that debate by saying that it justified Sartre's eventual exclusion from the realm of literary criticism. At the risk of simplifying a complex development, the rise of "la nouvelle critique" similarly accompanied an eclipse of Sartre and Sartrean modes of thought in the discussion of literature. This does not mean that Sartre himself stopped being interested in literature, or that people stopped reading him on the topic. It does mean that his answer to the question What is Literature? struck the *nouveaux critiques* as having very little to do with literature at all.[3] Sartre's distance from *la nouvelle critique* appeared so great that, as far as I can judge, no one noticed when he tried to engage some of its precepts. *L'Idiot de la famille*, for example, contains a potentially interesting treatment of semiology which has met with no echo. A situation developed in which there appeared to be no communication between Sartre's world-oriented philosophy of engagement and the theories of textuality that focused on defining "literariness," the distinctive property of literature as such.

If, however, bad faith marks a point of slippage between ethical and rhetorical questions, if it can be interpreted as the moment in Sartre's own philosophy where the aesthetic surfaces (Sartre's discussion of bad faith resembles the seventeenth-century discussion of the aesthetic as the "je ne sais quoi" that can only be recognized but not given a discursive definition), then perhaps the preceding scenario can be reconsidered. My thesis is that, with the Baudelaire debate, bad faith goes under cover, so to speak, and infiltrates the camp of the *nouveaux critiques*. It no longer bears Sartre's name, but it can be recognized. The site of its transformation, of its disappearance and reappearance, is Maurice Blanchot's essay, "Baudelaire's Failure." This is not surprising, since Blanchot is the one critic who claims not to be scandalized by Sartre but to find the latter's interpretation of Baudelaire perfectly natural. Blanchot's equanimity is due to the fact that he systematically rewrites bad faith, translating it from an ethically reprehensible conduct into the thing that gives literature "meaning" and "value," into something very close to "literariness." Thus, bad faith may be recognized in his definition of poetry:

> Poetry is a means of putting oneself in danger without running any risk, a type of suicide, of self-destruction, that conveniently makes room for the safest type of self-affirmation. It is fitting to remember the point, because *literature itself calls for this critique* [*of poetry*], and can have neither meaning nor value except as a Passion which the writer knowingly fakes [*une passion vécue par l'écrivain, dans l'imposture dont il se sent complice*]. (p. 142, emphasis added)

A decade later, Roland Barthes will give a similar definition of literature. This time, however, bad faith is summoned to serve against Sartre and the theory of engagement:

> [I]t is absurd to ask a writer to *engage* his work. . . . One can only ask that a writer be responsible, and even here it should be understood: if a writer is responsible for his opinions, that is insignificant, If he accepts with more or less intelligence the ideological implications of his work, that too is of secondary importance; true responsibility for the writer involves tolerating/upholding[4] literature as a *failed engagement*, like Moses' look upon the Promised Land of the real. ("Ecrivains et écrivants": 150, original emphasis)[5]

In Barthes' view, the writer's responsibility is to recognize that literature must distort any engagement with the world, no matter how sincere the writer may be: "[I]t follows that [literary language] can never explain the world, or at least, when it pretends to explain it, this is only the better to deepen its ambiguity: once the explanation has been fixed in a (finished) *work*, it immediately becomes an ambiguous product of the real, to which it bears a *distant* relationship" (p. 149, original emphasis).

The resulting uncertainty attending any epistemological claims about the world is no longer, for Barthes, due to the bad faith of the writer as an individual subject but to the latter's identification with literary language: "[B]y identifying with a discourse [*une parole*], the writer loses all claims to truth, since language . . . once it is no longer rigorously transitive, is precisely the structure whose purpose is to neutralize the true/false distinction" (pp. 149–50).

Thus disguised, bad faith becomes synonymous with literature and literary indifference to the epistemological values of truth and falsehood. Barthes clearly must struggle with Sartre's ghost in order to make the equation between bad faith and literariness, but with the passage of yet another decade that equation has become naturalized.[6] In the 1970s, without any allusion to Sartre, Paul de Man will define "fiction" in precisely the same terms, as indifferent to epistemological values and independent of authorial intention, sincere or otherwise.[7]

This critical development can be *read* and not simply acceded to: the methods of *la nouvelle critique* can be used, it seems to me, to understand the genesis of that criticism as a historical phenomenon. *La nouvelle critique* comes into being as an erasure and as a dissemination of Sartre (to speak in a Derridean vein): once Sartre loses his authorial claims to the structure of bad faith, bad faith can be reproduced everywhere. This observation should be possible now, in a way it might not have been twenty years ago, because we are no longer living *la nouvelle critique* in its newness and it has slipped rather suddenly from state-of-the-art criticism into historical artifact. As with aesthetic Modernism, there is a crisis in contemporary criticism where the new has grown old precisely at the point where its highly regulated structures of exclusion are exposed as aleatory.[8]

This presents an opportunity—of reading Sartre alongside Barthes, for example—for rethinking the critical landscape in a genuine way.[9] It would be a shame if that opportunity were lost because of an unwitting continuation of the same polemical exclusions—between historical and textual criticism, between old and new schools—that have underwritten critical thinking for the past fifty years. When I began work on this project, the ideological winds were not in Sartre's favor, and if my arguments often take the tone of an apology, it is due to this fact. Now the situation has changed, and the *nouveaux critiques* have only a vestigial influence on contemporary critical preoccupations. If I defend their methods and wish to suggest that these could be applied, not only to the close reading of texts, but also to the study of literary history, it is from a similar desire to avoid the kind of polemical polarization that can short-circuit understanding. I hope to have demonstrated with this book that, contrary to expectations, Sartre's extra-literary treatment of Baudelaire can be co-opted for a genuine reading of the poetry. This would be one small contribution to criticism in a post–cold-war period.

Reference Matter

Notes

Introduction

1. I consider Benjamin's reading of Valéry in Chapter 1.
2. Baudelaire's poem ends with the appeal to a "Hypocrite lecteur, —mon semblable,—mon frère!" (Hypocritical reader,—my kin,—my brother!).
3. For a discussion of the difference between bad faith and other self-negating modes of conduct (lying, irony, resentment, etc.), see chapter 2, part I of *L'Etre et le néant*.
4. The relationship between this and a more traditional analysis of stylistic mélange in nineteenth-century poetry would be well worth exploring, although I do not pursue the topic here.
5. "It was not the symbolists of 1885–1890 but the literary historians of the midtwentieth century who called attention to the sonnet 'Correspondences' and the critical articles collected in *L'Art romantique* and in *Curiosités esthétiques*" (*Symbolism*, 10).
6. See in particular Benjamin's discussion of the poem "Le Cygne" (The Swan) in *Charles Baudelaire: A Lyric Poet*, 82–83.
7. De Man's work on Rousseau has yielded a similar definition of the allegorical narrative. Rousseau's history of man, for example, in *Discours sur l'origine de l'inégalité parmi les hommes* (Discourse on the origin of inequality among men), is to be understood as an allegory because it is the story of a "scrupulously maintain[ed]" balance between progress and regress. See "Metaphor" in *Allegories of Reading*, 140–41.
8. For a discussion of the allegory/symbol distinction see Benjamin's *The Origin of German Tragic Drama*, 159–67. A more straightforward analysis can be found in de Man's "The Rhetoric of Temporality," 187–208. Benjamin emphasizes that allegory produces its effects through means

that are not essentially aesthetic, that the impact of an allegorical painting of fame, say, could just as well be communicated by the sight of "the word 'fame' in large clear letters on the wall." Were the painting to be aesthetically successful in its own right, "this is quite separate from and independent of what it achieves as allegory" (161–62). (Benjamin is here citing Schopenhauer's reflections on the subject of allegory.) The disjunction between poetic beauty and poetic meaning that I have traced in the architecture of *Les Fleurs du mal* is thus an allegorical characteristic.

9. This is the expression Sartre uses in his effort to characterize the world of Baudelaire's poetry. His analysis centers on a reading of the poem "Le Guignon" (Bad luck), and on the curious lightness of the final image:

> Mainte fleur épanche à regret
> Son parfum doux comme un secret
> Dans les solitudes profondes.
>
> Many a flower reluctantly gives off
> Its perfume, sweet like a secret
> In deep solitudes.

Sartre might have gone even further to note that this image of evanescent being replaces the opening figure of Sisyphus, pinned beneath his proverbial stone: "Pour soulever un poids si lourd, / Sisyphe, il faudrait ton courage!" (To lift up such a heavy weight, / Sisyphus, one would need your courage!). In other words, the poem itself casts off the weight of the curse it invokes at the outset. For Sartre's reading see *Baudelaire*, 220–21.

10. See "Spleen II" in *Les Fleurs du mal*.

11. Roughly speaking, a poetics involves the description of the literary object as such while an aesthetics takes account of that object's effect on a reader. Jauß' essay ("The Poetic Text Within the Change of Horizons of Reading: The Example of Baudelaire's *Spleen II*") and de Man's critique are both collected in *Toward an Aesthetic of Reception*.

12. On the relationship between allegory and the sign, see de Man's discussion in "Sign and Symbol in Hegel's *Aesthetics*," 773–75.

13. We might contrast this blood-letting with the one de Man attributes to an aphenomenal violence of the letter in "Spleen II." See his introduction to Jauß, xx–xxi.

14. This panic is expressed elsewhere in Baudelaire's corpus. The opening stanza of "La Fontaine de sang" (The fountain of blood) reads:

> Il me semble parfois que mon sang coule à flots,
> Ainsi qu'une fontaine aux rythmiques sanglots.

Je l'entends bien qui coule avec un long murmure,
Mais je me tâte en vain pour trouver la blessure.

It seems to me sometimes that my blood gushes forth,
Just like a fountain with rhythmic sobs.
I hear it quite plainly, flowing with a long murmur,
But I touch myself in vain to find the wound.

15. "I cannot say I" is de Man's rendition of "so kann ich nicht sagen was ich nur meine," from paragraph 20 of the *Encyclopedia*, where Hegel treats the cogito. See "Sign and Symbol in Hegel's *Aesthetics*," 768–69.

16. Even poems like "A une passante" (To a passerby) and "Les Sept vieillards" (The seven old men), which narrate a single event, or series of events, are not similarly located. "La rue assourdissante autour de moi hurlait" (The deafening road was howling all around me), only partially specifies the location of the first poem. Similarly, "Un matin . . . je suivais . . . le faubourg" (One morning . . . I was wandering . . . the outskirts of the city) leaves the locus of "Les Sept vieillards" in partial suspense.

17. This is not to say that Chambers' treatment of allegory per se is the most highly developed. In *Allegories of Reading*, for example, de Man is clearly grappling with the level of linguistic complexity that Chambers wishes to suggest with his notion of two allegories. For heuristic purposes, no doubt, Chambers has drastically simplified what he calls "de Manian allegory." I argue, however, that de Man's discussion of Baudelaire occurs at a simplified moment in the critic's exposition of allegory.

18. There are other poems in *Les Fleurs du mal* where the myth of returning home—"the heart full with one's beautiful, native lake"—is accompanied by a kind of estrangement. In "L'Invitation au voyage," for example, the dreamed-of destination is a place where everything would speak one's sweet native tongue (*la douce langue natale*) while glowing with a strange, oriental splendor. "La Vie antérieure" (My former life) displays similar characteristics, as does "J'aime le souvenir de ces époques nues." These "mythic" poems seem to celebrate the estrangement that "Le Cygne" presents as fatal. Wallace Stevens creates a comparable effect in "Tea at the Palaz of Hoon"—the exoticism there involves the invocation of a place/time in which the poetic subject may declare, "And there I found myself more truly and more strange." Baudelaire's insight was considerable when he equated this configuration of the subject with myth.

Chapter One

1. Cited in Friedrich, *The Structure of Modern Poetry*, 19.
2. Cited in Pichois and Ziegler, *Baudelaire*, 172. Further references to this work will be cited in the text.
3. Cited in George Saintsbury, "Charles Baudelaire" in *Miscellaneous Essays*, 216, New York: C. Scribner's Sons, 1892. I have not been able to find the remark in any of Asselineau's writings, and imagine from Saintsbury's comments that it is simply part of an oral tradition. Asselineau did write something similar (although more judicious) in his biography of the poet: "Those who had been irritated by his sarcasm and his mystifications, once they had only the poet and the writer to deal with [since Baudelaire's death], came around to his cause; once they no longer had to fear him, they could freely admire him. They began to understand him, some of them perhaps for fear of the ridicule one incurs in Paris for not appreciating what the social elite approves. Indeed, a man's opinions of an established work of art or talent are an excellent touchstone for his intelligence." *Baudelaire et Asselineau*, 152. I would like to thank Margaret Miner and Claude Pichois for helping me in this investigation.
4. There are many examples that could be cited of this tendency. One that I find intriguing, and to which I will return, involves Baudelaire's official rehabilitation by the Cour de Cassation (Supreme Court of Appeal) in 1949. The 1857 condemnation of *Les Fleurs du mal* as offensive to public morality was treated by the modern court as perfectly "arbitrary," so meaningless for twentieth-century readers that it could only be put down to the mystery of historical difference, to the unjustifiable turn of mind of the nineteenth-century reader.
5. There is a corollary to this observation: if Baudelaire's signature has drifted from the immediate production to the historical inscription of his work, then the work in its immediacy must acquire a kind of anonymity. I say "a kind" of anonymity since no one would go so far as to ascribe the production of *Les Fleurs du mal* to pure historical processes. Benjamin hints at this anonymity when he speaks of Baudelaire's "emancipation from experiences." It is possible to get a sense of what this might mean for a detailed reading of *Les Fleurs du mal* by consulting Hans Robert Jauß' "The Poetic Text" 155–61 and 167–70. Jauß discusses the status of the lyric "I" in the poem that begins "J'ai plus de souvenirs que si j'avais mille ans" (I have more memories than if I were a thousand years old). The "I's" attempts to identify itself fail repeatedly, leaving us with what de Man, in his introduction to the Jauß volume, calls "the grammatical

subject cut off from consciousness" (xxv). Such a grammatical subject has no signature.

6. For a brief history of the term *poésie pure* see Friedrich, 102–3.

7. The definition of Symbolism occurs in italics. Valéry is citing his own preface to Lucien Fabre's *Connaissance de la déesse* (Paris: Société littéraire de France, 1920), xii–xiii.

8. The French here retains a balance that is difficult to translate: Baudelaire, "par la curiosité de son esprit . . . [a] mérité la chance de découvrir . . . dans les ouvrages d'Edgar Poe un nouveau monde intellectuel." Baudelaire's intellectual curiosity earned him the good fortune of discovering Poe. The discovery involves both chance and necessity.

9. This observation has several potential implications. One is that practitioners of *poésie pure*, like Valéry himself, would have to misread the doctrine to some extent in order to make use of it. It is also possible that Baudelaire, while advancing a theoretical poetics akin to *poésie pure*, engaged in a very different poetic practice. In any event, the clear historical line, that would trace the development of *poésie pure* from Baudelaire through Mallarmé to Valéry, is hereby disturbed.

10. The homology between the story of Baudelaire's reception and that of his poetic production is illustrative: it shows the complicity between the historical and aesthetic modes of understanding at the very moment when the two are said to part ways.

11. The French reads "dans l'étendue de leurs effets." The word *étendue*, which can also be translated as "expanse," is the word Valéry uses to describe Baudelaire's effect on Poe's corpus.

12. Riffaterre, "L'Etude stylistique des formes littéraires conventionnelles" in *Essais de stylistique structurale*, 184–89.

13. Valéry may have taken his notion of a language within language from Percy Bysshe Shelley's poem *The Revolt of Islam*, Canto VII, xxxii:

> And on the sand would I make signs to range
> These woofs, as they were woven, of my thought;
> Clear, elemental shapes, whose smallest change
> A subtler language within language wrought . . .

14. This poetic dissatisfaction has many of the formal characteristics of Sartrean bad faith. Interestingly, Valéry's deferred poetic synthesis is described in terms that recall Baudelaire's "Correspondances":

> Comme de longs échos qui de loin se confondent
> Dans une ténébreuse et profonde unité,

Vaste comme la nuit et comme la clarté,
Les parfums, les couleurs et les sons se répondent.

Like long echos that mingle from afar
Into a somber and deep unity,
Vast as night and as the light,
Perfumes, colors, and sounds answer one another.

I will discuss the relationship between bad faith and Baudelaire's poetics in Chapter 2.

15. Cited in *Les Fleurs du mal*, critical edition by Jacques Crépet and Georges Blin, revised by Georges Blin and Claude Pichois (Paris: José Corti, 1968), 1: 475.

16. See Pichois' notes to Baudelaire, OC, 1: 1183.

17. Baudelaire used the expression, which he borrowed from Buffon, in a review of *La Double vie* by Charles Asselineau. See OC, 2: 87. Johnson has recently applied the expression *homo duplex* to Baudelaire as author of a dual corpus—*Les Fleurs du mal* and *Le Spleen de Paris*. *Défigurations*, 15.

Chapter Two

1. *L'homme et l'oeuvre* (the man and the work) is a term used to designate a systematic mode of literary criticism that is roughly attributed to Charles Augustin Sainte-Beuve (1804–1869) and was made part of the French scholastic system by Gustave Lanson (1857–1934).

2. "We touch here upon the original choice that Baudelaire made of himself, upon that absolute engagement by which each one of us decides in a particular situation what he will be and what he is." *Baudelaire*, 21.

3. From Baudelaire's letter to his mother, May 6, 1861. Cited in *Baudelaire*, 18–19.

4. Cited in *Baudelaire*, 20, original emphasis.

5. "To Sartre's credit—as alien as poetry is to him . . . —it must be said that he succeeded in bringing out some unnoticed harmonics [*pas encore mis en relief*] of Baudelaire's *oeuvre* . . ." See the preface to *Baudelaire*, 14–15.

6. The term *poète maudit* (accursed poet) was coined by Paul Verlaine in a small volume of critical essays devoted to several nineteenth-century poets whom Verlaine considered underappreciated. Baudelaire does not figure in the collection, but is thought to have inspired the title.

7. For a reading of the comic potential in the first poem, see Klein's "Bénédiction."

8. "La conscience est un être pour lequel il est dans son être conscience du néant de son être." The exact translation of existentialist prose is frequently unreadable.

9. These are the expressions Sartre cites as instances of bad faith: their catchy memorability is due to their condensing the conceptual structure of bad faith in a small linguistic parcel. The first is the title of a collection of reflections by novelist Jacques Chardonne. The second is the first line from Mallarmé's "Tombeau d'Edgar Poe." See *L'Etre et le néant*, 92–93.

10. "[H]e is the man who, experiencing most deeply his human condition, tried most passionately to hide it from himself" (*Baudelaire*: 50).

11. "De Maistre et Edgar Poe m'ont appris à raisonner," writes Baudelaire in *Hygiène* (De Maistre and Edgar Poe taught me how to reason) (1:668). Sartre paraphrases the citation somewhat and claims that Baudelaire said of De Maistre "It is he who taught me to think." See *Baudelaire*, 81.

12. See Blanchot's reading of this stanza, 137–38.

13. See Sartre's discussion of "Les Fenêtres" in *Baudelaire*, 26–28.

14. See Rivière, *Etudes*, 16–17.

15. This was the expression used by Barbey d'Aurevilly in the article he wrote for Baudelaire's defense at the 1857 trial. See Baudelaire, OC, 1:1196.

16. Jean-Pierre Richard calls this expansiveness "profondeur" and associates it with a redemptive reading of Baudelaire: "Critics have often spoken of Baudelaire's failure: in the following pages I wish to show a successful Baudelaire." See "Profondeur de Baudelaire," in *Poésie et profondeur*, 95.

17. See Richard Klein's "Straight Lines" and Johnson's "Les Fleurs du Thyrse" in *Défigurations*.

18. This is at least a reasonable assumption, when we consider the classicizing impulse of Leconte de Lisle, for example, whose poetry displays formally the qualities it advocates ideologically.

19. *The Oxford Classical Dictionary*, ed. N. G. L. Hammond and H. H. Scullard (Oxford: Clarendon Press, 1973), 773.

20. In the opening of *L'Ecole païenne*, Baudelaire develops a more explicit connection between Pan and Jesus Christ. At a banquet commemorating the 1848 revolution, a young man rises to give a toast to the god Pan, whom he considers the spirit of the revolution. The narrator takes offense

and inquires, "Hasn't [Pan] been dead for a long time? I thought a great voice had been heard floating over the Mediterranean, and that this mysterious voice . . . had said to the old world: THE GOD PAN IS DEAD!" (OC, 2: 44). The reference here is to an anecdote from Plutarch's *De Defectu Oraculorum*, which treats the question of mortality in divine beings. In Plutarch's text the mysterious voice announces the death of "Great Pan," and this will be echoed in "le grand Pan" of "La Muse malade." Pan's supposed death, like that of Jesus, occurred during the reign of Tiberius Caesar. The young man of *L'Ecole païenne* pursues this parallel as he answers the narrator's insinuation: "That's a rumor that has been going around . . . No, the god Pan is not dead! the god Pan is still living . . . He's coming back." When the narrator asks, "Are you pagan, then?" the young man replies, "Well yes, of course; don't you know that Paganism, properly comprehended, properly understood, is the only thing that can save the world? We have to get back to the true doctrines, *momentarily* obscured by the infamous Galilean" (OC, 2: 44, original emphasis). By alluding to a second coming of Pan and to the saving powers of Paganism, the young man extends the rivalrous/analogous relationship between the Arcadian deity and Christ. The figural play here may be of interest for a reading of "La Muse malade." It is not at all unusual for exegesis to oppose Greek and Christian figures. In one tradition, Greek myths and deities are interpreted as shadows or prefigurations of Christianity; when these shadows are fulfilled, they are supplanted by perfect or complete figures. Thus the Greek world is made "old" by the more perfect revelation that follows it. An alternate mode of opposing Greek and Christian worlds is to consider the former ever young, a Golden Age whose chronological "earliness" underwrites its ontological priority; like the figures on Keat's Grecian urn that can never "bid the Spring adieu," the Golden Age is impervious to corruption and, hence, bestows mortality upon subsequent epochs. In this view, Christianity would be "old" from the moment of its birth into the world. Although Baudelaire plays with both these exegetical options, he in fact subscribes to neither. The young man at the revolutionary banquet seems to argue for the ontological priority of the Greek—"We have to get back to the true doctrines, *momentarily* obscured"—but he does so by "completing" the figure of Pan with Christian characteristics, that is, by reversing the technique of prefiguration. This means that the shadowy figure, in this instance, Jesus, can never be abolished or supplanted, as it is in scriptural exegesis, because here the shadow *supplies* completion. Thus, the return to the pagan for Baudelaire is accomplished by a perpetual allusion to Christianity, an allusion that occurs with "le seigneur des moissons" of "La Muse malade." We should note how this figuration involves what can be identified in the thematics of the poem as bad faith.

21. See the letter dated January 28, 1854, in Baudelaire's *Correspondance*, 1: 256–62.

Chapter Three

1. Sartre cites, for example, the suspicions voiced by Jacques Crépet in his preface to *Les Fleurs du mal*: "Was his life marred by faults that time does not erase? That is difficult to believe after all the inquiries of which his life has been the object. Nevertheless he treats himself as a criminal, declares himself guilty 'in every way'." See *Baudelaire*, 54.

2. I am thinking of the way the aesthetic character of the poem is supplied by a wish in bad faith. See the discussion of "La Muse malade" in Chapter 2.

3. Valéry even goes so far as to suggest that one could "bring together the poetry of Victor Hugo and that of Baudelaire, with the intent of showing the former to be exactly *complementary* to the latter" ("Situation": 602, original emphasis).

4. See the preface to *Les Contemplations*.

5. Benjamin comments that "Le Soleil" is "probably the only place in *Les Fleurs du mal* that shows the poet at work" ("Motifs": 164). This may explain why the poem offers such an economic image of the poetry's *situation*.

6. See Baudelaire's letter to Armand Fraisse, February 18, 1860, in C, 1: 675.

7. See Sartre's well-known critique of surrealism in "Situation de l'écrivain en 1947" (The Situation of the writer in 1947) in *Qu'est-ce que la littérature?*, n. 6, p. 367.

8. For a discussion of the two uses of *comme* in the poem "Correspondances" see Paul de Man's "Anthropomorphism," 248–49.

9. I make this assertion not simply on the basis of a philosophical tradition, but because within the context of my discussion the ethical situation is, in part, determined by *external* circumstances.

10. In the discussion that follows I use the pronoun "he" in reference to Baudelaire's reader. This is because the reader whom Baudelaire's poetry invokes is specifically masculine. The reader Baudelaire desires is called a "brother," the one he doesn't want is called a "man of good will." In a projected preface to *Les Fleurs du mal*, Baudelaire asserts that he isn't writing for "mes femmes, mes filles ou mes soeurs" (my wives, daughters, or sisters) (OC, 1, 181). We should not assume that Baudelaire's attitude is typical of

male authors in nineteenth-century France. Honoré de Balzac, for example, at the beginning of *Père Goriot*, portrays the reader of his novel as a genteel woman. Something more than literary convention, therefore, is at stake in Baudelaire's exclusion of a female readership. Chambers addresses this issue in the fifth chapter of *Mélancolie et opposition*. He argues that the female reader excluded from "Au lecteur" resurfaces in "L'Invitation au voyage": the first poem is addressed to "mon semblable, mon frère" (my kin, my brother), whereas the second begins with an apostrophe to "mon enfant, ma soeur" (my child, my sister). Chambers links the question of gender to what I have called the dynamic of aesthetic difference in Baudelaire's poetry. In *Narrative as Performance*, Maclean uses Baudelaire's prose poems to refine reader-response theory and to argue that, along with an implied reader, literary works can inscribe an excluded reader (see pp. 38–41 and chapter four, "Scene and obscene: the constitution of narrative audiences and gendered reading"). Paradoxically, the excluded reader is included in the work as the one for whom reading is an act of transgression. Although I am not convinced that women read Baudelaire's poetry simply because he tells us not to, Maclean's argument makes it apparent that his exclusionary rhetoric is not straightforward, and may even be in bad faith.

11. Ibid., 155. See also pp. 156–57 in which Benjamin compares Baudelaire's reader to the Bergsonian philosophy of memory. The former becomes the figure for historical meaning by offering an "undistorted" picture of "the inhospitable, blinding age of big-scale industrialism"; the latter blinks before this picture of history and gives instead its "spontaneous afterimage."

12. "Baudelaire" in *Etudes*, 17. Rivière's emphasis. It is interesting to compare Rivière's detection of a poetic modesty with Sartre's description of the modest "faith of bad faith": "Bad faith seizes upon facts, but it is resigned from the beginning not to be convinced by them, not to be persuaded and transformed into good faith: it makes itself out to be humble and modest, it claims to understand that faith involves decision, and that after each intuition one must decide and *will what is*" (*L'Etre et le néant*: 105, original emphasis).

13. These are the concepts that play human transcendence against human facticity: "I become myself," "I am more than myself," etc.

14. "Role" here is not quite the right word, since the reader is not meant to play, but to *be* the hypocrite.

15. This is the sado-masochistic formulation of the Baudelairean subject as it is presented in the poem "L'Héautontimorouménos" (The self-tormentor) (1: 79).

16. Sartre's mother, Anne-Marie, was widowed when her son was still an infant, and remarried in 1917 when he was twelve years old. "My mother's remarriage led, on my part, to a clear rupture in our relationship; I felt it was a betrayal, even though I never told her so." Cited in Hollier, *Politique*, 109.

17. Collins, "Baudelaire and Bad Faith" in *Sartre as Biographer*, 78–79.

18. See the poem "L'Avertisseur" (The warning signal), 1: 140.

19. See Derrida's résumé of the problem of pity in Rousseau. *De la grammatologie*, 258–72.

20. A provisional list of these points might be: the verbs *occuper* (to occupy, inhabit) and *travailler* (to torment, obsess) of the first stanza; "Nous volons au passage un plaisir clandestin / Que nous pressons bien fort comme une vieille orange" (We steal in passing a clandestine pleasure / Which we press very hard like an old orange); "C'est que notre âme, hélas! n'est pas assez hardie" (It's because our, soul alas! is not daring enough); "C'est L'Ennui!—l'oeil chargé d'un pleur involontaire" (It is Boredom!—its eye laden with an involuntary tear); and, of course, the final line of the poem.

21. This persistence lies behind the mistaken classification of Baudelaire's poetry as symbolist poetry.

22. See Sartre's discussion in *Baudelaire*, 220–21.

23. Collins, *Sartre as Biographer*, 75.

24. Blin, *Le Sadisme*, n. 2, p. 120, original emphasis.

25. Joseph Halpern, *Critical Fictions*, 57.

Chapter Four

1. See Baudelaire's discussion of sculpture in the *Salon de 1859*, OC, 2: 677.

2. Baudelaire himself picked an engraved *danse macabre* for the frontispiece of the second edition of *Les Fleurs du mal*, thereby inviting us to suspect an emblematic intention.

3. Although I have translated the first line as "You answer, great skeleton, my dearest desire!" the French is literally, "You answer to my dearest *taste*!" The second line reads, "The charms of horror only intoxicate the strong!"

4. *L'Etre et le néant*: 102. Sartre's reflections on this topic are inspired by Valéry's criticism of Stendhal's excessive sincerity.

5. The difference between a blueprint (which precedes a work) and an

abstract (which follows it) is immaterial here: "that Art had already extracted," the always/already temporality is operative in this instance.

6. Georges Poulet, "Baudelaire," p. 327.

7. Benjamin, "Motifs": 181.

8. This is an expression cited to me by a French *lycée* student, as an example of the kind of thing good literature teachers say about Baudelaire. It sounds authentic.

9. I am using the second, 1861 edition of *Les Fleurs du mal* for my analysis. This is generally considered the most perfectly constructed edition of the poetry.

10. A similar phenomenon occurs in the opening stanzas of "La Chevelure." Jeanne's head of hair is both a point of departure and a destination for this poem, whose ironic reversals are truly vertiginous. Michel Deguy has plotted out some of these ironies in "Le corps de Jeanne" (Jeanne's Body), 334–347.

11. This is the closing chapter of the *Salon de 1846*, OC, 2: 493–96.

12. The temporal threat to the integrity of the self, implicit in Baudelaire, is most explicitly developed in Proust. At the beginning of *Combray*, for example, we read of the several Swanns: "Our friend's corporal envelope had been so stuffed (with the various ideas that the family had of him), that the Swann [of that time] had become a complete and living being, and that I have the impression of leaving one person and coming to a different one when I pass in my memory from the Swann I later knew with precision to that first Swann , , ," *A la recherche*, 1. 19.

13. Among his projected prefaces, Baudelaire made the remark that poetry can imitate any number of geometric figures—spirals, zigzags, and superposed angles—and that "by combining such a noun with such an adjective," it may express "every sensation of sweetness or bitterness, beatitude or horror." This kind of careful attention to poetic effect can prove fruitful when applied to Baudelaire's own corpus. See OC, 1: 183.

14. "Unravaged" is literally "pure of all outrage" and "flawless" is "virgin of flaws."

15. See Sartre's discussion in *L'Etre et le néant*, 107.

16. Time thus differs here from Bataille's concept of Baudelairean temporality, which occurs as pure expenditure. See Bataille's discussion of poetic participation in *La Littérature*, 47–8.

17. Rivière, *Etudes*, 16.

18. Other important examples of empty eternities occur in "Les Petites vieilles" (The little old women)—"Débris d'humanité pour l'éternité

mûrs!" (Debris of humanity, ripe for eternity!) (1: 91)—and in "A une passante" (To a passerby)—"Ne te verrai-je plus que dans l'éternité?" (Will I see you no more, except in eternity?) (1: 93).

19. See *OC*, 1: n. 2, p. 859.

20. This issue is developed in de Man's introduction to the work of Jauß, xxiii: "Allegory is material or materialistic, in Benjamin's sense, because its dependence on the letter, on the literalism of the letter, cuts it off sharply from symbolic and aesthetic syntheses. 'The subject of allegory can only be called a grammatical subject'; the quotation is not from Benjamin but from one of the least valued sections of Hegel's *Lectures on Aesthetics*, the canonical bible, still for Heidegger, of the phenomenalism of art. Allegory names the rhetorical process by which the literary text moves from a phenomenal, world-oriented to a grammatical, language-oriented direction."

21. De Man has also worked out some of allegory's temporal particularities: "In the world of the symbol, it would be possible for the image to coincide with the substance, since the substance and its representation do not differ in their being but only in their extension: they are part and whole of the same set of categories. Their relationship is one of simultaneity, which in truth, is spatial in kind, and in which the intervention of time is merely a matter of contingency; whereas, in the world of allegory, time is the originary constitutive category. The relationship between the allegorical sign and its meaning [*signifié*] is not decreed by dogma . . . We have, instead, a relationship between signs in which the reference to their respective meanings has become of secondary importance. But this relationship between signs necessarily contains a constitutive temporal element; it remains necessary, if there is to be allegory, that the allegorical sign refer to another sign that precedes it. The meaning constituted by the allegorical sign can then consist only in the *repetition* (in the Kierkegaardian sense of the term) of a previous sign with which it can never coincide, since it is of the essence of this previous sign to be pure anteriority . . . Whereas the symbol postulates the possibility of an identity or identification, allegory designates primarily a distance in relation to its own origin, and, renouncing the nostalgia and the desire to coincide, it establishes its language in the void of this temporal difference. In so doing, it prevents the self from an illusory identification with the non-self, which is now fully, though painfully, recognized as a non-self. It is this painful knowledge that we perceive at the moments when early romantic literature finds its true voice. "Rhetoric," 206–7.

Chapter Five

1. "I am not positively old, but I could shortly become so." See Baudelaire's letter to his mother, December 20, 1855, C, 1: 325.

2. In "The Work of Art in the Age of Mechanical Reproduction," Benjamin compares the cameraman to the painter. The cameraman's equipment "penetrates deeply" into the web of reality, but by this very token offers "an aspect of reality which is free of equipment." The painter, on the other hand, "maintains in his work a natural distance from reality" and this distance leaves its traces on the completed canvas. See *Illuminations*, 233–34.

3. The "mélange de cris, de détonations de cuivre et d'explosions de fusées" (the blend of cries, detonating brass and exploding rockets) that one may find in a Baudelairean carnival does not reveal revolutionary potential. Unlike Bakhtin's *carnavalesque*, Baudelaire's carnival days lie outside history and its conflicts: "En ces jours-là il me semble que le peuple oublie tout, la douleur et le travail; il devient pareil aux enfants. Pour les petits c'est un jour de congé, c'est l'horreur de l'école renvoyée à vingt-quatre heures. Pour les grands c'est un armistice conclu avec les puissances malfaisantes de la vie, un répit dans la contention et la lutte universelles." (On those days it seems to me that the people forget everything, sorrow and work; they become like children. For the little ones it is a day off, the horror of school being postponed for twenty-four hours. For the grown-ups it is an armistice concluded with life's maleficent powers, a respite from universal contention and strife.) See "Le Vieux saltimbanque" (The old circus player) (1: 295).

4. The expression is a bit difficult to render, but means something like "the school of shrill pedants." Crépet claims Baudelaire borrowed the expression from Nadar.

5. Louis-Philippe was nicknamed *la Poire* (the Pear), both because of his flaccid face and because the slang meaning of the word is "fathead." Charles Philipon, who founded several caricature journals (*La Caricature, Le Charivari*, etc.), was brought to court in 1831 for cartoons representing the king as a pear. He defended himself with a series of drawings that gradually transformed a realistic depiction of Louis-Philippe into a pear with a face. Then he asked the court by what logic they would condemn one of the drawings but not the others, since they all resembled each other. Philipon lost his case, but published his drawings and made more than enough money to cover the fines incurred.

6. See Baudelaire's discussion of the way in which Gavarni "has greatly

influenced manners [*les moeurs*]" in *Quelques caricaturistes français*, 2, 560.

7. I am speaking only of Benjamin's position in "Motifs." In the "Theses on the Philosophy of History," Benjamin is careful to distinguish between topical and dialectical transformations. See the fourteenth thesis, *Illuminations*, 261.

8. It is interesting that Benjamin is not inclined, even here, to retrieve beauty by allying it to inauthenticity. This would have been a perfect opportunity to set Baudelaire against himself by citing, for example: "Tes yeux, illuminés ainsi que des boutiques / Et des ifs flamboyants dans les fêtes publiques, / Usent insolemment d'un pouvoir emprunté, / Sans connaître jamais la loi de leur beauté" (Your eyes, lit up like shopfronts, / And outdoor lights on public holidays, / Make insolent use of a borrowed power, / Without ever knowing the law of their beauty), "Tu mettrais l'univers entier dans ta ruelle" (You'd put the whole world at your bedside) (1: 27–28). When Benjamin *does* cite this passage later in his essay, he omits the last line and with it the possibility of an inauthentic beauty.

9. Benjamin uses the verb *begünstigen*, "to encourage," or in the juridical sense, "to aid and abet" a criminal. The second meaning recalls Benjamin's description of Atget's photographs as scenes of a crime. Photography, then, seems to possess guilty intentions, if only by association—it does not remain an innocent accessory in the conspiracy against art.

10. According to *Le Petit Robert*, "cliché" entered usage as a synonym for the photographic negative in 1865, as a synonym for the commonplace in 1869.

Conclusion

1. I realize that this remark needs much defending. Writers can be extremely difficult or strange without being historically incoherent. We know what to think and say about them even if we find them hard to understand. Mallarmé might fall into this category (see de Man's closing comments in "Lyric," and Bénichou's recent book, *Selon Mallarmé*). On the other hand, Baudelaire challenges our ability to affirm that he is a radical poet, since he may in fact be quite conservative. The incoherency in this case is more thoroughgoing since our basic categories of appraisal cease to function properly.

2. Sartre's critical biographies of Flaubert and Genet might serve as models here. Both were written in part to correct the defects of the Baudelaire book, i.e., to show more clearly the historical pressures weighing

upon the individual life. The discussion of Flaubert's father is of particular interest, because Sartre depicts him as both a peasant of the Ancien Régime and a nineteenth-century man of science. According to Sartre, historical schizophrenia manifested itself in Flaubert's father as a character flaw. The effects of a similar historical rupture have yet to be traced in the case of Valéry.

3. I am leaving "la nouvelle critique" and "les nouveaux critiques" in French, so as not to confuse them with American New Criticism and New Critics.

4. The verb in French is *supporter* and Barthes seems to be exploiting its double meaning, which offers a condensed example of the problems of bad faith: Does the writer merely tolerate literature's failure, or is there some complicity involved?

5. The title of Barthes' essay has been translated as "Writers and Scribblers" or "Writers and Hacks," but these don't quite render the connotations of *écrivant* which is not pejorative and does not refer to commercial writing, but emphasizes a transitive process.

6. Although Barthes never mentions Sartre explicitly in the essay, the latter is present everywhere, both as the object of Barthes' polemic and, perhaps, as a model for the hybrid type of writer, the "écrivain-écrivant," that Barthes defines in his closing discussion.

7. See in particular pp. 290–93 of "Excuses" in *Allegories of Reading*. De Man here picks up on the concept of fiction that Rousseau elaborates in *Les Rêveries du promeneur solitaire* (the fourth "Promenade"). Rousseau is also a crucial figure for Blanchot, who considers him to be the first to live out the false passion of literature. See "Rousseau" in *Le Livre à venir* (The book to come). Sartre, curiously, absolves Rousseau of his literariness, or of his bad faith, and treats him as a signal example of successful engagement. See *Qu'est-ce que la littérature?*, 114–15. All this suggests that the interpretation of Rousseau should be another fruitful place for examining the kinds of questions I have raised with respect to Baudelaire.

8. The crisis takes the form of a kind of historical cacophony, which I am keenly aware of in my own writing and which marks much of current literary criticism in the United States. Is the critical language we are using old or new? Are we writing from within a living discourse, speaking a dead language, or dissecting a dead letter with living hands? Frequently, several of the options are operative at once. Barthes' critical discourse, to find a point of comparison, never reflected this kind of historical crisis. Baudelaire, on the other hand, seems to have been familiar with it.

9. For an example of the type of work I am thinking of, see Guerlac, 806.

She explicitly turns the new critical practice of reading to a consideration of Sartre's philosophy of engagement: "Thus although what we call 'theory' could be said to have emerged in reaction to engagement, engagement is now invoked in the name of a *dépassement* (going beyond) of theory. An imperative of engagement historically frames the thinking of post-structuralism. We have come full circle without ever having subjected this term to close scrutiny. Indeed, the familiar notion of engagement has hardly been read."

Bibliography

Adorno, Theodor. "Commitment." In *Aesthetics and Politics*, trans. ed. Ronald Taylor, 177–95. London: NLB [Verso], 1977.

Asselineau, Charles. "Charles Baudelaire, sa vie et son oeuvre." *Baudelaire et Asselineau*, eds. Jacques Crépet and Claude Pichois, 61–155. Paris: Nizet, 1953.

Austin, John Langshaw. *How to Do Things With Words*. Eds. J. O. Urmsen and Marina Sbisà. Oxford: Oxford University Press, 1976.

Barthes, Roland. *Critique et vérité*. Paris: Seuil [Collection "Tel Quel"], 1966.

———. "Ecrivains et écrivants." *Essais critiques*, 147–54. Paris: Seuil [Collection Points], 1964.

Bataille, Georges. *La Littérature et le mal*. Paris: Gallimard [Collection Idées], 1957.

Baudelaire, Charles. *Correspondance*. Eds. Claude Pichois and Jean Ziegler. Paris: Gallimard [Bibliothèque de la Pléiade], 1973.

———. *Les Fleurs du Mal*. Eds. Jacques Crépet and Georges Blin; rev. Georges Blin and Claude Pichois. Paris: José Corti, 1968.

———. *Oeuvres complètes*. Paris: Gallimard [Bibliothèque de la Pléiade], 1976.

Benedetto, L. F. "L'Architecture des *Fleurs du Mal*." In *Zeitschrift für französische Sprache und Literatur*, Vol. 39, 18–70. Chemnitz: Wilhelm Gronau, 1912.

Bénichou, Paul. *Selon Mallarmé*. Paris: Gallimard. 1995.

Benjamin, Walter. *Charles Baudelaire: A Lyric Poet in the Era of High Capitalism*. Trans. Harry Zohn. London: NLB, 1973.

———. "Fate and Character." In *Reflections*, ed. Peter Demetz, 304–11. New York: Harcourt Brace Jovanovich, 1979.

———. "On Some Motifs in Baudelaire." In *Illuminations*, ed. Hannah Arendt, trans. Harry Zohn. 155–200. New York: Schocken, 1969.
———. *The Origin of German Tragic Drama*. Trans. John Osborne. London: NLB, 1977.
———. "Short History of Photography." *Artforum*, 15: 6, (Feb. 1977): 46–51.
———. "Theses on the Philosophy of History." In *Illuminations*, ed. Hannah Arendt, 253–64. New York: Schocken, 1969.
———. "The Work of Art in the Age of Mechanical Reproduction." In *Illuminations*, ed. Hannah Arendt, 217–51. New York: Schocken, 1969.
Bersani, Leo. *Baudelaire and Freud*. Berkeley: University of California Press, 1977.
Blanchot, Maurice. "L'Echec de Baudelaire." *La Part du feu*, 133–51. Paris: Gallimard, 1949.
———. "Rousseau." *Le Livre à venir*. Paris: Gallimard, 1959.
Blin, Georges. *Baudelaire*. Paris: Gallimard, 1939.
———. *Le Sadisme de Baudelaire*. Paris: Corti, 1948.
Brunetière, Ferdinand. "Charles Baudelaire." In *Revue des deux mondes*, 81 (1 Jun. 1887): 695–706.
Burton, Richard D. E. *Baudelaire and the Second Republic: Writing and Revolution*. Oxford: Clarendon Press, 1991.
Chambers, Ross. "Mémoire et mélancolie." In *Mélancolie et opposition: Les débuts du modernisme en France*, 167–86. Paris: José Corti, 1987.
———. "Poetry in the Asiatic Mode: Baudelaire's *Au Lecteur*." In *Yale French Studies*, 74 (1988): 97–116.
Chase, Cynthia. "Getting Versed: Reading Hegel with Baudelaire." In *Decomposing Figures*, 113–38. Baltimore: Johns Hopkins University Press, 1986.
Cohen-Solal, Annie. *Sartre*. Paris: Gallimard, 1985.
Collins, Douglas. *Sartre as Biographer*. Cambridge: Harvard University Press, 1980.
Contat, Michel, and Michel Rybalka. *The Writings of Jean-Paul Sartre*, Vol. 1. Trans. Richard C. McCleary. Evanston: Northwestern University Press, 1974.
Deguy, Michel. "Le corps de Jeanne." *Poétique* 3 (1970): 334–47.
———. "L'Infini et sa diction: Ou de la diérèse (Etude baudelairienne)." *Poétique* 40 (1979): 432–44.
de Man, Paul. "Anthropomorphism and Trope in the Lyric." In *The Rhetoric of Romanticism*, 239–62. New York: Columbia University Press, 1984.

———. Introduction to *Toward an Aesthetic of Reception* by Hans Robert Jauß, vii–xxv. Minneapolis: University of Minnesota Press, 1982.
———. "Lyric and Modernity." In *Blindness and Insight*, 2d ed., 166–86. Minneapolis: University of Minnesota Press, 1983.
———. "The Rhetoric of Temporality." In *Blindness and Insight*, 2d ed., 187–228. Minneapolis: University of Minnesota Press, 1983.
———. "Sign and Symbol in Hegel's Aesthetics." In *Critical Inquiry* (Summer 1982): 761–75.
Derrida, Jacques. *De la grammatologie*. Paris: Minuit, 1967.
Feuillerat, Albert. "L'Architecture des *Fleurs du mal*." In *Studies by Members of the French Department of Yale University*, 221–330. New Haven: Yale University Press, 1941.
Fournier, Edouard. *Le Vieux-neuf: Histoire ancienne des inventions et découvertes modernes*. Paris: Dentu, 1859.
Friedrich, Hugo. *The Structure of Modern Poetry*. Trans. Joachim Neugroschel. Evanston: Northwestern University Press, 1974.
Girard, René, with Jean-Michel Oughourlian and Guy Lefort. *Des choses cachées depuis la fondation du monde*. Paris: Bernard Grasset, 1978.
Greenberg, Clement. "Modernist Painting." *Art and Literature* 4 (Spring 1965): 193–201.
Guerlac, Suzanne. "Sartre and the Powers of Literature: The Myth of Prose and the Practice of Reading." *MLN*, 108: 5, (1993): 805–24.
Halpern, Joseph. *Critical Fictions: The Literary Criticism of Jean-Paul Sartre*. New Haven: Yale University Press, 1976.
Hannoosh, Michele. *Baudelaire and Caricature: From the Comic to an Art of Modernity*. University Park: Pennsylvania State University Press, 1992.
Hegel, G. W. F. *Aesthetics: Lectures on Fine Art*, Vol. 2. Trans. T. M. Knox. Oxford: Clarendon Press, 1974.
Hollier, Denis. *Politique de la prose*. Paris: Gallimard, 1982.
Hugo, Victor. *Poésie*, Vol. 1. Paris: Seuil [Collection l'Intégrale], 1972.
Hyslop, L. B., and F. Hyslop, eds. *Baudelaire: A Self Portrait*. London: Oxford University Press, 1957.
Jauß, Hans Robert, "The Poetic Text within the Change of Horizons of Reading: The Example of Baudelaire's Spleen II." In *Toward an Aesthetic of Reception*, trans. Timothy Bahti, 139–85. Minneapolis: University of Minnesota Press, 1983.
Jameson, Fredric. "Baudelaire as Modernist and Postmodernist." In *Lyric Poetry: Beyond New Criticism*, ed. Chaviva Hosek and Patricia Parker, 247–63. Ithaca: Cornell University Press, 1985.

Johnson, Barbara. *Défigurations du language poétique: La seconde révolution baudelairienne*. Paris: Flammarion, 1979.
Kant, Immanuel. *Critique of Practical Reason*. Trans. Lewis White Beck. Indianapolis: Bobbs-Merrill, 1956.
———. *Groundwork of the Metaphysics of Morals*. Trans. H. J. Paton. New York: Harper and Row, 1964.
Kelley, David, ed. *Salon de 1846*. Oxford: Clarendon Press, 1975.
Klein, Richard. "*Bénédiction/Perte d'Auréole*: Parables of Interpretation." *MLN* 85: 4, (1970): 515–28.
———. "Straight Lines and Arabesques: Metaphors of Metaphor." *Yale French Studies*, 45 (1970): 64–86.
Leiris, Michel. Preface to *Baudelaire* by Jean-Paul Sartre. Paris: Gallimard [Collection Idées], 1947.
Maclean, Marie. *Narrative as Performance: The Baudelairean Experiment*. London: Routledge, 1988.
Mallarmé, Stéphane. *Oeuvres Complètes*. Eds. Henri Mondor and G. Jean-Aubry. Paris: Gallimard [Bibliothèque de la Pléiade], 1989.
Malraux, André. *L'Homme précaire et la littérature*. Paris: Gallimard, 1977.
Pascal, Blaise. *Oeuvres complètes*. Ed. Louis Lafuma. Paris: Seuil [Collection l'Intégrale], 1963.
Peyre, Henri. *Connaissance de Baudelaire*. Paris: José Corti, 1951.
———. *What Is Symbolism?* Trans. Emmett Parker. Tuscaloosa: University of Alabama Press, 1980.
Pichois, Claude, and Jean Ziegler. *Baudelaire*. Trans. Graham Robb. London: Hamish Hamilton, 1989.
Poe, Edgar Allan. "The Poetic Principle." In *The Complete Works of Edgar Allan Poe*, vol. 1. New York: AMS Press, 1965.
Poulet, Georges. "Baudelaire." In *Etudes sur le temps humain*, 327–49. Paris: Plon, 1965.
Proust, Marcel. *A la recherche du temps perdu*. Ed. Pierre Clarac and André Ferré. Paris: Gallimard [Bibliothèque de la Pléiade], 1954.
———. *Contre Sainte-Beuve*. Paris: Gallimard [Bibliothèque de la Pléiade], 1971.
Richard, Jean-Pierre. *Poésie et profondeur*. Paris: Seuil, 1955.
Riffaterre, Michael. "L'Etude stylistique des formes littéraires conventionnelles." In *Essais de stylistique structurale*, trans. Daniel Delas, 182–202. Paris: Flammarion, 1971.
———. "The Self-sufficient Text," *Diacritics* 3: 3, (Fall 1973): 39–45.

Rivière, Jacques. *Etudes*. Paris: Gallimard, 1936.
Rousseau, Jean-Jacques. *Emile*. Paris: Garnier, 1964.
Sartre, Jean-Paul. *Baudelaire*. Paris: Gallimard [Collection Idées], 1947.
———. *L'Etre et le néant*. Paris: Gallimard [Collection Tel], 1943.
———. *Les Mots*. Paris: Gallimard, 1964.
———. *Qu'est-ce que la littérature?* Paris: Gallimard [Collection Idées], 1948.
Shelley, Percy Bysshe. *The Complete Poetical Works of Percy Bysshe Shelley*. Ed. Neville Rogers. Oxford: Clarendon Press, 1975.
Stevens, Wallace. *The Palm at the End of the Mind*. Ed. Holly Stevens. New York: Vintage Books, 1972.
Suhl, Benjamin. *Jean-Paul Sartre: The Philosopher as a Literary Critic*. New York: Columbia University Press, 1970.
Swinburne, Algernon. "Charles Baudelaire." In *Poems and Ballads* followed by *Atalanta in Calydon*, ed. Morse Peckham, 308–17. Indianapolis: Bobbs-Merrill, 1970.
Thody, Philip, *Jean-Paul Sartre: A Literary and Political Study*. London: Hamish Hamilton, 1964.
Valéry, Paul. "Existence du symbolisme." In *Oeuvres*, vol. 1, 686–706. Paris: Gallimard [Bibliothèque de la Pléiade], 1957.
———. "Situation de Baudelaire." In *Oeuvres*, vol. 1, 598–613. Paris: Gallimard [Bibliothèque de la Pléiade], 1957.

Index

In this index an "f" after a number indicates a separate reference on the next page, and an "ff" indicates separate references on the next two pages. A continuous discussion over two or more pages is indicated by a span of page numbers, e.g., "57–59." *Passim* is used for a cluster of references in close but not consecutive sequence.

Adorno, Theodor: and cold-war criticism, 3, 4, 174, 178; "Commitment," 3
Aesthetic difference, 11, 20, 47, 51–52, 56, 84–88 *passim*
Aesthetics, 16–20 *passim*, 46ff, 74, 127, 129, 181n8; and indeterminacy, 8–10; and Hegel, 73; and indifference, 81, 83f
Allegory, 12–21 *passim*, 26, 143–49, 172, 181nn7, 8, 193nn20, 21; allegoresis, 16; and irrealization, 21; allegorical textuality, 22f
Alterity, 9; and solitude, 60–62
Ancelle, Narcisse, 7
Art for art's sake, 3
Asselineau, Charles, 30f, 38, 61, 186n17
Austin, J. L., 33
Authenticity, 4–6, 156–57, 195n8

Bad faith, aesthetic character of, 10–12, 77, 81, 92, 119, 125. See also Sartre
Bakhtin, Mikhail, 194n3
Balzac, Honoré de, 190n10

Barthes, Roland, 175f, 196nn4–6, 8
Bataille, Georges, 64–68 *passim*, 109, 192n16; on sovereign attitude of poetry, 69; on the prosaic, 70–79 *passim*, 83f
Baudelaire, Charles: on *modernité*, 1; on hypocritical reader, 8, 108; on poetic contract, 8; architecture of *Les Fleurs du mal*, 10f, 123–49 *passim*; rehabilitation at the Cours de Cassation, 54, 58, 184n4; trial of 1857, 79, 187n15; poetics of *correspondances*, 127–30 *passim*, 136f, 141; on *le lieu commun*, 160; on photography, 150–72 *passim*; on *cliché*, 171ff
—Works: "L'Albatros," 62; "Assommons les pauvres," 14, 24; "Au lecteur," 7–10 *passim*, 111, 117, 120, 190n10; "A une passante," 183n18, 193n18; "L'Avertisseur," 191n18; "Le Balcon," 80, 132, 147; "Bénédiction," 62; "La Chevelure," 130, 141, 192n10; "La Cloche fêlée," 80; "Correspondances," 10, 90, 127, 129f; "Le

Cygne," 16, 21f, 25, 75, 18¹n6, 183n18; "Danse macabre," 10, 123–30 *passim*; *De l'essence du rire*, 113; "De l'héroïsme de la vie moderne," 135; "L'Ecole païenne," 86ff, 187n20, 188; "Elévation," 82; "L'Ennemi," 11, 18ff, 141–47 *passim*; "Epigraphe pour un livre condamné," 8, 112–21 *passim*; "Les Fenêtres," 70, 72, 187n13; "Les Feuilles d'automne," 99; "Le Flacon," 75; "La Fontaine du sang," 182n14; "Les Foules," 61–62; *Fusées*, 61; "Le Gouffre," 63, 67ff; "Le Guignon," 62, 119f, 140, 182n9; "Harmonie du soir," 140; "L'Héautontimorouménos," 9, 190n15; "L'Horloge," 131f, 148; "L'Invitation au voyage," 121, 183n18, 190n10; "L'Irrémédiable," 25, 131, 148; "J'aime le souvenir de ces époques nues," 11, 133–38 *passim*, 140–46 *passim*, 183n18; "J'ai plus de souvenirs que si j'avais mille ans," 184n5; "Le Léthé," 63; "Madrigal triste," 120; "Le Mauvais moine," 140; *Mon coeur mis à nu*, 60f, 74, 115, 135; "La Mort," 148; "La Muse malade," 81–91 *passim*, 97, 124, 139ff, 188, 189n2; "La Muse vénale," 143; "La Musique," 81–84 *passim*, 148; *Le Peintre de la vie moderne*, 1; "Les Petites vieilles," 192n18; "La Pipe," 148; *Le Poème du hachisch*, 18, 124; *Projets de préface*, 97f; "Le Public moderne et la photographie," 153; *Quelques caricaturistes français*, 164, 195n6; "Recueillement," 48, 55; "Le Reniement de Saint Pierre," 69, 102; "Rêve parisien," 16, 76; *Salon de 1846*, 150, 192n11; *Salon de 1859*, 12, 127, 150–72 *passim*, 191n1; "Les Sept vieillards," 183n16; "Le Soleil," 15, 98, 101–7 *passim*, 189n5; *Le Spleen de Paris*, 16, 47, 63, 186n17; *Spleen et Idéal*, 82, 131ff, 140, 143, 148; *Tableaux Parisiens*, 124, 148; "Le Thyrse," 84; "La Vie antérieure," 47, 140, 183n18; "Le Vieux saltimbanque," 194n3

Benedetto, L. F., 148
Bénichou, Paul, 195n1
Benjamin, Walter, 6, 11, 47, 74f, 107f, 111, 131, 150–72 *passim*, 181n6, 193n20; Baudelaire criticism after Benjamin, 14–28; on self-reflexivity, 159
—Works: "Fate and Character," 162; "On Some Motifs in Baudelaire," 2, 12, 36ff, 74, 99, 156ff, 167f, 171, 189n5, 190n11, 192n7, 195n7; *The Origin of German Tragic Drama*, 181n8; "The Paris of the Second Empire in Baudelaire," 12, 14; "Short History of Photography," 156, 167; "Theses on the Philosophy of History," 195n7; "The Work of Art In the Age of Mechanical Reproduction," 194n2
Bergson, Henri, 190n11
Blanchot, Maurice, 63, 175, 187n12, 196n7
Blin, Georges, 94ff, 186n15, 191n24
Breton, André, 29, 32
Brunetière, Ferdinand, 30f
Burton, Richard, 14, 24

Canonization, 33–35
Caricature, 8, 15, 94–126 *passim*, 131, 164–72 *passim*
Chambers, Ross, 21–27 *passim*, 183n17, 190n10
Christophe, Ernest, 123f
Cohen-Solal, Annie, 7
Cold-war criticism, 3, 174, 178
Collins, Douglas, 191nn17, 23

Index

Contat, Michel, 57f
Context and situation, 15, 21–28, 43f, 99–102, 107, 159f
Correspondances versus *spleen*, 47, 80
Crépet, Jacques, 186n15, 189n1, 194n4

Daguerre, Jacques, 156, 161
D'Aurevilly, Barbey, 10, 80, 92, 187n15
Deguy, Michel, 192n10
Delacroix, Eugène, 151f, 170, 172f
De Man, Paul, 16–20 *passim*, 177, 181n7, 182n12, 183nn15, 17, 189n8, 193nn20, 21, 195n1, 196n7
Derrida, Jacques, 23, 177, 191n19
Dialogic structure, of *Les Fleurs du mal*, 9, 20
Du Bos, Charles, 31
Du Camp, Maxime, 30, 152

Eliot, T. S., 29

Fabre, Lucien, 185n7
Feuillerat, Albert, 147
Fietkau, Wolfgang, 16
Flaubert, Gustave, 143
Fournier, Edouard, 163ff
Friedrich, Hugo, 184n1

Gautier, Théophile, 42f
Gavarni, Paul, 165, 194n6
Greenberg, Clement, 4f
Guerlac, Suzanne, 196n9

Halpern, Joseph, 191n25
Hegel, G. W. F., 17–20 *passim*; on historiography and oratory, 73–75 *passim*, 193n20
Historicity, 24, 99, 163
Hollier, Denis, 191n16
L'homme et l'oeuvre criticism, 58, 63f

Hugo, Victor, 31ff, 40, 49–53 *passim*, 97ff, 107, 189n3

Imagination, 13
Indeterminacy, 10
Irony, 7

Jameson, Fredric, 24
Jauß, Hans Robert, 16–20 *passim*, 182n11, 184n5
Johnson, Barbara, 9, 186n17, 187n17

Kant, Immanuel, 4; post-Kantian aesthetics, 13, 15, 65, 80, 91
Klein, Richard, 187nn7, 17

Lamartine, Alphonse de, 97
Lanson, Gustave, 186n1
Leconte de Lisle, Charles-Marie, 187n18
Leiris, Michel, 61
Louis Napoléon, 14, 16, 100

Maclean, Marie, 21, 190n10
Maistre, Joseph de, 67, 187n11
Mallarmé, Stéphane, 29, 32, 39, 42ff, 52, 174, 187n9, 195n1
Malraux, André, 1
Manet, Edouard, 5
Memory, 11; voluntary and involuntary, 169
Modernism, 2f, 6, 12, 23–27 *passim*, 32, 150, 155, 173
Molière, 154
Musset, Alfred de, 97, 102

Pascal, Blaise, 115ff
Peyre, Henri, 10, 31, 38, 57
Philipon, Charles, 164, 194n5
Photography, 12, 24; and authenticity, 156f, 167f; and voluntary memory, 157, 167–69
Pichois, Claude, 30, 54, 86, 123, 144, 184n2, 186nn15, 16

Pity, and reading, 114–18
Poe, Edgar Allan, 38–44 *passim*, 52, 185n8, 187nn9, 11
Poète maudit ideology, 62
Poetics, 16f
Poulet, Georges, 192n6
Proust, Marcel, 31, 58, 132, 157, 168, 192n12
Pure poetry (*poésie pure*), 5, 39, 41, 45, 49f

Raymond, Marcel, 29, 35
Relational essence, of *Les Fleurs du mal*, 111, 129
Richard, Jean-Pierre, 187n16
Riffaterre, Michael, 49, 55, 106, 185n12
Rimbaud, Arthur, 29, 32, 39, 44
Rivière, Jacques, 75, 109, 141, 187n14, 190n12, 192n17
Romanticism, 4, 13, 31, 43, 52, 151, 155, 170
Rousseau, Jean-Jacques, 116f, 174, 181n7, 191n19, 196n7
Rybalka, Michel, 57f

Sainte-Beuve, Charles-Augustin, 58, 186n1
Saintsbury, George, 184n3
Sartre, Jean-Paul, 2–5 *passim*, 27f, 57–93 *passim*, 111, 113, 118, 186n5; on bad faith, 6, 8, 66, 77, 81, 92, 109, 118, 125f, 143, 174f, 181n3, 185n14, 187n9, 190n12; self-negation, 8; *L'Etre et le néant*, 10, 57, 65f, 76, 85, 97, 100f, 109f, 125, 189n7, 191nn16, 4, 192n15, 195n2, 197; on situation, 15, 101, 103; on solitude, 58–62; convertibility, 62; on evil, 67; on *transcendance*, 71, 76; on ethical challenge to the aesthetic, 85; *Les Mots*, 114; *L'Idiot de la famille*, 175
Second Empire, 26f
Semiosis, 23
Shelley, Percy Bysshe, 185n13
Stevens, Wallace, 122, 183n18
Subject: as alien, 9; as grammatical, 17f; decentered, 25; and consciousness, 26; modern, 26f
Suhl, Benjamin, 7
Surrealism, 103, 107, 109, 189n7
Symbol, 11, 20
Symbolism, 11–14 *passim*, 42, 52, 54, 174, 185n7

Temporality, 11, 13, 132–42 *passim*
Thody, Philip, 7

Valéry, Paul, 10–15 *passim*, 29–56, 97, 107, 114, 150, 174, 185n7, 9, 189n3; "Situation de Baudelaire," 3–6 *passim*, 13, 35–54 *passim*, 99; and *charme*, 48f
Verlaine, Paul, 39, 186n6
Vernet, Carle, 165
Violence, 8f

Wiertz, Antoine, 156, 167

Library of Congress Cataloging-in-Publication Data
Blood, Susan.
  Baudelaire and the aesthetics of bad faith /
Susan Blood.
      p. cm.
  Includes bibliographical references and index.
  ISBN 0-8047-2809-7
  1. Baudelaire, Charles, 1821–1867—Aesthetics.
  2. Modernism (Literature)—France.   3. Aesthetics,
  French—19th century.   I. Title.
  PQ2191.Z5B554 1997
  841'.8—dc20   96-27397
                                                        CIP

⊚ This book is printed on acid-free, recycled paper.

Original printing 1997
Last figure below indicates year of this printing:
06 05 04 03 02 01 00 99 98 97